Crime and Criminal Justice

Crime and Criminal Justice

Edited with an Introduction by

Donald R. Cressey

A NEW YORK TIMES BOOK

Quadrangle Books
CHICAGO

Library of Congress Catalog Card Number: 71-130380
SBN Cloth 8129-0178-9
SBN Paper 8129-6144-7

The publishers are grateful to the contributors herein for
permission to reprint their articles.

Acknowledgments

I wish to thank Martha Jean Cressey—daughter, critic, art historian, accountant, and *dactylo extraordinaire*—for her help with this book, which I dedicate to her.

Particular thanks are also due James P. Driscoll of the University of California, Santa Barbara, who helped in many ways. Finally, I am grateful to Morris Janowitz of the University of Chicago, and to my wife.

D. R. C.

Contents

3. The Wheels of Justice

4. Some Experiments in Change

5. Some Proposals for Change

Crime and Criminal Justice

Introduction

THE SERIOUSNESS of the crime problem hardly needs description. President Johnson's National Crime Commission in 1967 estimated that each year the citizens of the United States lose at least $15 billion to criminals—about three times the amount they spend on all education, from kindergarten to medical school. Another $6 billion goes each year to crime prevention, police, courts, and corrections.

The financial losses from fraudulent business transactions are much greater than the losses from "street crimes." Each working day trusted employees make off with more than $8 million of their employers' cash or merchandise, a total annual loss of more than $2 billion. In comparison, crimes against the person (homicide, assault) cost about $800 million in lost earnings and medical expenses each year, while robbery, burglary, larceny, and automobile theft—the most publicized and feared crimes—cost about $600 million. Organized criminals, however, are responsible for the greatest economic impact of crime. They derive about twice as much income from gambling and the sale of other illegal goods and services as unorganized criminals derive from all other kinds of criminal activities combined.

The cost of crime cannot of course be measured in dollars alone. A price tag cannot be put on lost or damaged lives, fear of suffering, or frustration arising from an inability to control critical events. An eighty-year-old lady who loses fifteen dollars to a purse snatcher or mugger loses much more than the contents of her purse. She loses, at least in her mind, the freedom to walk the streets in safety. The victim of a rapist may lose status in the community, as may persons not ordinarily considered the victims of crime, such as the relatives of the murderer, the embezzler, the child molester, or the thief.

In recent years fear of crime has become a problem as serious as crime itself. An uneasiness about crime and even terror of criminals now possess the residents of most of our large cities, and a large proportion of our suburban and rural residents. The general public or the taxpayer who experiences these fears is thus a victim of crime. Moreover, the general public or the taxpayer must bear the costs of administering criminal justice, and for that reason is further victimized by crime.

Some observers take the view that crime makes certain social contributions which partially offset the losses it causes. For example, some sociologists suggest that crime promotes the solidarity of the society, just as does war. While it is true that a community might be welded together by certain spectacular murders and rapes, it is probable that most other crimes both stem from and promote dissension, suspicion, and divisions in society. Moreover, the solidarity aroused by crime is generally rather futile—it is an emotional expression which serves only to outlaw criminals and otherwise drive them into conflict with the dominant society.

Again, it has been urged that we must have crime in order to prevent morality from going to extremes. If all criminals were eliminated, the idea goes, standards would be set a little higher, and a new crop of deviants would be created. This argument too is not entirely convincing. Many primitive groups have retained essentially the same moral standards without many serious violations over long periods of time. It is true, however, that the high standards of morality fixed in concrete criminal laws are slowly lowered as community standards are lowered. Often the statutes reflect a morality no longer widely prevalent—as in current prohibitions against homosexuality between consenting adults—so that criminality is in effect *created* by the outmoded statute.

Although the criminal law changes only slowly, administration of that law is characterized by a flexibility that permits police, prosecutors, judges, and correctional personnel to adjust the "law on the books" to the "law on the street." The key characteristic of criminal justice administration is discretion. For many centuries philosophers of jurisprudence have attempted by deductive reasoning to determine some invariant principle or set of principles underlying the criminal law. Divine order, the will of the sovereign, nature, reason, community consensus, and other principles have been presented. More than a half-century ago Roscoe Pound, in *Interpretations of Legal History,* argued convincingly that a final answer to the question "What is law?" is impossible because law is a living, changing thing. The criminal law, Pound noted, may at one time be quite uniform and at another time give much room for administrative discretion, may at one time be very general in its proscriptions and at another time quite specific, may at one time be based on divine order or sovereign will and at another time on juristic science.

Pound's statement is a call to consider "law in action." Pound maintained that the law regulates social interests and arbitrates conflicting interests, claims, and demands. He saw the criminal law as a body of norms that are binding on all who live within the political boundaries of a state, and are enforced through the coercive power of the state. But he went on to suggest that the specific character of these legal rules depends upon the character and interests of those groups in the population that influence legislation and criminal justice administration. Because the norms embodied in the criminal law change as the dominant groups change, what is "crime" varies from time to time and place to place. Further, the "law on the street" or the "living law" (the law as it is perceived by the police and other criminal justice administrators) may change drastically as the morality of the dominant interest groups changes, even while the "law on the books" remains unchanged.

Obviously, the governmental devices established for enacting criminal laws and for securing adherence to them are devices aimed at maximizing the degree of conformity in a society. Yet criminal statutes and the various cogs in the wheels of justice— police, courts, jails, and prisons—are more than mechanisms for coercive enforcement of an agreed-upon morality. They are also mechanisms for dispensing justice. Put another way, they are mechanisms for establishing and maintaining the consent of the governed.

Legislators and criminal justice administrators, like the rest of us, must constantly seek effective measures for controlling individual citizens whose criminal conduct indicates that they have withdrawn, at least partially and temporarily, their consent to be governed. This fact of life has led, rather sadly, to figures of speech which picture criminals as if they were entirely without civil liberties or even human attributes. For example, we speak of a "war on crime," and we label criminals as "enemies of society" and even as "mad dogs."

But if the matter were merely one of repression, to be conducted like war or pest control, then the declared criminal "enemies" or "pests" would simply be deposed or exterminated without regard for their rights and liberties as citizens. When "due process of law" is respected, the matter of crime control is not merely a matter of making war on enemies. It is a matter of dealing appropriately with members of society who, as members, are entitled to considerations not accorded to enemies. This means simply that official punishments must be ordered and executed in accordance with agreed-upon rules.

Moreover, if intentionally inflicted suffering—be it the pain of a fine or the pangs of imprisonment—is to be accepted by the recipients and by citizens generally, it must be imposed in degrees suitable to correcting serious deviation without stimulating rebellion. "Justice" serves to maintain the consent of the governed. Maintaining the consent of the governed, in turn, requires that the system of punishments for law violation be accepted as legitimate by those being governed. Rigid enforcement of criminal statutes is not enough, even if the enforcement process does not tamper with the rights summarized in the phrase "due process of law." There must be flexibility, change, common sense, adjustment, and compromise in the criminal code itself, and in the administration of the code in specific cases.

Because of this need for flexibility, criminal justice administrators are more than law-enforcement officers. They are, above all, diplomats who must constantly balance the demands and claims of various interest groups. They must help establish unwritten and sometimes unspoken agreements and understandings among various segments of society, which means that they must be negotiators and arbitrators. It is this diplomatic functioning of criminal justice administrators that serves to maintain the consent of the governed in a society. It is this diplomatic functioning, also, that makes policemen, prosecutors, and judges—among others—administrators of justice rather than mere agents of coercion.

The discretionary character of all criminal justice administration can readily be observed in the activities of the police, who are the principal diplomats in the criminal justice system. Policemen are asked to "combat" or "fight" crime, as if we had just declared war on it. But they are not given the money, manpower, equipment, or constitutional authority to go to war with criminals. These limitations are society's way of asking the police to overlook some crimes and to settle others out of court. Because the restrictions on police power are not usually recognized, the police often appear to be more inefficient crime-fighters than they are. Some police departments consider themselves successful merely because they have survived.

The solution to so-called police inefficiency does not lie in measures that would enable the police to take all suspects into custody. No amount of money, manpower, or equipment will make the police into automatons that strictly follow the coercive directives of criminal statutes. Strict law enforcement—in the sense of total enforcement of the directives contained in criminal statutes—cannot be purchased, no matter what the resources of a community or nation. Because rules of law necessarily must be quite general, gross injustices would be done if the police were not given room for flexibility, diplomacy, and discretion. For example, a statute defining robbery is likely to cover the behavior of a hold-up man—but it also is likely to describe the act of a boy who forcibly takes a basketball away from the children on a playground. The police, as diplomats, must decide whether injustice would be done by dealing with the boy as if he were a hold-up man. Thus police and other criminal justice administrators are not being inefficient when they function as diplomats rather than as law-enforcement officers, when they exercise discretion rather than following some strict set of rules, when they operate as administrators of justice rather than as inflicters of punishments. They are doing their jobs.

Citizens do not want to hear that their police, prosecutors, public defenders, judges, and correctional officials make "deals" by explicitly or implicitly negotiating with criminals. Nevertheless, "dealing" is as essential to criminal justice as it is to international relations. Judge Charles Breitel of the New York Court of Appeals has recently written, "If every policeman, every prosecutor, and every post-sentence agency performed his or its responsibility in strict accordance to the rules of law, precisely and narrowly laid down, the criminal law would be ordered but intolerable." It is this "intolerable" condition that is avoided when criminal justice administrators function as diplomats. Unfortunately, however, when "deals" with criminals become public they are likely to be taken as evidence of corruption, even if no money has changed hands.

So far as "law and order" are concerned, a community is never *a* community. It is a collection of competing interests. Legislators and criminal justice administrators—including the justices of the United States Supreme Court—rather precariously try to develop practices and procedures that will maintain an optimal degree of consent to be governed among the various interest groups. In every community there are interests in puritanical behavior, efficiency, and law enforcement. But every community also includes interests in a compromised morality, reciprocity, favors, domestic tranquility, and justice. When these two sets of interests are both powerful, as they are in most contemporary communities, criminal justice personnel cannot merely "enforce the law." They must, as diplomats, see that a balance is struck, that understandings are operationalized. They must help to establish and preside over a negotiated social order.

Consider the idea of using punishment to deter and reform criminals. Our forefathers were convinced, and most of us are convinced, that conduct described by criminal statutes can be minimized by swift, certain, and uniform punishment of those who deviate. Everything is to be reasonable. Each criminal law stipulates that a certain type of conduct is punishable, thus serving to warn citizens that such conduct will be punished. If criminal justice administrators calmly, rationally, swiftly, and certainly impose punishments on those who do not heed the warnings, the deterrence argument goes, the undesirability and impropriety of the prohibited behavior is emphasized. Imposition of punishment in a disinterested manner teaches both the offender and the onlookers a lesson.

This idea, which is one of the pillars of modern systems of justice, assumes that appropriate punishment can be stipulated in advance of any display of the violation. It views the criminal justice system as a huge computer that scans its memory bank for the correct punishment, then imposes it. The idea also incorporates the assumption that the computer programmers—the legislators—will rapidly change both the kinds of behavior prohibited and the prescribed punishments whenever the "law on the books" is inconsistent with the "law on the street." In other words, the assumption is that the persons being governed always want the law to be what is contained in the statutes. This is rarely the case.

Criminal statutes necessarily deal in generalities. A machinelike set of precise stipulations covering all varieties of crime and punishment cannot be set down, even by an omnipotent legislature. Punishments which seem appropriate in one time or place are too severe, or not severe enough, in another time or place. Whether the punishment stipulated for robbery is appropriate or not depends upon the circumstances of the offense and the characteristics of the offender. Nowadays, punishments that are considered "on the street" as too lenient can rarely be made tougher unofficially. Too many civil libertarians are watching. Fortunately, however, when statutory punishments are viewed as too severe, they can unofficially be mitigated in various ways. The police can overlook offenses, prosecutors can dismiss cases or reduce the charges, judges and juries can refuse to convict, and judges can rather blatantly change the law.

As criminal justice personnel unofficially modify the "law on the books," they become diplomats. Perhaps punishments are unofficially mitigated as a measure to prevent riot, revolt, and rebellion when intransigent legislators or cumbersome legislative processes block changes in the criminal statutes themselves. So that law and order are maintained, the administrators unofficially (but not necessarily corruptly) negotiate a series of compromises between those who want a uniform set of crimes and punishments and those who do not. A balance is struck, understandings are operationalized, and a negotiated social order prevails. Peace reigns.

A second important idea underlying contemporary legislation about criminal matters also must be considered. Our forefathers were convinced of the efficacy of deterrence, but they also were convinced that law violations and law violators must be handled individually, so far as punishment is concerned. This second conviction led to a "principle of adjustment" which asks criminal justice administrators to be *official* diplomats in matters of law and order. The "adjustment principle," like the "law-enforcement" or "deterrence principle," is a second pillar of contemporary systems of justice. The precisely stated stipulations of criminal statutes give advance notice that convicted wrongdoers will be punished in prescribed ways. But laws providing for suspended sentences, indeterminate sentences, probation, and parole—among others—stipulate that these penalties may be officially mitigated.

The mechanical system of equal justice promoted by Jeremy Bentham, Cesare Beccaria, and other members of the "classical school" of criminology was almost immediately modified at two points. First, children and "lunatics" were exempted from punishment. Second, penalties were fixed within narrow limits, rather than absolutely, so that judicial discretion was possible. The basic idea behind these modifications was, and is, that punishments should be "individualized," meaning that they should be adjusted to the circumstances of the offense and the character of the offender. Justice requires that, in some criminal cases, there shall be no punishment at all. Morris Cohen long ago pointed out, in *Reason and the Law,* that the idea of individualization and adjustment of penalties was but a reassertion of the old idea of equity as a corrective of undue rigor of law, "a corrective to the injustice which results from the fact that the abstract rule cannot take into account all the specific circumstances that are relevant to the case."

In the last analysis, the authorization of judicial discretion and, more generally, of individualization and adjustment of punishments was an attempt to implement penal theory that is in basic contradiction to deterrence theory. The deterrence or law-enforcement principle asks criminal justice personnel to maximize conformity by swiftly and uniformly punishing nonconformists. But the individualization or adjustment principle asks the same personnel to maximize conformity by *overlooking* some instances of nonconformity. The simplest and oldest application of the adjustment principle is found in the pardoning power. Indeed, as Cohen emphasized, in some religions God's *forgiveness* is His most glorious attribute.

The two contradictory directives for maximizing conformity, then, ask criminal justice administrators to play a game they cannot win. They are charged with enforcing the law in such a way that a measured amount of pain will be inflicted on each deliberate lawbreaker. They also are charged with enforcing the law in such a way that some crimes are forgiven, or partially forgiven, thus ensuring that a maximum number of citizens will continue to give their consent to be governed. Police, court officials, and correctional personnel must try to strike the delicate balance between severity and leniency of punishments, between imposing punishments uniformly and imposing them irregularly or not at all. In recent times we have, in addition, asked these personnel to "treat" criminals. To the degree that treatment is an alternative to punishment, not a supplement to it, its introduction into the legal process was, like introduction of the adjustment principle, an attempt to mitigate the penalties prescribed by statutes. Probation, prison, and parole workers, especially, are expected to modify the official punishments so that offenders will be "cured" or "corrected," and the degree of conformity thereby increased. As criminal justice administrators try to arrange these balances, they diplomatically implement the interests of many different community groups. They are not at war with criminals. On the contrary, like other diplomats they are constantly trying to avoid war.

A review of decisions handed down by the United States Supreme Court during the last decade suggests, in fact, that the

Court has been insisting that efforts to control crime become less warlike. The adjustment principle has made it possible for criminal justice workers to mitigate penalties and even to overlook some crimes, officially or unofficially. The discretion granted under this principle has also made it possible for the same personnel to ignore due process procedures in order to get a maximum number of nonconformists behind bars. The Supreme Court has declared the latter, but not the former, to be unconstitutional. Although the police and others are expected to control crime, they must do so within the legal framework of constitutional law and criminal procedure.

There are strong pressures on the police and other officials to manage the criminal justice process in such a way that a maximum number of crimes are deterred or discouraged. Stanford's Professor Herbert Packer has called this a "crime-control model" of the criminal justice process. But Packer also identifies a "due process model," and this is the model the Supreme Court has been following in defining the limits of the various stages in the criminal justice process, thus enhancing the capacity of accused persons, rich and poor alike, to challenge the operation of the process on the ground that it invades their rights to privacy, liberty, dignity, and equality.

For example, in the *Mallory* case (1957) a defendant was tried for rape and sentenced to death. Under procedures consistent with the "crime-control model," he had been detained from early afternoon until the next morning at police headquarters without being taken before a magistrate, although magistrates were available nearby. He was not told of his right to remain silent, to have counsel, or to be arraigned before a magistrate. By the time he had been arraigned, he had made a confession, which was used as evidence to convict him. The Supreme Court reversed the conviction, holding in essence that only the courts can decide that a person should be deprived of his liberty (as in pretrial detention and imprisonment), and that an illegal detention for "investigation" invalidates an otherwise legal confession.

In a second important case, that of *Mapp* (1961), the defendant was convicted of possessing lewd and lascivious pictures and books. She had refused to admit the police to her home, so they entered forcibly, without a search warrant, and seized the illegal material. In reversing the conviction, the Supreme Court held that "all evidence obtained by searches and seizures in violation of the Constitution is, by the same authority, inadmissible in a state court."

The *Gideon* (1963) and *Miranda* (1966) decisions also stressed the importance of due process. Gideon was charged with breaking and entering a Florida pool room. At his trial he asked the court to appoint a lawyer for him, but the judge refused. The Supreme Court reversed his conviction, stating, "The right of one charged with crime to counsel may not be fundamental in some countries, but it is in ours." Miranda was charged with rape, and his confession was admitted as evidence against him, but he had not been informed of his constitutional rights to remain silent and to have legal counsel. The Court reversed the conviction on the ground that he should have been so informed. Now the police must inform suspects of their right to counsel and their right to remain silent.

The Supreme Court's *Gault* decision (1967) also narrowed the area of discretion in the criminal justice process. Traditionally, the juvenile court has operated according to the adjustment principle. The basic idea is that juvenile court officials should look to the needs of the child rather than to his delinquent conduct. Elements of guilt, responsibility, criminal intent, and punishment are, theoretically, not considered. The assumption is that the results of contact with a juvenile court are beneficial, not harmful or punitive, and that, consequently, precise descriptions of prohibited acts are not necessary. In practice, of course, juvenile courts label delinquents as junior criminals and deprive them of their liberty, as do criminal courts.

The *Gault* decision, noting the difference between theory and practice, ruled that juvenile courts must grant to children many of the procedural protections required in criminal trials by the Bill of Rights. It specified that the child and his parent must be given notice in writing of the specific charges that must be met at the juvenile court hearing; that the child and his parent must be notified of the child's right to be represented by counsel; that a lawyer must be appointed if the parents cannot afford one; that children and their parents must be advised of the child's privilege against self-incrimination, such as the right to remain silent rather than be a witness against himself; that an admission or confession obtained from a child without the presence of counsel must be given the greatest scrutiny in order to insure reliability; and that, in the absence of a valid confession, confrontation and sworn testimony by witnesses available for cross-examination are essential for a finding of "delinquency."

The extension of these rights, long available to adults, would seem to require overnight transformation of juvenile court procedures. But a 1968 study of hearings in three urban juvenile courts indicated that the Supreme Court's directives were being avoided (*Law and Society Review,* 1969). In those hearings in which children were charged with delinquency, were subject to commitment to an institution, and were not represented by an attorney, the three courts were not systematically applying the principles of the Supreme Court's decision. The investigators concluded: "Despite the Supreme Court's concern for protecting youths in jeopardy of losing their liberty, juveniles were at the time of this study and presumably still are remanded to penocustodial institutions without being afforded their constitutional rights."

In light of the discretion that is essential to seeing that punishments are justly administered, this conclusion is not surprising. We have seen that criminal justice workers—from policemen to parole agents—often modify the "law on the books" by mitigating prescribed penalties. Since discretionary judgments are thus used informally to soften the harsh effects of criminal statutes, it is not surprising to find that they also are used informally to deprive suspects and defendants of their constitutional rights. The discretion granted for the achievement of good ends may also produce bad results. This paradox has in recent years been discussed by at least a dozen legal scholars, almost always in connection with analyses of so-called "plea bargaining" in the criminal courts.

Except in very serious cases, such as those involving capital offenses, a plea of guilty makes a trial unnecessary in the American courts. If the defendant pleads not guilty he is entitled to a jury trial, but he can waive this right and stand trial before a judge. Recent statistics show, however, that jury and court trials play a very small part in criminal justice processes. While there is variation from state to state, about 85 to 90 per cent of all persons convicted in American courts are now convicted on pleas of guilty.

Many of the guilty pleas are pleas to offenses calling for lighter penalties than the one originally charged. A defendant charged with grand larceny may be allowed to plead guilty to petty larceny; a man charged with theft of an automobile may plead guilty to tampering with the automobile or to theft of a tire; a person charged with murder may be permitted to plead guilty to manslaughter, and so on. Because a plea of guilty saves the state the expense of a trial, and for other reasons, the prosecutor may bargain by offering to reduce the original charge to the lesser offense. A plea of guilty to a lesser offense satisfies the prosecutor, for he has an immense burden of work and cannot go to trial on all cases. Further, he may know that a defendant committed an offense but question his ability to prove it beyond a reasonable doubt. He usually is anxious to bargain for a guilty plea in cases in which proof would be difficult. The defendant and the defense attorney are often satisfied by the plea of guilty to a lesser offense because the pleading enables the defendant to escape a severe penalty which might have been inflicted had he gone to trial on the original charge. Even if the defendant is guilty, he has a legal and moral right to plead not guilty if he believes the state cannot prove its case against him. By pleading guilty to a lesser offense he eliminates the risk of being wrong in that belief.

In a second general form of plea bargaining, the defendant enters a plea of guilty to the offense charged, but he does so in exchange for the prosecutor's promise of probation or a lighter sentence. It is the prosecutor's privilege to recommend a light or a heavy sentence to the judge. While the judge need not follow the recommendation, judges usually go along with agreements made between the defendant and the prosecutor, since considerable saving to the state is effected by a guilty plea.

The principal danger of plea bargaining, the National Crime Commission concluded in 1967, "lies in the fact that it is so informal and invisible that it gives rise to fears that it does not operate fairly or that it does not accurately identify those who should be prosecuted and what disposition should be made in their cases." Viewed in its best light, however, plea bargaining is part of the system for adjusting the general criminal law rules to the circumstances of specific offenses and the characteristics of individual offenders. Much so-called "plea bargaining," in fact, has very little to do with either pleas or bargaining. The matter is not merely one of explicitly negotiating a guilty plea in exchange for a reduced charge or a sentencing concession. Instead, it is one of implementing the adjustment principle discussed earlier. Tacit negotiations and understandings based on the prosecutor's sense of justice play as great a part in determining the outcome of criminal cases as does explicit bargaining.

Accepting or making a plea to a lesser offense, or exchanging a light sentence for a guilty plea, is not necessarily inimical to justice. Often the arrangement enables court personnel to modify the law informally so that it best meets the needs of an individual offender. For example, a severe sentence for robbery can be mitigated by the prosecutor confronted with the case of a boy who took a basketball away from the children on a playground. He only has to reduce the charge to, say, malicious mischief. Moreover, there are practical advantages in disposing of most cases without trial. The results are more prompt and certain, and pleas of guilty conserve resources for the most important cases.

In sum, one aspect common to the decisions of criminal justice agencies is their discretionary character. Important decisions made by the police, courts, and correctional agencies are not necessarily made in the formal settings and processes established by law. Instead, each of the agencies operates on the expectation that informal adjustments will occur. Discretionary decisions begin as the police encounter suspects in the field. They extend through the administrative and judicial actions occurring at each subsequent stage in the official history of a criminal case—including charge, trial, conviction, sentence, probation, imprisonment, discharge from prison, and parole. Conviction and punishment may, but need not, follow from official notice that a person has committed a crime. Conviction for crimes of different seriousness, and different punishments for the same crime, are at the core of the entire process.

The disparity between "law-enforcement" expectations and practices in the criminal justice system is becoming a source of both public and legal concern. The realities of our discretionary system of justice present us with the challenge of reshaping the whole system and its goals. Proposals for eliminating discretion at one stage or the other—be it at the arrest stage or the guilty plea stage or the paroling stage—do not seriously face the fact that justice will not be done if the "law on the books" is administered routinely, without the human judgments necessary to making the law come alive.

Part 1

THE CRIME PROBLEM

RECENT INCREASES in the sale of hand guns, watchdogs, burglar-proof locks, and other protective devices suggest that Americans' fear of crime is now greater than it has been at any other time during the current century. Everyone seems to have a cousin or an acquaintance who was mugged in Central Park or on the streets of Washington, D.C. Yet the increased level of fear may well be without a solid foundation. In the first article in this section, Fred J. Cook, a free-lance writer specializing in crime and politics, gives numerous examples of the relative safety of contemporary American streets as compared with the violence of times past. In 1967, President Johnson's Commission on Law Enforcement and Administration of Justice also pointed out that the American public never has been as safe from violent crime as it is at present.

Mr. Cook's basic concern is with the reliability of crime statistics. Everyone agrees that there is a difference between the amount of crime committed and the amount of crime tabulated in any set of crime figures. Many crimes are not reported to the police. Of those reported, many are not recorded. And of those recorded, many are not summarized in statistical tables. Any increase in the crime rate, then, can occur either because more crimes are being committed or because more crimes are being recorded and tabulated. The statistical problem is to determine whether an apparent increase or decrease in the crime rate is a real change, reflecting changes in the incidence of criminal behavior.

Crime statistics are probably the most difficult of all social statistics. In the first place, they are subject to political manipulations. A police chief, mayor, governor, or even a President is likely to be accused of neglect, incompetence, or corruption if the crime rate goes up during his term in office. Consequently, office holders are almost always interested in keeping the crime rate low, while office seekers are interested in demonstrating that the rate is high. When these demonstrations cannot be made objectively, they sometimes are accomplished statistically. In order to "prove" that crime rates are indeed much lower or higher than they appear to be, competing politicians develop their own sets of figures.

But crime statistics also are affected by honest variations in recording practices. The range of police discretion is so great that a "crime wave" can be created merely by a change in a police department's arresting and booking policies. A reasonable guess is that the general crime rate of a large city like Los Angeles, New York, or Chicago can overnight be made to go up or down by about 40 per cent—by honest shifts of the bases for statistical recording. Further, variations in official definitions of statistical "crimes" greatly affect the apparent incidence of those crimes. For example, some police departments mark up an automobile theft as soon as they receive a report that a car has been stolen. Other police departments wait twenty-four hours before recording the car as stolen—cars recovered during the waiting period are not recorded as automobile thefts. Since most stolen cars are recovered within a few hours, a shift from one statistical system to the other can alter the automobile theft rate by as much as 75 per cent.

Despite such flaws in crime statistics, it seems reasonable to assume, as Mr. Cook does, that crime is on the rise in the United States and other industrialized nations. In the years since World War II, it appears that "the crime problem" has most seriously touched the most urbanized, industrialized, and affluent societies rather than the developing ones. Marshall B. Clinard, a sociologist-criminologist at the University of Wisconsin, attempts to account for this difference. Why should the crime rate be rising faster among the "privileged" than among the "underprivileged"? Mr. Clinard suggests that as the individualism accompanying increased urbanization and mobility has increased in industrialized nations like the United States, old-fashioned morality has broken down. Years ago Thorstein Veblen, the distinguished economist, developed a theory similar to Clinard's. He argued that industrialized countries have high crime rates because the economic individualism of the businessmen operating in such societies is in some ways similar to the individualism of the criminal who takes what he wants. Crime rates are bound to rise when increasing numbers of urban dwellers consider themselves obligated to obey only those laws they "believe in."

Some observers are convinced that high American crime rates can be checked by police power—without altering economic, political, and social conditions and attitudes. Consistently, it has become commonplace to attribute high crime rates to inadequate defensive and repressive measures. During the last decade, especially, the dominance of this view has led to tremendous increases in appropriations for police equipment, ranging from airplanes, helicopters, and tanks to MACE, two-way radios, and plastic handcuffs. Much of the money has come from the federal government.

The notion that crime is caused by inadequate defenses also is reflected in attacks on the United States Supreme Court. In the Introduction, I reviewed most of the recent "due process" decisions of the Court, and these decisions will be discussed again in Part 2. The issue here is whether the apparent rise in the American crime rate can properly be attributed to the Court's emphasis on due process of law. By following the deterrence argument, discussed in the Introduction, many writers have concluded that if the police were just allowed to get tough with criminals, the crime rate would go down. The article by Yale Kamisar, professor of constitutional law and criminal law at the University of Michigan, treats this issue statistically.

Rather than arguing that recent Supreme Court decisions have or have not "handcuffed" the police, Professor Kamisar takes it for granted that the police have been "handcuffed." He then goes on to ask the basic statistical question: Is the crime rate really higher now, when the police are using a due process model of criminal justice procedures, than it was in the "good old days" when they were permitted to use, to a greater extent than at present, a crime control model? His answer to this question is an emphatic "No." Long before the current controversial Supreme Court decisions, critics were attributing crime to official leniency and official respect for individual freedoms.

While most members of democratic societies do not want their police to repress crime at the cost of suppressing individual liberty, it is clear that no modern, urbanized society can function without police. During the Nazi occupation of Denmark during World War II, the Copenhagen police department was dissolved, thus setting up the conditions of a natural experiment dealing with the question, "Will crime increase in a community if the police withdraw completely?" The Danish experience suggested an affirmative answer. During the seven months Copenhagen was without police, its general crime rate increased dramatically. But the rates for personal crimes like rape, assault, and murder did not increase—suggesting that such crimes occur rather independently of the formal mechanisms of social control. In 1969, Gerald Clark, editor of the *Montreal Star,* observed the results of a similar natural experiment when the Montreal police department suddenly went out on a one-day strike. His report suggests that the effects on the crime rate were similar to those which had occurred in Copenhagen twenty-five years earlier. There were no reported rape cases, but robberies increased dramatically, looting was common, and old grudges were settled. Clearly, the centralized power of the state must be used to set limits on individual actions. The enduring problem is that of determining just how far the restrictive power should extend.

There's Always a Crime Wave

by Fred J. Cook

ALL PUBLIC pulse-taking these days shows that average Americans—and this applies to residents of ghetto areas as well as to the more affluent, living in the suburbs—want better guarantees for personal safety and protection of property. They are wrought up by the menace of "crime." But just what do they mean by the word? There are, of course, all kinds of crime. There is organized crime, a colossal, multi-billion-dollar-a-year conspiracy that has invaded almost every stratum of American life but seems virtually ignored in the present preoccupation with the kinds of everyday crime that most directly affect the average citizen.

The man in the street today seems most concerned with ghetto riots, the violence, the burning and looting, and with the robberies and muggings that threaten his personal safety on the streets, in the subways, in the hallways of apartment houses. To the public mind, it all seems connected; it's all "crime." The reality, of course, is not so simple.

The politicians of the day, responding to this mood sometimes in outright demagoguery, sometimes in genuine concern, are making law and order the battle cry of the 1968 Presidential campaign.

The Republican candidate, Richard M. Nixon, touched it all off in his acceptance speech at Miami, charging that "some of our courts in their decisions have gone too far in weakening the peace forces as against the criminal forces." He added that, "if we are to restore order and respect for law in this country, there's one place we're going to begin: we're going to have a new Attorney General of the United States of America. . . ."

Vice President Hubert H. Humphrey, the Democratic nominee, responded by promising to halt "rioting, burning, sniping, mugging, traffic in narcotics and disregard for law." But he argued that law enforcement must proceed hand in hand with justice and held that "the answer lies in reasoned effective action by the authorities, not in attacks on our courts, our laws or our Attorney General."

Former Alabama Gov. George C. Wallace, the odd man out of this campaign, was the real rabble rouser on the law and order issue. The United States Supreme Court was his *bête noire,* and his solution was simple: free the police of all restraint. The pat Wallace speech, repeated everywhere he goes, contains a passage that usually brings down the house. It goes like this: "If you walk out of this hotel tonight and someone knocks you on the head, *he'll* be out of jail before *you're* out of the hospital, and on Monday morning they'll try the *police*man instead of the criminal. . . . That's right, we gonna have a *police* state for folks who burn the cities down. They aren't gonna burn any more cities."

Even to begin to understand what the shouting is all about, one must come to grips first with the basic reality of the crime situation as it exists today. To the fundamental question (Just how bad is it?), the answer is paradoxical to a considerable degree. Experts agree that crime today is a major problem, that it is bad and is getting worse—and yet it is perhaps no worse than it has been in some unruly eras in our past, and much of the public agitation about it results from an exaggerated idea of the degree of menace.

The President's Commission on Law Enforcement and Administration of Justice, in its report "The Challenge of Crime in a Free Society," tried last year to put the problem and some of the irrational fears about it into clear perspective. Taking a broad historical view, it found little justification for the widespread popular belief that these are the worst of times. It wrote:

"A hundred years ago contemporary accounts of San Francisco told of extensive areas where 'no decent man was in safety to walk the street after dark; while at all hours, both night and day, his property was jeopardized by incendiarism and burglary.' Teen-age gangs gave rise to the word 'hoodlum'; while in one central New York City area, near Broadway, the police entered 'only in pairs, and never unarmed.' A noted chronicler of the period declared that 'municipal law is a failure . . . we must soon fall back on the law of self preservation.' 'Alarming' increases in robbery and violent crimes were reported throughout the country prior to the Revolution. And in 1910 one author declared that 'crime, especially in its more violent forms, and among the young is increasing steadily and is threatening to bankrupt the nation.' "

The commission emphasized that there is an ebb and flow in the tide of crime much like the ebb and flow of the sea. Its study of crime statistics showed that, in the number of offenses per 100,000 population, the year 1933 in some respects rivaled our own. "The willful homicide rate has *decreased* somewhat to about 70 per cent of its high in 1933, while robbery has fluctuated from a high in 1933 and a low during World War II to a point where it is now about 20 per cent above the beginning of the postwar era," the commission wrote. "The over-all rate for violent crimes, primarily due to the increased rate for aggravated assault, now stands at its highest point, well above what it has been throughout most of the period."

Turning from the past to an analysis of the present, the commission cited Federal Bureau of Investigation statistics and other studies to show that "about 70 per cent of all willful killings, nearly two-thirds of all aggravated assaults and a high percentage of forcible rapes are committed by family members, friends, or other persons previously known to their victims." The chance that the average American will suffer from a crime of violence is still relatively minimal. Robert M. Cipes, a consultant to the commission, put it this way in his recent book, "The Crime War": "The risk of death by murder is one out of 20,000, about the same as the risk of drowning. The chances of being killed in an accidental fall are twice as great as those of being murdered, and the chances of being killed in a car accident more than four times greater!"

In view of such facts, one may well wonder how the American people as a whole have become possessed by the idea that we are faced with a veritable crime crisis. Most experts agree that much of this mood stems from the riots in recent years; the violence, the burning and looting excited fears that we were verging on anarchy. These fears have been fed by the indisputable fact that many categories of crime have been increasing steadily from year to year—a rise that, on its face, seems shocking and sensational. It is only when one examines the basis for such statistics and tries to relate the circumstances of today to those of troubled eras of the past that one becomes aware of the built-in delusions in many alarming headlines.

The one accepted crime barometer for the nation is the Uniform Crime Report of the F.B.I. But the F.B.I. started to accumulate such data only in 1930, and it has steadily expanded the number of police departments reporting and the comprehensiveness of their reports. This means, as the President's crime commission found, that a lot more crime is being *reported* today, but it does not mean that more crime in the same proportion is being *committed*. The commission found that there has always been—and there is still today—a vast reservoir of unreported crime. The fact that much more of this previously hidden crime is being reported today inflates crime statistics and distorts the comparative averages.

There are at least two major causes for such distortion. In the past, in many cities, the official attitude was that ghetto crimes did not matter much; either they were not reported at all, or only sketchily reported, unless all hell broke loose. Yet it is in precisely these areas, all studies show, that crime rates soar to their highest peaks, and so today, when ghetto crime is being much more fully recorded, it is inevitable that over-all statistics reflect much more crime.

A second major distortion has resulted from the practice of some police departments in the past of deliberately understating the volume of crime in their jurisdictions, so as to make themselves look good, to cultivate the public impression that they have crime under control.

In one city, the President's commission found a secret "file 13" containing a catalogue of citizens' complaints that were not included in the official crime record. At one time, in Philadelphia, a single precinct actually had 5,000 more complaints than it officially recorded.

The F.B.I., when it becomes aware of such practices, cracks down on offending departments by refusing to publish their statistics. When this happens, reporting techniques are usually changed—and the official crime index in the particular city rises in an almost perpendicular line.

In 1949, the F.B.I. refused to accept New York Police Department statistics because it no longer believed them. The department changed its procedures, and the next year it showed a jump of 400 per cent in the number of robberies reported, and an incredible 1,300 per cent rise in the number of burglaries. But then, in the late fifties, the department again adopted a "look good, don't rock the boat" policy and began watering down the number of officially reported crimes.

"The unwritten law was," one high department official says, "that you were supposed to make things look good. You weren't supposed to report all the crime that actually took place in your precinct—and, if you did, it could be your neck. I know captains who actually lost their commands because they turned in honest crime reports."

The Lindsay administration changed all this and insisted on truth, no matter how much it hurt. The result of this change in official policy was dramatic. Reported robberies leaped from between 7,000 and 8,000 a year to about 23,000, burglaries from 40,000 to 120,000. Anyone who was not aware of the figure juggling that had previously taken place had to assume that the city was confronted with an unprecedented crime crisis.

The high public fever over the crime issue may be traced, in part, to such distortions and exaggerations. This does not mean that crime is not a serious problem. It is. It is on the rise in this country—and also, as the President's commission found, in nearly every highly industrialized society of Western Europe. "Since 1955," the commission wrote, "property crime rates have increased more than 200 per cent in West Germany, the Netherlands, Sweden and Finland, and over 100 per cent in France, England and Wales, Italy and Norway."

What the commission found was that an industrialized, affluent society increases the incentives for crime. There is the urbanized life in which everyone is a stranger to everyone else—and so crime may be committed with less fear of detection, the unknown criminal melting into the anonymous crowd. There is the tempting spate of products that an affluent society produces, goods that clutter the shelves of the supermarkets and discount stores, a lure to the shoplifter—and shoplifting has become one of our fastest growing crimes. There is the ever-crying need for money and more money to enjoy the bounties of the affluent society—and so white-collar thefts, the looting of a store's inventoried stock or embezzlements from the till, have become another of our fastest growing crimes. Threaded through such misdeeds is a Robin Hood–like rationale—that it is not so great a sin for the little fellow to steal from the great, big, impersonal —and wealthy—corporation. Or, as the crime commission put it: "Restraints on conduct that were effective in a more personal and rural society do not seem as effective in an impersonal society of large organizations."

This urbanization, this affluence, this impersonalized bigness help push the crime rate upward, and they have another partner: youth. All crime studies show that most crime is committed by persons in the young age groups; the United States is now a nation in which, by 1970, half the population will be 27 or younger. Adding this element of youth to all the other factors, the President's crime commission forecast that there would probably be a continuing rise in crime rates for some years to come.

The accuracy of this prediction has now been underlined by the latest F.B.I. and city police department reports. The annual F.B.I. Uniform Crime Report, issued Aug. 26, showed a 16 per cent rise in violent crimes in 1967 over 1966, and city police department figures, compiled now on a similar basis for both years, reflected a comparable increase. Another police department computation showed that murders in the city rose in the first six months of 1968 from 346 to 436, a jump of 26 per cent.

"In recent years," says Vincent O'Leary, now a professor at the new Graduate School of Criminal Justice in Albany and until recently director of research and special services for the National Council on Crime and Delinquency, "there has been a real upsurge in ghetto crime. Now, the riots came out of the same whirlpool—out of the same poverty-stricken, ghetto areas —but, to me, the two are quite different things. The motivations, I feel sure, are not the same at all. There is this tendency today to lump all kinds of crime together—just to denounce 'crime,' as if it was all the same thing—and then to seek one certain, simple, quick solution. To me the most dangerous thing in the whole situation is this simplistic idea."

The individual mugger, burglar or sneak thief, O'Leary points out, takes to crime as the only means available to him to get his "piece of the system." Riots, on the other hand, he sees as a form of social protest. "Here, there is a suggestion of a desire to overthrow or change the whole system," he says. "This is the difference. And we've got to do something quick about this one, about this issue of collective behavior. We've got to get that one fast. We've got to wet down the fever."

The tragedy, as O'Leary and many other experts see it, is that the public's unrealistic vision of one monolithic "crime menace" leads most easily to cries for harsher law enforcement, for more sweeping and rigid anticrime measures, rather than to the broader and slower programs that might possibly get at some of the root causes—the kind of programs advocated in the much-praised but virtually ignored Kerner report.

O'Leary is an expert in the corrections-prison field, and after the wave of prison riots in the fifties, he was one of the major experts testifying before Congressional committees. From the work of years in trying to rehabilitate individual criminals, he has become convinced that, if you are to work a great reformation in the man, you must work equally great changes in the society of which he is a part.

"We used to have the idea in corrections," he says, "that you could deal with the individual; you sat down with him in prison, you tried to get his confidence, you tried to change him and then send him out. But we have learned that you don't get very far with that system. I have talked to these guys. I know. Oh, they'll play the game with you, they'll con you along—but change them? Not very often.

"What we have discovered is that there are definite subcultures in our society in which violence exists, in which violence is a way of life. You can talk to men who come out of such subcultures, and you can almost see them thinking, 'This is the way to go, man. This is the way it is. What you trying to do? Change me? What do you think I am—crazy?'

"If you are really going to change things, you are going to have to change, not just the man, but the whole of that violent subculture of which he is a part. You know Robert Kennedy talked about bringing business into the ghettos and rebuilding, remaking the ghettos; Gene McCarthy talked about moving the ghetto residents out into the countryside and establishing jobs and homes for them there. I don't know which is the better method, but I'm convinced that you are going to have to get at that subculture; you have to break it up and change it."

This brings us back to the imperatives set forth in the Kerner commission's report on urban riots—to the need for a massive attack on the intertwined problems of poverty and race, the ghetto and crime. Even if the nation moved in this direction, which it has shown little disposition to do, the struggle is one for the years, not for the days and months immediately ahead; and an American public, in typically impatient American mood when once aroused, seems to be demanding action now. What about the prospects for "action now"? Realistically, what can be done?

One high-ranking Federal law enforcement official argues that a vast increase in the army of policemen on city streets would help. "The best thing that has happened in Washington recently was the assignment of 1,000 extra policemen to street patrols," he says. Washington is also making use of a computerized crime-fighting system. All information about crimes, the time and place of their occurrence, is fed into a computer which sifts out the mass of data and pinpoints the major trouble spots and the times at which crimes are most likely to be committed. Police are then able to concentrate on these areas. This system, plus the presence of that extra 1,000 patrolmen on the streets, is having an effect in Washington, the official believes. "There is no deterrent like that of the cop in uniform visible on the street corner," he says. "This is such a simplistic idea that it is often overlooked."

Other experts are less optimistic. Prof. Henry S. Ruth Jr., of the University of Pennsylvania Law School, who served as deputy director of the President's crime commission, doubts that even a doubling of present police forces would produce the kind of quick solution Americans want. "Not enough research has been done on this to show its value," he says. "There have been a few experiments in specific areas of our cities, like more patrolmen on the New York subway system, for instance, and in some cases crime in those areas has dropped. But what has happened in the rest of the city? Have criminals just moved their activities somewhere else? [Professor Ruth was speaking *before* the latest release of Police Department crime figures, showing an over-all increase in crime.] The commission's crime report makes one important point in this regard, and that is that you can't make any correlation between the number of policemen per 100,000 population and the incidence of crime. Washington, D.C., for example, is one of the most heavily policed cities—and yet it has one of the highest crime rates.

"It is foolish to talk about doubling policemen and catching more criminals under the present system—that is, unless you think the situation is so bad that you are just going to stick people away behind bars for 30 years. And that is a thing we are not prepared to accept."

Professor Ruth, who probably has as comprehensive a view

of the problem as anyone as a result of his crime commission role, says frankly: "I don't see anything anyone can do to reduce crime in a year or two." There are, as he sees it, two major roadblocks to really effective action.

"First," he says, "our criminal justice system has received too little attention in planning and resources, and so it is unable to cope realistically with the problem; and, second, the public refuses to take any responsibility to do anything about it."

Expanding on the second point, Professor Ruth gives these illustrations:

"The businessman, if you ask him to hire a one-time offender, to give an ex-con a chance, refuses to have anything to do with him. I don't see how you can scream about crime and then say, 'I won't hire any man who has been in prison.' If a first-offender comes out of prison and can't get a job, he has only one alternative: to go back to crime. He has to live.

"Or, take another situation, try to get a small correctional institution established in a rural-suburban area maybe 10 or 15 miles away out in the country; at once, the public is up in arms, they don't want it. Yet, unless you can do something along these lines, you aren't going to make much progress. In the same way, try to hire more policemen and give them the kind of salaries that will attract high-caliber men—and the public howls about increased taxes."

Unrealism haunts the whole issue, as Professor Ruth and many other experts see it. There is unrealism in the public frenzy about the crime menace—"The actual fear is exaggerated among people who have the least cause to worry about it," Professor Ruth says. "The most indignant letters come from people who live in the suburbs and rural areas, but all statistics show that people who live in the central cities are the ones who are most in danger." There is unrealism in the expectations now being aroused by campaign oratory that something swift and sure can be done; unrealism concerning the public's own role and the price it will have to pay to get what it wants, and, finally, unrealism concerning the whole complicated system of American criminal justice.

There is widespread agreement among the experts that the

criminal justice system itself is archaic, inept and badly in need of top to bottom overhaul. The nation spends between $4- to $5-billion annually on its criminal justice system—an all-inclusive term that embraces police, corrections, courts and prisons. It is, most experts agree, a splintered and chaotic system that often serves to perpetuate the very evils it is supposed to correct.

Eliot Lumbard, who served this year as chief counsel to a New Jersey legislative committee investigating the state's criminal justice system, puts the issue in this perspective: "The structure of our criminal justice system dates back to the 17th and 18th centuries. Crime was then a neighborhood problem. Everybody in small towns knew everybody else. People often prosecuted their own cases. Today that same system continues in an entirely different world—the world of modern, urban America where everyone is a stranger to everyone else. The basic American assumption is that the system, if not perfect, is at least pretty good simply because it is ours; but, in fact, it may be inefficient and inept and unable to cope with current problems."

Lumbard cites the fantastic splintering of police jurisdictions. He points out that Westchester County, for example, has some 46 separate police departments; in New Jersey, the state inquiry showed, there are 430 police chiefs and only 12,000 policemen. "Now, if you subtract the big-city forces like those in Newark, Jersey City and Camden from this total, you find you have a situation in the rest of the state where you have a lot of chiefs and virtually no Indians," Lumbard remarks. "It's a ridiculous situation."

The evils that begin with splintered police forces spread throughout the system. The lower courts—the night courts, the so-called "people's courts," those most intimately and directly involved with crime the instant an arrest is made—are inundated by a tidal wave of prisoners held for every imaginable kind of offense. Drunkards and derelicts are there in staggering numbers. So are narcotics users. Prostitutes. Bookies and numbers' runners. Mafia gangsters. Thugs and holdup men. All are dumped in an indiscriminate welter on the heads of the lower court magistrates. Some cases involve health and psychological problems, not crime, and never should come into court as criminal cases in the opinion of most experts; others involve all kinds and degrees of potential social menace. But how is one to sort these out from the welter? The answer is that one doesn't.

"To deal sensibly with crime," Lumbard says, "you have to break it down into manageable terms and deal with individual units. You can't use the same techniques in dealing with all of these problems. Specific programs must be addressed to specific problems. And one of our great problems today is that our present system of law enforcement doesn't reflect any such refinement."

The result is a hurried, haphazard processing of the always cluttered, always overflowing criminal calendar. Richard H. Kuh, who spent 12 years as an assistant district attorney in the office of District Attorney Frank S. Hogan, has made a special study of the manner in which potentially dangerous criminals are sped through the revolving doors of the lower courts, copping pleas to offenses far less serious than those they had committed, receiving slap-on-the-wrist penalties that are, in effect, licenses to go out and sin some more.

"The prosecutors and the courts are both to blame," Kuh says. "Basically, their obsession is that the only way to clear the calendar is to give away the courthouse."

In an article he wrote for the Bar Bulletin of the New York Bar Association, Kuh pointed out that, in New York County, "only about 3 per cent or less of the felony indictments go through to a jury verdict annually." The rest get off by copping a plea to a far less serious offense. Kuh argues that this "crime-plea gap" fosters crime by letting really dangerous criminals loose on society again and again. In his article, he cited several cases illustrative of the point. Here is one of them:

"William Townes, one April half-a-dozen years ago, at knife-point forced a woman he accosted in her building hallway to admit him to her apartment. Once there, he forced her to undress, speeding the process by cutting part of her clothing from her body. When, at the moment he ordered her into the bedroom, footsteps were heard, he snatched the watch from her wrist and fled. The victim went to phone from a neighbor's apartment—and Townes, during her absence, re-entered her apartment. She screamed on returning and he fled waving a knife—into the arms of waiting police.

"His prior record included 19 arrests over a 20-year period, showed an appreciable history of addiction, and embraced at least three prior reduced felonies. Charged with robbery in the first degree and cognate crimes (and so subject to imprisonment for a minimum of 10 years and a maximum of 30), he, too, was permitted to plead guilty to attempted grand larceny in the second degree, as a first felony offender; the maximum term under that plea was two and a half years in state's prison. His sentence, in fact, was one of 15 months to two and a half years, making him eligible for release in about 10 months, less credit for time served while awaiting disposition of the charges."

Cases like this, endlessly repeated, cause Vincent O'Leary to make this summation: "The most immediate and important problem is our system of criminal justice. We've got to get that under immediate control. The lower courts are where the action is, and they are the poorest financed and have, on the whole, the least competent judges. Some 40 per cent of the people who come before them are drunks who don't belong in the system in the first place; there are an incredible number of pot and kettle disputes. The first thing we have to do is to unclog these courts; we must build up our other resources and get out of the system the people who don't belong there. Then we must have trials damn fast. If a man is held on a serious charge, try him quickly, give him the sentence he deserves—and then try to work with him. But all of this is what we are not doing today."

How far we are from doing it, ironically enough, is illustrated by a case involving one of O'Leary's own co-workers in the National Council on Crime and Delinquency. Miss Sally Niklas, who is employed in the council's public relations office, went home from work to her apartment at 162 West 85th Street one day last November. She had some packages in her arms, and she paused in the vestibule to pick up her mail. She sorted quickly through it, standing there, and as she did, she heard the hall door open behind her. Fumbling with her packages, she got out her key and was trying to unlock her apartment door when a man behind her said:

"Here, let me help you."

"Oh, thank you," Sally said.

Then she became aware that the man, instead of helping her, was trying to snatch her pocketbook.

"I forgot everything they tell us here," she says. "You know, don't fight; let him have your pocketbook and your money. Well, I fought. He slammed me up against the wall and wrenched the pocketbook from my hand. It fell open and the wallet dropped out. I made a last grab at him as he ran and tore out a piece of his coat."

Sally reported the incident to the police, and in just a few minutes two cops called at her door. They already had the suspect. They had been cruising in their prowl car when they saw him running down the street, a piece missing out of his flapping coat. "I have the missing piece," Sally told them—and a fit on the coat of the suspect showed she did.

In the struggle with the robber, Sally had had her head bruised when she was banged against the wall, and a small bone in her right hand had been fractured, so that she had to wear a cast for six weeks. Her assailant was a young Puerto Rican. He had been arrested twice before on similar charges, but each time the complainants had been persuaded to drop the case and he had gone free. The youth's mother and sister were both working, and so they raised the money to hire a lawyer and get the youth out on bail. Let Sally tell the rest of the story.

"At first," she says, "they tried to get me to drop the charges as the other complainants had. His sister tried to talk to me, and then his lawyer tried to give me the argument that he was just a young boy, you know; he'd never been in trouble; he deserved a chance. I asked the lawyer what about the two previous charges, and that ended that; he didn't raise that issue again.

"But in all the months since this happened, the case has gotten nowhere. I have been in court 11 times—and it hasn't even come up yet. First, the lawyer needed time to prepare his case. Then, the boy was sick. Then, the lawyer was sick. Then, the lawyer still needed more time, after six months, to prepare his case. The judges seem to take little interest; each time it's a different judge, each one just passes it along.

"In the meantime, the police tell me, the youth had been arrested on two other charges. The last time, it was for stealing a grand piano. He had repainted it, apparently figuring this would disguise it the way you would a stolen car, and the police spotted him, all alone, pushing his camouflaged piano down the middle of the sidewalk. They don't think he was a narcotics addict at the time he tried to rob me, but they think he is now; they've noticed needle marks on his arms.

"Still the case hasn't come up. One time, I wasted a whole day in court, and the case wasn't even called: the calendar was too cluttered. If it wasn't that I work here and it's really almost a part of the job, I would have given up long ago and dropped the charges the way the other complainants did. I'm ready to do my patriotic duty, I want to, but how much are you supposed to take? You go to court, you waste a whole day, or most of it—and nothing happens. Over and over again. After a time, you begin to lose faith in the system."

Corruption Runs Far Deeper Than Politics

by Marshall B. Clinard

THERE IS SO much talk about corruption in all phases of our society that it is difficult to appraise what has been happening. We need some perspective. We must separate symptoms from ultimate causes. Political corruption, crime, immorality, athletic scandals, the current disorders of our society, cannot be diagnosed as independent, isolated phenomena. All are common consequences of a general social disruption in the ways we live and work and think together as human beings.

Are things today really as bad as they seem? Corruption in government, to take one example, is certainly no recent innovation—witness the scandals of the Grant Administration eighty years ago, or the railroad "Robber Barons," or Teapot Dome. It is not easy to draw a sound conclusion that government dishonesty is vastly worse today. Our Federal agencies operate in an urbanized and industrialized nation of 150,000,000 people as compared to the 40,000,000, for example, in Grant's time; there are now 2,000,000 Federal employes rather than 56,000. It is well to keep in mind that more people are handling larger public funds than ever before in our history. While the disclosures in Washington have shocked the country, the possibility remains that the actual rate of corruption in public service might not have increased nearly as much as people believe.

This great increase in the number of Government employes comes partly from our population growth but even more from extension of governmental services. Today there are many agencies of government dispensing huge sums of money through contracts, subsidies and loans, and constituting lucrative sources for favors by politicians and business men, which either did not exist or were relatively unimportant many years ago. Even the degree of influence on tax questions is fairly recent, for income taxes were never before as important a part of the Federal revenue structure.

In addition, any problem of this type, be it public graft or organized crime, becomes a "social" problem only when the people are aware that the condition exists. Awareness not only makes such things as illegal gambling, tax bribery or athletic fixes social problems, but arouses the public to correction of the evils. Modern press, radio and television, as well as the facilities at the disposal of contemporary Congressional committees, make the exposure of corruption much more likely than ever before.

The fact remains, nevertheless, that there is a present-day pattern in our society of dishonesty, illegal advantage, loss of integrity and moral indifference. It is unfortunate that the problem of corruption is so often identified exclusively with politics and politicians. Actually it has no such specific connection. The state of affairs is much more general and serious, for not only can politics and government be "corrupt" but also business, labor, the professions and even the general public.

Political corruption itself cannot be explained solely by the presence of certain corrupt officials or political machines in either major party. The belief that if we only "clean the rascals out" of selected spheres of American life we will have no more corruption is a false assumption. Although widely believed, the solution is never as simple as that.

Who is to blame? Lincoln Steffens asked himself this same question at the turn of the century. Originally, he says in his autobiography, he believed that "bad men" caused "bad government." But he found "politicians to be not bad men; they were pretty good fellows. They blamed the bad business men who, they said, bribed them." Steffens then went to see the "bad business men" and found they were not so bad either. The business men maintained it was the politicians who solicited bribes or campaign contributions. They said they did not approve of the system.

Dr. H. H. Wilson, a political scientist, in writing a recent book about political crimes, declares: "the record indicates that the political morality reflects, rather than shapes, the society in which it operates and that, more pertinently, it is naïve in the extreme to expect from politicians a far different ethical standard from that which prevails throughout the country. Indeed, were today's politicians to adopt such a standard they would almost certainly be rejected by the voters as idealists, dreamers, crackpots or visionaries."

What are some of the factors which lie behind what appears to be an increasing breakdown of ethics and integrity in our society? Chief among them has been the widespread, rapid development of urban ways of life which are changing our hitherto predominantly rural country. These urban ways include extensive physical and mental mobility, impersonality in relations with others, excessive individualism and materialism and pronounced differences over fundamental values.

To understand corruption one must recognize the role that our extensive mobility plays in breaking personal ties and producing value conflicts. During the period from 1947 to 1950 one out of five of the population changed residences. Earlier, between 1940 and 1947 some 70,000,000 persons, exclusive of the armed forces, settled in different homes or different parts of the country. This was approximately one-half the people of the United States.

Now mobility has many effects which are by no means beneficial. Close relations with relatives and neighbors are broken, so that one's family and personal reputation comes to have less importance. One is thrown into contact with large numbers of strangers who mean little personally to one. (This is particularly the case in Washington, as in many of our other large cities.) Finally, mobile individuals are often exposed to modes of conduct which might not have been acceptable to them in their former locality.

Extensive mobility and impersonality, therefore, have meant that contemporary individuals have increasingly tended to regard their own interests as paramount. Many persons today, some of whom have appeared before Congressional committees, do not think in terms of social objectives but rather personal success. To counteract such an emphasis on the "I" rather than the "We" there has been an increase in the enactment of formal laws.

It is only a step from individualism to the emphasis on materialism. The extent to which a society places the measure of success on an individualistic basis can be seen in the attitude, held by many, that a poor man financially, even if he possesses great personal integrity, is a failure. Material possessions become an important way of displaying one's position in society.

Thus men will steal, bribe and accept bribes to get additional wealth and the status that comes with it. The "fast buck," the "something for nothing" philosophy become pandemic. It is not surprising to find under such conditions that tax collectors have added to their social prestige by accepting considerable sums of money with which to purchase more expensive houses and automobiles, or that other Government officials have been willing to display their social position through that perennial symbol of what Veblen called "conspicuous consumption," the mink coat.

What does all this add up to? For one thing we have tended to lose agreement on desirable personal objectives and at the same time to be in conflict over the fundamental objectives in our society. An example of this is provided in the development of what might be called selective obedience to law. One does not obey *all* laws but only certain types of law, according to one's occupation, social class or the nature of the law.

Extensive bribery of politicians, public officials, sheriffs, police officers or others was found by the Kefauver Committee to be virtually the only way that widespread organized crime could really exist in a large number of our cities. The police who accept bribes from organized criminals to protect gambling, for example, believe this type of graft to be "clean ice" since the public wants it under any conditions.

And, in fact, while our citizens are likely to complain ardently about corruption in the Federal Government, they often permit such behavior to continue as a matter of course in their own back yards. This public apathy is recognized by our politicians and organized criminals and serves them, in part, as a rationalization for their illegal behavior.

Likewise, many politicians see nothing wrong with such graft since it is comparable to what is often offered them by various groups, from organized criminals to business men, or is easily solicited as campaign funds or other contributions in return for political favors.

Government officials operate in a situation where bribes and favors are offered, and where politicians, including Congressmen, exert influence for special interests. Influence is applied to Federal employes by business men through many of the manufacturers' representatives, the public relations, or "Washington relations," men, the 2,500 registered lobbyists, the expediters, the Five Percenters, the "fixers," or the "fellow who knows his way around."

Many business men claim that laws regulating the conduct of banking, pure foods, securities, taxes, labor practices, restraint of trade, misrepresentation in advertising, bribery and price and rationing controls are not nearly as binding on the individual as laws prohibiting burglary, robbery and other such laws in our society.

The public can well recall the extensive black market which existed in the United States during World War II. The Government found price and rationing violations in over 1,000,000 cases and imposed heavy sanctions in about 260,000 cases, most of them business concerns. Illegal profits ran into billions of dollars, and at least one in every fifteen business concerns was dealt with by Government action.

Some labor union leaders see no reason why they should obey laws prohibiting labor "racketeering" or laws affecting the conduct of labor relations and strikes if it is not to their advantage to obey the law.

Farmers have been known selectively to disobey the law, as in failure to pay proper income taxes, and in their intimidation of farm auctioneers or in dumping milk trucks to keep up the price of milk in the last depression.

What is central to all this selective disobedience to law by politicians, business men, Government employes, and others is the idea that such behavior may be illegal but it is not necessarily "immoral" or "criminal." Indeed, lawbreaking is often divided into two neat categories: the conventional crimes of burglary and larceny which are frequently punished by imprisonment, and those violations of law which have come to be known as "white collar crime."

Many people believe that the terms "crime" and "criminal" should be restricted to the more overt acts like burglary and robbery which not only fit the common stereotype but which they themselves would never do. Their illegal behavior might make them minor "lawbreakers" but certainly not "criminals." How a society can expect to control ordinary crime with one set of standards while allowing violations of law under another set of definitions is incomprehensible.

Recently Willie Sutton, the robber, was quoted as saying: "Judy Coplon is free to go as she pleases. Others, accused of defrauding the Government of hundreds of thousands of dollars, merely get a letter from a committee in Washington asking them to come in and talk it over. Maybe it's justice, but it's puzzling to a guy like me."

It is doubtful, however, if a broader definition on the part of the public as to what constitutes crime or more adequate enforcement of our laws is the entire answer to corruption. A democracy can only function on the assumption that laws are being supported by the citizenry who believe it is their duty to obey these laws and not the responsibility of government to force them to obey through fear of apprehension.

What is needed to deal effectively with corruption in our society is the devising of ways to encourage greater citizen participation in neighborhood, community and welfare activities.

We need to substitute more social for personal objectives and to find satisfactions in life that are not based so extensively on merely the possession of material goods. In this regard many educators have rightly criticized the excessive competition, rather than cooperation, that is encouraged in our contemporary school system with its emphasis on grades and other marks of individual distinction.

Ethical standards of what constitutes right conduct likewise must be promoted among politicians, Government officials, business men, the professions, labor and the public. The bribery of public officials can only be prevented by the development of higher standards in business, especially through trade associations. Organized crime cannot be controlled without public agreement on the immoral consequences of widespread gambling, particularly as it leads to the bribery of public officials and police officers. Graft cannot be controlled among Congressmen and Government employes without agreement on what is proper official conduct, the indoctrination of new members and employes into such a code of ethics and expulsion of those who deviate.

Last year Senator Douglas' Committee on Ethical Standards in Government set forth a series of proposals which bear directly on the issues. They include (1) mandatory disclosure of income, assets and certain business transactions by members of Congress, Government officials and leaders of political parties; (2) definitions of what constitutes improper behavior by officials, and (3) proposals for the punishment of delinquent officials (at present we often allow them simply to resign), and punishment of persons who bribe public officials.

More fundamental was Senator Douglas' proposal for a citizens' organization to work for better government at the national level and a commission on ethics in government which would have as its purpose the investigation of "the moral standards of official conduct of officers and employes of the United States; the effect thereon of the moral standards in business and political activity of persons and groups doing business with the Government or seeking to influence public policy and administration; and the moral standards generally prevailing in society which condition the conduct of public affairs or which affect the strength and unity of the Nation."

In the light of all the hue and cry about corruption in government it is unfortunate that these sound proposals by Senator Douglas' committee have attracted so little attention. The solution to corruption is not a hopeless task. We have only to remember that the British, a hundred years ago, were widely known for the extensive corruption in their Government as well as other areas of life—a reputation which, unfortunately, has been passed on to us.

When the Cops Were Not "Handcuffed"

by Yale Kamisar

ARE WE LOSING the war against crime? Is the public getting a fair break? Has the pendulum swung too far to the left? Do the victims of crime have some rights, too? Are the courts handcuffing the police?

If there were a hit parade for newspaper and magazine articles, speeches and panel discussions, these questions would rank high on the list. Not only are they being raised with increasing frequency, but they are being debated with growing fury.

Last year, probably the most famous police chief in the United States, William H. Parker of Los Angeles, protested that American police work has been "tragically weakened" through a progressive "judicial takeover." These are strong words, but Boston District Attorney Garrett Byrne, then president of the National Association of District Attorneys, easily topped the chief with the cry that the Supreme Court is "destroying the nation." (Despite this rant, Mr. Byrne has since been appointed to the President's newly established National Crime Commission, which has been assigned the task of making a systematic study of the entire spectrum of the problems of crime.)

From the *New York Times Magazine,* November 7, 1965, copyright © 1965 by the New York Times Company.

This year, Michael J. Murphy, former Police Commissioner of New York, is the leading contender for anti–Supreme Court honors. Mr. Murphy's pet line is: "We [the police] are forced to fight by Marquis of Queensberry rules while the criminals are permitted to gouge and bite."

Not infrequently, one who dares to defend the Court, or simply to explain what the Court is doing and why, is asked which side he is on: the side of law and order—or the side of the robber, the dope peddler and the rapist. Any defense of the Court is an attack on the police. And any attack on the police (to quote Mayor Sam Yorty of Los Angeles, and he is not alone) is an "attack on our American system," perhaps even part of "a world-wide campaign by Communists, Communist dupes and sympathizers."

Today, the course of the Court is clear. Once concerned with property rights much more than with human liberty, it is now, as Anthony Lewis wrote several years ago, "the keeper, not of the nation's property, but of its conscience." If that role constitutes lending aid and comfort to the criminal element, then the Court is guilty.

As Judge Walter Schaefer of the Illinois Supreme Court pointed out in his famous Holmes Lecture of a decade ago, however, many of those safeguards of criminal procedure which we now take for granted came surprisingly late. Whether a state had to appoint counsel for an indigent defendant was a question which did not confront the Court until 1932, and it held then that counsel had to be provided only when the defendant was facing possible death sentence. Whether the state could convict a defendant on the basis of a coerced confession was an issue first presented to the Court in 1936, and all the Court was asked to do then was ban confessions extracted by brutal beatings.

What was it like in 1910 and 1920 and 1930 when the effectuation and implementation of criminal procedural safeguards were pretty much left to the states themselves? What was it like in the days when, as Dean Erwin Griswold of the Harvard Law School recently pointed out, "some things that were rather clearly there" (in the Constitution) had not yet "been given the attention and effect which they should have if our Constitution is to be a truly meaningful document"? Or, if you prefer, what was it like in the "good old days" before the Supreme Court began to mess up things?

In 1910, Curtis Lindley, president of the California Bar Association, declared the need for an "adjustment" in our criminal procedures "to meet the expanding social necessity." "Many of the difficulties," he continued, "are due to an exaggerated respect for the individual. . . ." He proposed (1) that a suspect be interrogated by a magistrate and, if he refused to answer the inquiries, that the state be permitted to comment on this fact at the trial; and (2) that the requirement of a unanimous verdict of guilty be reduced to three-fourths, "except possibly in cases where infliction of the death penalty is involved." This, he pointed out, would still "give the defendant three-fourths of the show."

The following year, 1911, in a hard-hitting Atlantic Monthly article entitled "Coddling the Criminal," New York prosecutor Charles Nott charged that "the appalling amount of crime in the United States compared with other civilized countries is due to the fact that it is generally known that the punishment for crime in America is uncertain and far from severe." Where lay the fault? According to Nott, the two law-enforcement obstacles which had to be cleared were the protection against double jeopardy and the privilege against self-incrimination.

Eight years later, Hugo Pam, president of the Institute of Criminal Law and Criminology, also addressed himself to the "crime problem," one which had been greatly aggravated by "the advent of the automobile." As he viewed the situation in 1919, "the boldness of the crimes and the apparent helplessness of the law have embittered the public to the extent that any advance in treatment of criminals save punishment is looked upon with disfavor." Law-enforcement officials, he noted, "have repeatedly charged that in the main these serious crimes have been committed by people on probation or parole." It followed, of course, that there was a strong movement afoot to curtail or completely repeal these provisions.

The following year, 1920, and again in 1922, Edwin W. Sims, the first head of the newly established Chicago Crime Commission, added his voice to the insistent demands "for action" that would reduce crime. He had the figures: "During 1919 there were more murders in Chicago (with a population of three million) than in the entire British Isles (with a population of 40 million)." Moreover, the prosecution had obtained only 44 convictions as against 336 murders. The situation called for strong words and Mr. Sims was equal to the occasion:

"We have kept on providing criminals with flowers, libraries, athletics, hot and cold running water, and probation and parole. The tender solicitude for the welfare of criminals publicly expressed by social workers conveys to 10,000 criminals plying their vocation in Chicago the mistaken impression that the community is more interested in them than it is in their victims. . . .

"There has been too much mollycoddling of the criminal population. . . . It is time for plain speaking. Murderers are turned loose. They have no fear of the police. They sneer at the law. It is not a time for promises. It is a time for action. The turning point has come. Decency wins or anarchy triumphs. There is no middle course."

If Edwin Sims were still in fine voice today, he would be much in demand. At home and on the road, he would probably outdraw even Messrs. Byrne, Murphy and Parker. About all Sims would have to do would be to strike "social workers," insert "Supreme Court," and maybe add a paragraph or two about recent Supreme Court decisions. But his era, I repeat, was 1920.

The nineteen-twenties were troubled times. In speaking of the need for a National Crime Commission, The New Republic of Aug. 26, 1925, declared: "It is no exaggeration to assert that the administration of criminal justice has broken down in the United States and that in this respect American state governments are failing to perform the most primitive and most essential function which society imposes on government." At about the same time, the great criminologist Edwin H. Sutherland reported: "Capital punishment has been restored in four states since the war, and in many places there is a strenuous demand for the whipping post. . . . Crime commissions are recommending increased severity and certainty of punishment."

By 1933, the public had become so alarmed at an apparent increase in professional criminality that a U.S. Senate investigating committee, headed by Royal S. Copeland of New York, scoured the country for information which could lead to a national legislative solution.

The Detroit hearings brought out that the murder rate in the United States was nine times higher than in England and in Wales, "where they have basically the same Anglo-Saxon institutions," and even twice as high as Italy's, "the home of the Mafia, the 'Black Hand.'" In New York, a witness solemnly declared that "the crime situation in this country is so serious that it approaches a major crisis in our history, a crisis which will determine whether the nation is to belong to normal citizens or whether it is to be surrendered completely to gangster rule."

In Chicago, drawing upon his 20 years of experience as a lawyer, prosecutor and municipal judge, a witness concluded that "there is entirely too much worry, consideration and too many safeguards about the criminal's constitutional rights." He recommended for the Senate committee's consideration Illinois's new "reputation vagrancy law, which provides that all persons who are reputed to habitually violate the criminal laws and who are reputed to carry concealed weapons are vagrants." "Under this law," he reported, "we have harassed and convicted . . . numerous mad dogs of the West Side." (The following year, the Illinois Supreme Court struck down the law as unconstitutional.)

Senator Copeland told assembled witnesses of his desire for "a frank expression of opinion, no matter how critical you may be of existing institutions." Most of the witnesses were equal to the challenge.

A Maj. Homer Shockley urged that "constitutional and statutory guaranties, applicable to the average citizen, be suspended by special court procedure for the person who is known to be an habitual criminal . . . or who habitually consorts with criminals, to the end that the burden of proof of innocence of any fairly well substantiated charge be squarely placed on the accused; that he be tried without the benefit of a jury; and that, if convicted, all of his property and wealth be confiscated except such portions as the accused can prove were honestly gained by honest effort." The presumption of innocence is "fair enough" for the normal person, but not "for the dirty rat whom everybody knows to be an incurably habitual crook."

(Lest the major be peremptorily dismissed as a nonlegally trained commentator, it should be noted that two years earlier the dean of a Middle Western law school was reported to have advocated the establishment of a commission empowered to convict persons as "public enemies" and fix terms of their removal from society without convicting them for any specific offense, as historically required.)

Citing Toronto, where whippings were said to have broken a wave of jewelry-store stick-ups, another witness at the 1933 hearings, New York Police Commissioner Edward Mulrooney, came out for 30 or 40 lashes to be applied at the time a criminal entered prison, others every six months thereafter.

Lewis E. Lawes, the famous warden of Sing Sing prison, exclaimed: "Strip our hysterical reaction in the present emergency and what have you? A confession that our agencies are not keeping step with crime, are falling short of their mark. Yesterday it was robbery, today it is kidnapping, tomorrow it will be something else. With every new crime racket will come a new hysteria." After delivering these refreshingly sober remarks, Warden Lawes proceeded to disregard his own advice:

"I think I am a liberal, but at the same time, in case of war I would fight for the country, and this is war. I believe if they do not have some form of martial law against this particular group [racketeers and kidnappers] that there will come in . . . lynch law and from lynch law they will have the martial law. . . . It seems to me that this is a war to be stamped out quickly and could be stopped in 60 days if all the authorities get together honestly and let the public know exactly what they are doing. . . . If I were Mussolini I could do it in 30 days."

Even renowned defense attorney Sam Liebowitz, honored "to

be called upon to speak from the viewpoint of the criminal lawyer," seemed to get into the swing of things. He proposed a "national vagrancy law," whereby if a well-dressed crook "cannot give a good account of himself" to a police officer who spots him on the street or in his Cadillac "you take him into the station house and question him, and then take him before a judge. The judge says, 'Prove you are earning an honest living.'

"No honest man need rebel against a thing like that," contended the great criminal lawyer. "If you are earning an honest dollar, you can show what you are doing. . . . It is the crook that sets up the cry of the Constitution, and the protection of the Constitution, when he is in trouble."

Detroit prosecutor Harry Toy agreed that "a national vagrancy act—we call it a public-enemy act—is a wonderful thing." Mr. Liebowitz had assumed that a national vagrancy act would require an amendment to the privilege against self-incrimination, but the Detroit prosecutor insisted that such an act "could be framed under the present Federal Constitution as it now stands." (His own state's "public-enemy" law was held unconstitutional by the Michigan Supreme Court a few months later. The following year New Jersey made it a felony, punishable by 20 years' imprisonment, to be a "gangster"; the U.S. Supreme Court struck the law down in 1939 on the grounds of vagueness and uncertainty.)

Chicago Municipal Court Judge Thomas Green plumped for an amendment to the Fourth Amendment permitting searches of persons "reputed" to be criminals and to be carrying firearms. The reason the framers of the Constitution stressed personal liberty, he explained, was that "there were no gangsters" then. "I think personal liberty is a wonderful thing," he hastened to add, "but today the man who takes advantage of personal liberty is the gangster, the gunman, the kidnapper."

Virtually every procedural safeguard caught heavy fire in the Senate hearings. One witness called "the right to the 'shield of silence'" (the privilege against self-incrimination) "the greatest stumbling block to justice and incentive to crime in all common-law countries." Another maintained that "the present provisions against self-incrimination were intended to protect the citizen against the medieval methods of torture, and they have become obsolete in modern life."

A report of the International Association of Chiefs of Police listed as "contributing factors to our serious crime problem . . . the resort to injunctions, writs of habeas corpus, changes of venue, etc., all with a view of embarrassing and retarding the administration of justice." The "founders of the Republic," it was argued, "never intended that habeas corpus and bail should be granted to a thug or serious thief."

Judge William Skillman of Detroit Criminal Court, known as "the one-man grand jury," maintained that permitting the state to appeal an acquittal "would do much to insure to society, represented by the state, a fair break in the trial of a lawsuit" because "the so-called 'former jeopardy clause' . . . has many times been used as a shield by a weak or timid or even venal judge." Capt. A. B. Moore of the New York State Police proposed that an "expert adviser" or legally trained "technician" sit with and retire to the jury room with the jury "to advise them [on] those technicalities that had been implanted in their minds by a very clever attorney."

So much for the teens and twenties and thirties, the so-called golden era when the U.S. Supreme Court kept "hands off" local law enforcement.

When Chief Parker warns us in our time that "the police . . . are limited like the Yalu River boundary, and the result of it is that they are losing the war just like we lost the war in Korea," I wonder: When, if ever, weren't we supposedly losing the war against crime? When, if ever, weren't law enforcement personnel impatient with the checks and balances of our system? When, if ever, didn't they feel unduly "limited"? When, if ever, will they realize that our citizens are free *because* the police are "limited"?

When an official of the National District Attorney's Association insists in our time: "This country can no longer afford a 'civil-rights binge' that so restricts law-enforcement agencies that they become ineffective and organized crime flourishes," I wonder: When, if ever, in the opinion of law-enforcement personnel, could this country afford a "civil-rights binge"? When, if ever, wasn't there a "crime crisis"? When, if ever, weren't there proclamations of great emergencies and announcements of disbelief in the capacities of ordinary institutions and regular procedures to cope with them?

When Chicago's famous police chief, O. W. Wilson, stumps the country, pointing to the favorable crime picture in England, and other nations "unhampered" by restrictive court decisions, and exclaiming that "crime is overwhelming our society" (at the very time he is accepting credit in Chicago for a 20 per cent drop in crimes against the person), I am reminded of a story, apocryphal no doubt, about a certain aging promiscuous actress. When asked what she would do if she could live her life all over again she is said to have replied: "The same thing—with different people."

I venture to say that today too many law-enforcement spokesmen are doing "the same thing—with different people." They are using different crime statistics and they are concentrating on a different target—the Supreme Court rather than the state courts, parole boards, social workers and "shyster lawyers"—but they are reacting the same way they reacted in past generations.

They are reconciling the delusion of our omnipotence with the experience of limited power to cope with the "crime crisis" by explaining failure in terms of betrayal. To borrow a phrase from Dean Acheson, they are letting a "mood of irritated frustration with complexity" find expression in "scapegoating."

Secretaries and ex–Secretaries of State know almost as much about scapegoating as Supreme Court justices. If the task of containing or controlling "change" in Africa or Asia is beyond our capabilities, to many people it means simply, or at least used to mean simply, that the State Department is full of incompetents or Communists or both. Here, as elsewhere, if things seem to be going wrong, but there is no simple and satisfactory reason why, it is tempting to think that "the way to stop the mischief is to root out the witches."

Crime is a baffling, complex, frustrating, defiant problem. And as James Reston once pointed out in explaining Barry Goldwater's appeal to millions of Americans: "The more complicated life becomes, the more people are attracted to simple solutions; the more irrational the world seems, the more they long for rational answers; and the more diverse everything is, the more they want it all reduced to identity."

As the Wickersham Report of 1931 disclosed, the prevailing "interrogation methods" of the nineteen-twenties and thirties included the application of the rubber hose to the back or the pit of the stomach, kicks in the shins and blows struck with a telephone book on the side of the victim's head.

These techniques did not stem the tide of crime. Nor did the use of illegally seized evidence, which most state courts permitted as late as the nineteen-forties and fifties. Nor, while they lasted, did the "public-enemy" laws, or the many criminal registration ordinances stimulated by the Copeland hearings.

If history does anything, it supports David Acheson, who, when U. S. Attorney for the District of Columbia (the jurisdiction which has borne the brunt of "restrictive" court rules), dismissed the suggestion that "the crime rate will go away if we give back to law-enforcement agencies 'power taken from them by Federal court decisions' " with the assurance that "the war against crime does not lie on this front. Prosecution procedure has, at most, only the most remote, casual connection with crime. Changes in court decisions and prosecution procedure would have about the same effect on the crime rate as an aspirin would have on a tumor of the brain."

Unfortunately this speech was not given the publicity it deserved. Nor were the refreshingly cool, thoughtful remarks of the new Deputy Attorney General, Ramsey Clark, who last August pointed out:

"Court rules do not cause crime. People do not commit crime because they know they cannot be questioned by police before presentment, or even because they feel they will not be convicted. We as a people commit crimes because we are capable of committing crimes. We choose to commit crimes. . . . In the long run, only the elimination of the causes of crime can make a significant and lasting difference in the incidence of crime.

"But the reduction of the causes of crime is a slow and arduous process and the need to protect persons and property is immediate. The present need for greater protection . . . can be filled not by . . . court rulings affirming convictions based on confessions secured after hours of questioning, or evidence seized in searches made without warrants. The immediate need can be filled by more and better police protection."

Chief Parker has expressed the hope that in searching for answers to our crime problem the new National Crime Commission "not overlook the influencing factor of the judicial revolution." The greater danger is that too much attention will be paid to this "revolution."

Critics of the courts are well represented, but not a single criminologist or sociologist or psychologist sits on the 19-man commission. These are conspicuous omissions for a group asked "to be daring and creative and revolutionary" in its recommendations. These are incredible omissions for those of us who share the views of the Deputy Attorney General that "the first, the most pervasive and the most difficult" front in the war on crime "is the battle against the causes of crime: poverty, ignorance, unequal opportunity, social tension, moral erosion."

By a strange coincidence, the very day the President announced the formation of the Crime Commission, the F.B.I. released new figures on the crime rate—soaring as usual—and J. Edgar Hoover took a sideswipe at "restrictive court decisions affecting police prevention and enforcement activity." And at their very first meeting, last September, the commission members were told by Mr. Hoover that recent court decisions had "too often severely and unfairly shackled the police officer."

Probably the most eminently qualified member of the President's Commission is Columbia Law School's Herbert Wechsler, the director of the American Law Institute and chief draftsman of the recently completed Model Penal Code, a monumental work which has already had a tremendous impact throughout the nation. The commission would have gotten off to a more auspicious start if, instead of listening to a criticism of recent court decisions, its members had read (or reread) what Mr. Wechsler, then a young, obscure assistant law professor, once said of other crime conferences in another era of "crisis" (those called by the U. S. Attorney General and a number of states, including New York, in 1934–36):

"The most satisfactory method of crime prevention is the solution of the basic problems of government—the production and distribution of external goods, education and recreation. . . . That the problems of social reform present dilemmas of their own, I do not pretend to deny. I argue only that one can say for social reform as a means to the end of improved crime control what can also be said for better personnel but cannot be said for drastic tightening of the processes of the criminal law—that even if the end should not be achieved, the means is desirable for its own sake."

What Happens When the Police Strike

by Gerald Clark

ON THE DAY Montreal became a city without policemen, Gilles
Madore unsuspectingly left his home as usual at 9:30 A.M. to
drive to work. Madore, a 32-year-old bank inspector, had been
filling in for the past few months as manager of the City &
District Savings Bank branch at the corner of St. Denis Street
and St. Joseph Boulevard, almost entirely a French-speaking
residential area with only a splash of English and Italian. It was
a perfect October day—clear and crisp—and during the 15-
minute drive Madore noted that the trees were at their peak
of gold and crimson. He was listening to the car radio, but since
it was an FM all-music station, he caught no bulletins. Madore,
in fact, did not know the police had walked off the job until
he arrived at the bank and a nervous teller greeted him with the
news that the city was wide open to criminals. "Don't worry,"
Madore said reassuringly. "We're a small branch. Holdup men
won't come here." Besides, this was a Tuesday, by experience the
quietest day in the week for bank robberies.

Madore was not alone in his ignorance of the strike. Most
Montrealers were only now beginning to hear of it, for there had

been no forewarning, no build-up. The morning newscasts had carried, as a routine item, the report that police were to meet in the Paul Sauvé Arena at 9 A.M. to hear the results of an arbitration board's findings on wages and other issues that had remained unsettled for almost a year. But no one had anticipated a walkout; it was illegal for policemen and firefighters to strike.

At about the time Madore was learning of the development, another tall—and rather rugged—Montrealer, René St. Martin, was also receiving a sketchy fill-in. St. Martin, 25, was a patrolman, first class, assigned to cruisers. He had worked the 4 P.M.-to-midnight shift and, after a few hours' sleep, had now arrived at court as a witness in a stolen-car case. But, St. Martin discovered, no cases were being heard; few police witnesses had shown up. Shop stewards of the union, the Montreal Policemen's Brotherhood, had made the rounds of 25 station houses around 7:30 A.M.—and calls had gone out over police radio bands—to get men to leave their posts at once, to assemble in the arena even before the planned session. Men arriving for the 8 A.M. shift also were told that the arbitration board's decisions were so distasteful that everyone had better head for the meeting. Even members of the Sûreté, the detective branch, turned in their sidearms and took off.

To St. Martin it was a surprise—and shock—to realize that a full strike was under way. He got into his car and drove the 10 miles to the arena in the northeast end of the city. By now scores of blue-and-white police cruisers were double- and triple-parked, along with scores of motorcycles. St. Martin arrived at about 11 A.M. and, as it developed, stayed there until midnight. With him were almost all of the other 3,780 men of the Montreal police force.

Thus, on Oct. 7, the largest city in Canada, and one of the most civilized cities in the world, found what it was like to be without police protection during a day and night. Before the ordeal was over, a psychologist would shoot and kill a burglar; another man—a provincial police corporal—would be slain, and 49 persons would be wounded or injured in rioting. Nine bank holdups, almost a tenth of the total for the whole of last year, would be committed, along with 17 other robberies at gunpoint.

Ordinarily disciplined, peaceful citizens would go wild, smashing 1,000 plate glass windows in the heart of the city and looting shop displays. The losses and damage would exceed $1-million.

But the gray statistics alone would not be very meaningful. It was on the social and psychological levels that the story held its horror. For the real message was about the "thin blue line"—the phrase used by Sgt. Guy Marcil, president of the Policemen's Brotherhood—that separates civilization from chaos and anarchy.

Essentially, it was not the rise in professional crime—12 times the normal—that counted. It was the way political grievances, and private and group frustrations, shot to the surface when no one was around to enforce the law. These included: an attack by taxi drivers on a company holding an exclusive franchise to provide limousine service at Montreal's International Airport; an attack by French-Canadian separatists on symbols of the "English Establishment"; an attack on the Mayor's property by social agitators who contend that not enough is being done for the poor; an attack on the United States Consulate by anti-Americans; and then, simply, an attack on a code of ethics and behavior by conventional men and women who chose to join a mob.

At the outset, a few of Montreal's English-speaking people, who number about one-fifth of the population, thought the Quebec revolution had commenced. But for most people the day itself was reasonably calm. Apart from traffic tie-ups, the public experienced few inconveniences. At first there was a fear that accident victims might suffer, since police handle the cruising ambulances. Early on, a radio dispatcher tried to get an ambulance to respond to a call. The driver, instead, asked the dispatcher for directions to the Paul Sauvé Arena. Minutes later the radio went dead as dispatchers themselves left for the North End. But by then hospitals and private ambulance services had begun to take over.

It was not even accurate to say that the city was entirely without police. At headquarters, 47 officers—all of them ineligible for membership in the union—remained on duty, relaying distress calls to the Quebec Provincial Police (Q.P.P.) who started to send their own cruisers into city districts. By 10 A.M. 200

members of the Q.P.P. were mustered, and 40 brown-and-yellow alien cruisers were on the streets. It was not quite the same as the city force's 686 cars, motorcycles and other vehicles, but it was comforting nonetheless. Then a news bulletin at 10:30 A.M. alarmed the public: firemen, disgruntled over an arbitration board decision affecting them only a day earlier, were walking out of 45 stations and joining police at the arena. Yet even here there soon came an encouraging note. The city would not be completely vulnerable; the firefighters had decided to leave behind emergency teams of nine men in each of Montreal's 10 districts, enough to operate a pump and ladder truck.

Soon, however, it was apparent that the provincial police— most of them drawn from the local administrative office or brought in from outlying areas and unacquainted with city streets —could not keep pace with the kind of alarms municipal police handle as routine. Gilles Madore, at his branch, heard rumors that the banks would be ordered to close and the army summoned. As the morning progressed, he began to feel some apprehension. Customers paused to relay reports of holdups elsewhere. While Madore still believed his branch was safe (after all, it kept none of the large sums that downtown branches must keep for business firms), the first holdup of the day, at 11:15 A.M., had been at a Bank of Montreal branch in Pointe St. Charles, a slum district. Three men had entered the bank, two of them wearing Halloween masks and carrying pistols, the other wearing a brown paper bag with eye holes and carrying a shotgun. The nine employes kept their hands in the air while one of the bandits fired two shots at the lock of a teller's cash drawer. The haul was not large—a little more than $3,000—and the men were out of there in two minutes. It took the Q.P.P. 10 minutes to arrive. This was to form the pattern of the day. Time was on the side of the lawless.

The regular professional bank robbery in Montreal runs frequently to smoothly choreographed trios, with one man—usually armed with an impressive weapon like a submachine gun or shotgun—covering the staff while the other two leap over the counter to grab the money. The entire operation is supposed to be over within 30 seconds, at the most 45 seconds, because experienced hands know that an alert teller or manager will press a silent alarm connected to a protection service which in turn is linked with police headquarters. It takes 30 seconds from the moment the alarm is pressed until the message reaches the police; usually the nearest cruiser is not more than a minute or a minute and a half away. So, two minutes is the most any bandits can figure on; to give themselves a reasonable margin they rarely spend more than a quarter of that time.

René St. Martin, after 10 months on radio cars, was familiar with the technique of bank robbers. But his mind was elsewhere. He was listening to the speeches of union leaders, and he was in a quandary. While he supported the case made by the union, he believed essential services should not be allowed to strike. St. Martin likes being a policeman, and he does not feel—or at least did not until this moment—that the Montreal public is particularly hostile to the department or ungrateful to it. Fringe groups may shout "pigs" or "fuzz," but generally one does not hear such derogatory terms about Montreal policemen. On the contrary, there is an admiration for the way they have developed over the past few years into a remarkably good force: young, clean-cut recruits, efficient, honest, with the most rigorous training in the country and, until the walkout, a high level of discipline.

Certainly there was little public awareness of discontent in the ranks. During Expo 67 the Brotherhood went along with a city request for labor peace and accepted an unfavorable contract. Since then, however, the union had felt itself ignored, cut off by an administration that would not acknowledge the argument that Montreal patrolmen were entitled to at least the same income as police in Toronto, Canada's second largest city. St. Martin did not need reminders of how difficult his job was, though speaker after speaker pointed to the hazards in Montreal. It has the usual student troubles; last February rioters at Sir George Williams University barricaded themselves in a computer center and destroyed it. In addition, police must contend with a distinctive political situation: secessionists who are determined to break the Province of Quebec away from the rest of Canada often engage in terrorism. More than 100 bomb incidents have been recorded in the past two years, while street demonstrations, increasing in ferocity, have tested the 110-man riot squad. A senior observer from the Toronto Police Department who had studied several American riot squads in action said publicly that he had seen none to compare with Montreal's for deftness and effectiveness.

The plain fact was that Montreal police—who are expected to be bilingual on top of everything else—sustained in the line of duty three times the number of injuries of Toronto police and were paid considerably less. St. Martin, with five years' experience, received $7,300 a year, while his counterpart in Toronto received $9,112. The Brotherhood had demanded $9,200. Now—after 11 months of costly negotiation, conciliation and arbitration—it was told it would get $8,480. "Public garbage!" cried President Marcil. The smoky, noisy arena fell silent when the policemen's veteran chaplain, the Rev. Bertrand-Marie Boulay, a 50-year-old Dominican, exhorted them to keep to their fight: "You must stand shoulder to shoulder with your president and your negotiators, and your chaplain will be there, near the head of the line."

Now the men were just going to stay there—not "on strike" but in a "study session"—until they got what they were after. Carloads of sandwiches were brought in. Men pushed their folding chairs into squares and played a popular police card game called "pitch." Reminiscing about it later, St. Martin said he was hoping the decision to settle or not to settle would be taken from him. He was sure that in a matter of a few hours the provincial government would enact legislation compelling the strikers to go back to work, or that prominent industrialists would say, *"C'est assez ça,"* and persuade municipal authorities to offer improvements.

But there was no sign of either. Instead, there was simply a vague promise from the chairman of the city's executive committee, Lucien Saulnier, that the administration would reassess the findings of the arbitration board. Saulnier arrived at the Paul Sauvé Arena at midday, spoke for a few noncommittal minutes and left while some strikers jeered and others cheered. St. Martin thought it took a man *"qui a du guts"* to enter the arena.

Saulnier, though an elected councilor, in effect is city manager. While he is the cool and adroit administrator, Jean Drapeau, the Mayor since 1960, is the colorful and imaginative impresario who has transformed Montreal—always attractive but rather backward—into a lively and urbane and advanced metropolis. When financial experts said Montreal could not afford a subway, Drapeau not only built one; he made the Métro a showplace, with each of its score of stations of different artistic motif. Town planners from around the world came to admire and study the rejuvenated center of the city with its skyscrapers and underground plazas consisting of hundreds of shops and dozens of fine restaurants and theaters.

Montrealers, who possessed San Franciscans' sense of superiority and pride in their city, would deny Drapeau nothing. It was Drapeau who sold a skeptical Canada on staging, on manmade islands in the St. Lawrence River, what turned out to be the highly successful Expo 67. And later, when he threatened to resign if the one-season Expo was not continued as the annual Man and His World, townspeople rallied in such strength that the Federal and provincial governments agreed to a scheme underwriting part of any deficit. This year, Drapeau, at 53, hardly slowed down. His showmanship was unerring when he helped promote a National League franchise for a town with no obvious proclivity to baseball. Drapeau saw his Expos, of bush-league caliber, establish a first-season record by drawing 1.2 million fans.

But all of this effort took money and a distorted sense of priorities. The city fell notoriously behind in slum clearance, low-cost housing, social service and better pay for civic employes. There was growing resentment that the Mayor was too busy with frills to pay attention to routine affairs. Strikers at the Paul Sauvé Arena held aloft placards saying, *"Drapeau au poteau"* ("Drapeau to the gallows"). Drapeau, in fact, was at this moment of crisis on his way home from St. Louis, Mo., where he had gone to participate in a Canadian trade show. Only a month earlier he had attended another opening—of his own restaurant, Le Vaisseau d'Or, Ship of Gold.

Even though many people wondered what a Mayor was doing moonlighting, this was no ordinary restaurant. In characteristic

Drapeau style, he defined it as a concert hall where one could, incidentally, dine. A 16-member orchestra played Bach, Vivaldi and Mozart while patrons ate a seven-course meal in the re-created opulence of a Montreal mansion's living room of the eighteen-nineties. A dinner for two, with drinks and wine, cost about $40. The figure was not entirely lost on social agitators who pointed out that the maximum allowance for a family of four on welfare was $40 a week. In an area with almost 7.5 per cent unemployment, the city had 27,000 welfare cases representing 70,000 men, women and children. But more graphically, a Montreal Labor Council study indicated that 38 per cent of the total population lived in poverty or near the poverty line.

Three weeks after the opening of Le Vaisseau d'Or, a bundle of dynamite, estimated at 15 sticks, exploded outside Drapeau's two-story home in the East End of Montreal. No one was injured, but the house was demolished. Investigation failed to show whether the terrorists were political foes, social fanatics, labor extremists, Maoists or separatists who resented Drapeau's efforts to make Montreal an international capital rather than a unilingual French-Canadian haven.

One could almost be sure, in view of the absence of police from the streets, that Le Vaisseau d'Or would now be a target. But at the moment a more prosaic crime was in the making. Shortly before 1 P.M. a man about 23 years of age walked into a branch of the Canadian Imperial Bank of Commerce on Mount Royal Avenue East, stood in line at a teller's position and shoved across the counter a note: *"Silence. Ceci est un holdup."* The teller was an English-speaking woman who could not read French. But she could understand "holdup." Moreover, she saw what looked like the handle of a gun sticking from the man's pocket. He collected close to $1,000, in the process striking a blow for bilingualism.

By now some of the outlying bank branches were closing down in self-defense. Downtown branches, which had brought in private security guards, were untouched, but holdups were taking place with greater frequency in the residential districts. At 1:45 P.M. Gilles Madore received a phone call from the head office telling him to allow in only known customers. His branch is modern and, with the exception of garish brown tile covering the side of the counter, quite attractive; the glass front gives it an appearance of spaciousness. Madore double-locked the glass door himself. Five minutes later, as he was preparing to go to lunch, he saw from the big window of his office three hooded men—one carrying a shotgun—running toward the bank.

Madore instinctively pressed the silent alarm. The men banged on the door and then, frustrated, retreated to an adjacent lane. They were obviously professionals. The hoods they wore—knitted ski masks, covering the entire head, face and neck, with slits for the eyes and mouth—are favored by old hands. Seconds later, they were back. This time the man with the shotgun smashed the butt against the door. The glass fell away, and the men stepped inside. By now half of the staff of 12 had fled to the tiny kitchen. The other six waited, Madore beside the entrance to the manager's office. The man with the shotgun told him, *"Bouges pas, toi—je vais te descendre"* ("Don't move—or I'll bring you down"). As Madore remembers it, "I didn't move."

The other men, clutching revolvers, advanced to the other side of the counter. There was little conversation, but when a teller hesitated in handing over the key to his cash drawer, one of the bandits slapped his face. The yield from all the cash drawers came to $2,000. Under normal circumstances, the bandits should have made their escape by now. But the shotgun man, the lookout man, did not even bother to glance into the street to see if anyone had spotted them. Nor did he trouble to count aloud to 30—a common practice to warn that time is up. Instead, he instructed the cashier to open the cash box, kept for tellers, in the big vault. The men scooped up $4,000 in U.S. banknotes, $7,000 in Canadian funds and $15,000 in travelers' checks, making a grand total of $28,000—the biggest haul of the day. On the way out, the man with the shotgun paused at the water fountain and took a long drink. The duration of the operation was between four and five minutes. Provincial police arrived at 2:10 P.M., 20 minutes after Madore had sounded the alarm.

The delays were not always due to the heavy pressures on the provincial police or their unfamiliarity with Montreal's streets. Some of the strikers, after monitoring the Q.P.P. radio, ambushed and seized seven provincial cruisers responding to calls. The number was selected deliberately, for the Q.P.P. drew on seven radio bands and the strikers were able to muddle all of them with the cruisers' transmitters. For a while this strategy forced the provincial police, whom the strikers regarded as strike-breakers, to keep only two-thirds of their cars on the road. The rest remained at headquarters to take orders directly.

Most of the men at the arena were unaware of the ugliness outside, and when René St. Martin managed to reach a phone, he found his wife Andrée in a mood of dejection. Their 22-month-old son, Stéphane, was asleep, but their 3-year-old daughter, Josée, was looking at televised scenes of the arena and saying, "My daddy is there." It was not easy to get along on take-home pay of $105.42 a week, and Andrée knew the men were entitled to a better deal. But, as she later recalled it, "I am a mother, and I thought of the agony of some other woman whose child might be lying bleeding on the street, or who might be lost. . . ."

The afternoon was surprisingly tranquil. Holdups, though plentiful, were of a routine nature. At 3:05 P.M. two men with submachine guns entered the jewelry store of Roland Handfield on Jean Talon Street East and announced: "This is a holdup. Lay down on the floor." Handfield and his two clerks obeyed without hesitation. The men proceeded to fill a bag with rings, bracelets and other items valued at from $3,000 to $4,000—and then one of them said, "Three minutes. Let's go." A car, the motor running, was waiting at the corner.

At another small jewelry store, Bijouterie Borduas, a 23-year-old clerk, Pauline Deschambault, thought it was so dull and orderly in the streets and in the shops that surely the police must be back at work. Then she heard the bell tinkle as the front door opened, and she saw two young men walk in, unmasked but holding revolvers. She screamed and ran to the back of the store. The lone male clerk was told to flop behind the counter. A few minutes later, the men departed with about $6,700 in rings and watches.

The Perrette Dairy Ltd., with its chain of 40 shops in the city, reported five holdups, compared with the usual average of one a month. At 6:50 P.M., at the branch at 6030 Sherbrooke

Street West, a customer selected a package of cheese and, instead of paying for it, pulled a pistol from his pocket. The solitary clerk emptied the till of $107, forgetting the manager's injunction to keep ginger ale bottles within reach and heave them at any thief. Before the day ended, there had been a total of 26 armed robberies in all districts.

By early evening the provincial police had 500 men in action; another 300 were en route to Montreal from posts as far as Sept-Iles, 510 miles away. Lucien Saulnier made a radio and television appeal for people to "be calm and vigilant," stay home and protect their property. One woman said she had not worried about the situation until she heard this dramatic message. Another woman, young and pretty, was afraid to walk to the bus stop after a dental appointment; she thought she might be attacked or raped (there were no reported rape cases). She set about to make herself look old and uninteresting by dropping her glasses to the tip of her nose; she also covered a fresh coiffure with a pocket rain bonnet and tried to add inches to her miniskirt by pulling it low on her hips. It was only much later, when she had recovered from her moments of terror, that she was able to say wryly: "Have you any idea what it's like trying to walk in an extended miniskirt?"

Most people appeared relaxed, even if some behaved irrationally. Metropolitan Montreal numbers 2.5 million inhabitants, but only half live in the city proper, where the strike was taking place. The others live in separate municipalities—some of them, like Westmount and Outremont, enclaves surrounded by the City of Montreal—with their own police and fire services. None of these was on strike. However, a Westmount resident, arriving home at 7 P.M. from work, found his way barred by the door chain, a device never before used by his wife. "What's the idea?" he asked her. She replied that Saulnier had told people to be on guard. Another man returned from work to find that every light in his home in Outremont had been switched on; his wife was certain this would ward off intruders.

As it happened, the population, at the start, did heed Saulnier. It kept away from the downtown areas. A visitor driving along

Ste. Catherine, the biggest shopping and entertainment street, would have thought it a Sunday rather than Tuesday evening. Theaters, cinemas and restaurants functioned. It was just that the traffic was light and shushed. But not everywhere. Around City Hall, in the old quarter of Montreal, several taxis started hooting their horns before forming a procession and driving west to Barré and Mountain Streets. At that point, approximately 7:30 P.M., began the buildup for a night of havoc.

Other cabs headed downtown to join the cavalcade, and by the time it reached its objective, the garage of Murray Hill Limousine Service Ltd., it numbered 75 vehicles—carrying not only cabbies but political extremists. An alliance had been formed between the Mouvement de Libération du Taxi, which could claim a membership of no more than 100 of Montreal's 10,000 cab drivers, and the Front de Libération Populaire, a small group of Maoists and student radicals who charged that a "fascist Drapeau-Saulnier administration had sold out taxi drivers' interests to the capitalists." In fact, it was a Federal concession that had given Murray Hill the sole right to pick up passengers at Montreal's airport, in return for guaranteed service. But the grievance was an old one among drivers of city taxi associations.

For separatists and terrorists, with no riot squad to restrain them, this was obviously a night to make political gain in the wider goal of removing Quebec from "English domination." Murray Hill, as an example, was owned by an English-speaking Montrealer, Charles Hershorn, whose home had been bombed a year ago.

At 8:03 P.M. a Q.P.P. radio dispatcher sent four cars to Murray Hill. They fumbled through unfamiliar back streets flanked on the north by railway yards and on the south by the waterfront. At 8:08 P.M. another four cars were told to get there in a hurry. By now demonstrators were chanting, *"Québec aux Québécois,"* and throwing rocks and Molotov cocktails. The targets of the fire bombs were four Murray Hill buses and four cars in the parking lot, and quickly they were aflame. Demonstrators pushed one of the burning buses down an incline to crash into the barred garage doors. The tactics were terrifying to the Murray

Hill employes inside; they were sitting above underground storage tanks containing 18,000 gallons of gasoline. Firemen, forced back by the rioters, were compelled to set up hoses at a distance. Then a guard on the roof of the two-story building opened fire on the crowd with a 12-gauge shotgun. "How big is the crowd?" a Q.P.P. dispatcher asked over the radio. "Over 200," replied a cruiser, "and impossible to control." A city police striker, using a hijacked car transmitter, cut in—and a Q.P.P. man cursed him.

By now a second guard was shooting from the garage roof, and there was return fire from a tenement roof across the road. It was the first time that street war of this type had ever struck Montreal, and when it was ended, a provincial plainclothesman, Cpl. Robert Dumas, 35, was its chief victim. Dumas, a member of the Q.P.P. antisubversive squad, had been one of the first police on the site. He entered the Murray Hill garage to phone for reinforcements; then, racing out to try to halt rioters tossing Molotov cocktails, he was fatally wounded by a shotgun blast. Another 19 persons—some cabbies, some youths—were taken to hospitals with buckshot wounds. Thirty more suffered injuries at Murray Hill and in the subsequent bouts that took place as the crowd began moving, around 10:30 P.M., up the hill.

The next destination was the Queen Elizabeth Hotel, chosen because Murray Hill had a concession there; thus it deserved to have its storefront windows smashed. From here it was a short and logical step to the Sheraton–Mount Royal Hotel, for the same reason. But on the way, the demonstrators paused at the Windsor Hotel, where Mayor Drapeau's restaurant was located in the basement level. Drapes were ripped down, glassware smashed and small fires set. By now Drapeau, having landed from St. Louis an hour and a half earlier, was in City Hall receiving reports of the growing violence.

The streets in Drapeau's beloved heart of the city—the complex around Place Ville Marie and the Ste. Catherine Street area —were beginning to fill with more than the original couple of hundred separatists and agitators who had started out with an organized line of attack. Arriving from all directions, looters and vandals were hitting out indiscriminately. A provincial police officer radioed headquarters: "Send help to the corner of Peel and Ste. Catherine. People are breaking windows at the Bank of Nova Scotia." Minutes later: "We need more help. We are 25 against 500."

For two uninterrupted, chaotic hours the plunderers went to work, barely touched by the undermanned and bewildered Q.P.P. At one point young people surrounded a parked cruiser, rocking it and blocking the doors so the occupants could not escape. All along central Ste. Catherine Street, for a stretch of 21 blocks, the shattering of $300,000 worth of plate glass windows was hardly heard above the roar of the mob and the incessant ringing of unanswered alarm bells. In the distance sirens sounded. Their screech receded, however, as a new touch was added. Provincial police were receiving more and more calls about other riots in widely scattered parts of the city, only to find them fictitious. Later, Q.P.P. Director Maurice St. Pierre was to suggest the calls came from strikers.

In all, something like 156 shops had windows smashed and display contents hauled away—stereo units, radios, fur coats, dresses, an assortment of goods. The major department stores—Eaton's, Simpson's, Morgan's—were hit, along with lesser ones. Pink Poodle, a medium-priced women's specialty shop, caught it from two directions. While the ordinary looters were content to strip Pink Poodle's window mannequins of $3,000 worth of garments, professional burglars entered the premises through a back door and made off with 150 fur and cloth coats valued at $20,000.

There were riffraff out that night and maybe some poor people; but also there were so-called respectable, middle-class people. A well-dressed man, with a fur coat over each arm, scampered down Ste. Catherine Street shouting, "One for my wife, one for my girl friend." There were some orderly people, too. A middle-aged man, seeing a young man reaching for a fur coat, tried to talk him out of it—whereupon he was set upon by two other looters for interfering. At Seltzer Drugs, where the window offered transistor sets, hair dryers and other fairly expensive items, a woman reached for a yellow box of Kleenex, ripped away the wrapping and stuffed the tissue into her hand-bag. She laughed aloud, for no one in particular to hear, as though to proclaim that suddenly she had a license to break the rules.

Or maybe she simply needed to blow her nose, and in the spirit of gaiety took the Kleenex. For in a sense there was also a carnival atmosphere, a pre-Christmas festivity about the street. There was nothing furtive in the stealing. Many of the people who now descended on Ste. Catherine Street, drawn by radio and television accounts, were content to stand by as spectators; but some, when they saw windows smashed, helped themselves to what was inside. Often they seemed to wait for just the right window to be smashed. But with no bothersome police around —at one stage a busload of Q.P.P., arriving from out of town, drove along Ste. Catherine Street without any pause in the looting—a sense of fear was absent.

At the Paul Sauvé Arena, René St. Martin heard the Brotherhood president, Guy Marcil, announce that the Quebec Legislature had ordered the strikers back to work by one minute past midnight, or they would face severe fines and loss of accreditation as a trade union. Some men hissed. "We must obey," said Marcil. St. Martin was glad that the decision was, at last, made for him. But he felt it was not the Government's threat alone that got the men back on the beat. "It was," he said, "the way the rioters and looters were tearing our city to ribbons."

At 12:57 A.M. Montreal city police calls returned to the air. The 17-hour trial was over, and people cheered the first familiar blue-and-white cruisers that arrived at the corner of Peel and Ste. Catherine Streets. The police grinned back and began the business of chasing off the remaining looters and, along with the Q.P.P., making 104 arrests.

Many angles were left for later examination. Political extremists, after leaving the Sheraton–Mount Royal Hotel, shattered windows at nearby McGill University. But this was predictable, since separatists consider McGill a bastion of the English Establishment. Equally foreseeable was the small routine march on McGregor Avenue, where demonstrators threw stones through the windows of the United States Consulate while they left untouched in the same block consulates of Israel, West Germany,

Switzerland and Italy. Nor was there any special significance to the other crimes—except, as might be expected, that there were more than usual.

For instance, 456 burglaries were reported for 17 hours, compared with the normal 350 for a whole week. The pattern and timetable suggested that professionals, rather than amateurs, were at work. From 9 A.M. to 11 A.M., before criminals could be assured a police strike was indeed underway, no major incidents were logged. Then the signals began to come in from banks. After the banks closed, four jewelry stores in succession were held up. When jewelers shut down, at 6 P.M., the drug stores and food stores raised the alarm. The police, in making their analysis, did not believe that a single, massive gang was involved. Rather, several compact groups were thought to be operating, independently but with a common and logical program of attack based on known schedules of business establishments.

It was the behavior of ordinary people at night that caused the most perplexity and anxiety. No special denominator tied together the shops they looted: some were owned by Catholics, some by Protestants, some by Jews; some represented "English" interests, others "French" interests. Men and women of every kind and variety flocked to the Ste. Catherine Street area because it was here that the action, set off initially by organized extremists, was taking place. And then they abandoned inhibitions.

A German-trained psychologist, Dr. Paul Fircks, received a visitor in his home and explained the phenomenon. He did so by citing from a volume that is now a classic, "The Crowd: a Study of the Popular Mind," written in 1897 by a French psychologist, Gustave Le Bon. The crowd—the mob—is amoral, and if the law relaxes, the people in the crowd act out their impulses. Morals and ethics are externalized by the presence of the police; if the police are not there, the mob does as it pleases. It is the believer in individuality who stands back, who refuses to join the mob, who rejects looting, who behaves in a civilized fashion. "But the majority of people," adds Fircks, "join mobs when given an opportunity. Germany has shown this. Hitler was a genius who created out of supposed individuals a crowd, a mob."

Fircks, who is 67 and Russian-born, lived in Germany from 1934 to 1947. His own story is directly related to what happened in Montreal on what has come to be known as "Black Tuesday." A widower, Fircks lives alone with his cat, Baroness, in a large home in a high-income residential district where burglaries are frequent. Shortly before midnight he prepared to retire; but having heard the late news, and of the troubles downtown, he decided to take extra precautions.

Fircks, who practices psychotherapy, including hypnosis, remembered that in his office in the basement was a .32-caliber revolver that he had recently taken from a patient. He fetched it, went upstairs to his bedroom, bolted the door and slipped into bed—the revolver on the table next to him. When he awoke, it was to the sound of someone jimmying the bedroom door. Fircks fired three times, and when he descended found at the foot of the stairs the body of a man who, it turned out, was a 39-year-old habitual burglar.

What was Fircks's reaction? "I went through two world wars and the Nazis. No burglar is going to frighten me. Besides, I teach my patients to be aggressive. If you have an aggressive attitude, you cannot be afraid."

But shooting and killing even a burglar? "I looked at the man lying there, and I cursed him. I thought: How does he dare? Who does he think he is to threaten me, to come into my home this way?"

The day after the strike a Montreal editor received a phone call from an American newspaper friend in Washington. "What was the final toll up there?" asked the Washingtonian. When the answer was, "Two men killed, one a policeman, the other a burglar," the reaction was quick and astonished: "My God, if that happened here in Washington, if the police went on strike, the private hate lists would come out so fast we'd have a blood bath."

It was only in retrospect that Montrealers sensed how close a grim experience had come to gross tragedy. During the rioting and looting many people, sitting in suburban homes and watching television, thought it must be happening to a city in a foreign country. The awakening the next morning was acute when they traveled to downtown offices and saw the debris and damage. But the awful part was the realization that terrorists had selected relatively few targets, and that by and large the mob that later emerged was a good-natured one rather than vicious. No explosive bombs were thrown, no one cried out in a crusade of personal vendetta or racial or religious war. But if there is a next time with more targets and objectives, the thin blue line might indeed prove thin.

Each person had his own particular message to remember. For Dr. Fircks it was short and clear: "Never allow a policeman to strike, because then the mob comes together."

For Jean-Paul Gilbert, Montreal police director, there was no need for the harsh reminder that "a municipal force is a must in our society." A comparatively small number of men, familiar with local geography and conditions, can maintain peace in a city. Despite the good intentions and resources of the Q.P.P., who ultimately pressed 100 cruisers into service, Montreal was virtually without protection. Even the effectiveness of the army— a token force of the Royal 22d Regiment arrived as the strike was ending and mounted guard at City Hall—is questionable, according to Gilbert, unless soldiers are trained in crowd control. Thus he is a firm advocate of intensive coordination, in training and deployment, among forces on the national, state or provincial and municipal levels. The concept arouses misgivings among civil libertarians who fear growing police powers.

What did Black Tuesday teach Constable St. Martin? "That some people are like animals. You can expect teenagers to be undisciplined and wild, but it was shocking to see adults behave this way."

To his wife, Andrée, the police were wrong in striking or, worse still, were guilty of bad public relations, of spoiling an image: "They could have demonstrated how bitter they were if perhaps 1,000 at a time had assembled in the arena while the rest continued to protect the city."

Gilles Madore, the bank inspector, thinking not only of the illegality of the strike but of the way strikers ambushed cars of the Q.P.P.—in effect, committing such crimes as kidnapping and stealing—says: "If I had a priest who sinned and then asked me not to sin, I would hardly have faith in him. It is the same for the police. They have no right to go against the law and then expect others to obey it."

But Madore also believes that Montreal police are hard-working and efficient, and deserve to be paid more. There was little public opposition, in fact, when Lucien Saulnier announced 16 days after policemen were back on the job that a contract agreement had been reached. The city would boost a first-class constable's salary to $8,750—$270 above the arbitration board's award and, taking into account fringe benefits, effective parity with Toronto. If there was any over-all public indictment, it was against the Drapeau-Saulnier administration for failing to anticipate the mood of policemen.

The lesson for many people, apart from discovery of their vulnerability, was that society cannot legislate against strikes among civil servants unless it is prepared to guarantee that they will have no cause to feel aggrieved. Here was a body of men with a strong sense of discipline and responsibility, yet it felt impelled to lash out. The huge inflow of letters to the press contained the expected words of condemnation—the strike was illegitimate, misguided, shocking. Yet, curiously, the letters also showed a remarkable sense of fairness, of soul-searching, as though each man and woman was peering into his or her own background and values to find reasons for the walkout.

"Our police forces," wrote one woman, "are underpaid and underarmed. Yet society demands that they do their duty. I say society has a duty to them first. That entails our trust, our respect, our support and maintenance to match their dangerous task of protecting society."

Part *2*

LAW AND ORDER

IN THE introductory note to Part 1, we briefly discussed the widespread feeling in the United States that civil liberties decisions by the United States Supreme Court have handcuffed the police in their efforts at law enforcement. What follows in this section is a more detailed discussion of this charge by four experts. In 1966–1967, Professor James Vorenberg was director of the President's Commission on Law Enforcement and Administration of Justice. He was on leave from the Harvard Law School, where he now is director of the Center for the Advancement of Criminal Justice. (Mr. Vorenberg's article is adapted from a tape recording of a forum in which James Q. Wilson also participated. See "Police Work" in Part 3.) Daniel Gutman is Dean of the New York Law School, an independent school located in Manhattan. Anthony Lewis, now chief of the London bureau of the *New York Times,* won a Pulitzer Prize for his reporting in 1954, and Alan F. Westin, an expert on the Supreme Court, is professor of political science at Columbia University.

Since only a small proportion of crime is reported to the police, and since only about a fourth of the crimes reported result in any arrest, it is hard to believe that the crime rate has been profoundly affected by the Supreme Court's *Miranda* decision. As we pointed out in the Introduction, this decision requires policemen to warn suspects in custody of their rights to remain silent and to have counsel. If the police fail to follow the *Miranda* rules, the conviction rate goes down. Any defense attorney worth his salt now closely examines the conditions of his client's arrest and has the detainment declared unconstitutional if the rules have not been followed to the letter. Further, prosecuting attorneys are likely to dismiss all charges or to settle quickly for a plea of guilty to a lesser offense if they suspect that the detention and arrest of a defendant has not been without *Miranda* "flaws."

As Vorenberg observes, however, the *Miranda* rules do not decrease the criminal's risk of apprehension. The requirement that police give warnings to men in their custody can scarcely affect any calculation of risk in which a criminal or potential criminal might engage. No one ever committed a crime believing that doing so was safe because he might get caught by a policeman who might forget to read the *Miranda* warning. Dean Gutman is unhappy because the Supreme Court's procedural rules—announced in a series of decisions prior to the *Miranda* case—favor the criminal. But even Gutman does not argue that the apparent recent increase in the crime rate is due to the Court's decisions. His basic point is the one made by Vorenberg with reference to the *Miranda* procedures: when charges against admittedly guilty criminals are dismissed on technicalities, the conviction rate is bound to go down.

Perhaps a negligible conviction rate would adversely affect the crime rate, just as a negligible rate of apprehension and arrest (as during a police strike) affects it. But in ordinary circumstances, neither arrest rates nor conviction rates are so low as to affect the behavior of large parts of the population. The probabilities of arrest and conviction are not calculated by most potential criminals. If they were, the crime rate would skyrocket, because the calculations would show that the probabilities are very low. Everyone is a potential criminal, in the sense that all citizens frequently encounter objective opportunities to steal or commit other offenses. Knowing that there is a slim chance of arrest for any crimes they might commit, why do these citizens nevertheless refrain from crime? When stated this way—in terms of risk calculations—the problem becomes one of explaining why so *few* persons commit crimes, not why so many do so. After all, only a small minority of the population commits crimes, even during a police strike. Most citizens do not refrain from crime because they fear arrest, conviction, and punishment. Rather, they refrain because criminality is unthinkable. They are restrained by a sense of morality and decency.

The problem of finding proper remedies for police misconduct is a separate matter. Dean Gutman is rightfully indignant because the criminal law's remedy for police conduct that violates the Constitution is the freeing of obviously guilty persons. He cites the case of a man who three times confessed to the murder of his wife but went free because the police had violated procedural rules. Why, we may ask, are not ordinary economic and criminal law remedies used when the police are guilty of misconduct or law violation? If a policeman illegally detains a confessed murderer, why not fine the policeman, or discharge him, or imprison him, rather than letting the murderer go scot-free? The answer to such questions is to be found in the American distrust of police and our tolerance of only weak police power.

In matters of civil rights and due process of law, Americans have never relied on the police to police themselves. Instead they have, through the rulings of the Supreme Court and other appellate courts, made it impossible for the police to gain a legal advantage over suspected criminals by behaving illegally. The need for a judicial "exclusionary rule"—which prohibits the police from legally using evidence they have obtained illegally— becomes clear when wiretapping cases are considered. In 1934 Congress made it a crime for anyone, including policemen, to intercept a telephone conversation and divulge its contents. The law was frequently violated, both by policemen and by private parties. But in the thirty-five years the law was on the books— it was superseded by the federal Omnibus Crime Control Act of 1968—no policeman was ever convicted of violating it. In fact, only one or two policemen were even accused of violating it. In view of this failure of the police to prevent crime in their own ranks, the Supreme Court decided to make illegal police wiretapping useless and unprofitable. It held that illegally obtained wiretap evidence cannot be used as evidence in courts.

This "exclusionary rule" of course pertains to all evidence obtained illegally, not merely to evidence obtained by illegal taps. When illegally obtained evidence—including confessions—is excluded from the judicial process, a few guilty persons go free. The Supreme Court knowingly lets them go because in so doing it hopes to teach the police that, in matters of obtaining evidence at least, crime does not pay.

Some police have always argued that any method used to deal with suspects and criminals is absolutely essential to crime control. This conservative position eschews research, experimentation, and change. The Supreme Court's position, on the other hand, has been "liberal," in the sense that it has demanded changes in the system. Against the "necessity" stipulated by the police (and others), the Court has weighed other values. For example, in the 1930's the police maintained that third-degree methods of torture were necessary to keeping crime rates minimal, but the Court nevertheless outlawed such methods, principally on the ground that they were unreliable. The police should not need a method which might unreliably force a confession from an innocent man. The Court has more recently weighed the values of equality, human dignity, and privacy against the need for strict crime control. Even if a police method is "necessary," the Court has maintained, it is not necessary enough to justify violations of fundamental democratic rights.

Currently, one raging debate is between the advocates of the necessity for wiretapping and electronic surveillance on the one hand, and the advocates of privacy on the other. The Omnibus Crime Control Act authorized the police to engage in wiretapping and bugging, under carefully circumscribed and controlled conditions, in organized crime and national-security cases. Many officials were opposed to this authorization, and now they believe the law should be repealed. They acknowledge that the need to control organized crime and to protect national security is very great indeed. But, the argument goes, this need is not great enough to offset the actual and potential invasions of privacy stemming from authorized bugging and tapping.

The pros and cons of this issue are analyzed both by Mr. Lewis, who calls wiretapping a "dismal art," and by Dean Gutman, who asks Congress for legislation permitting wiretapping "for evidence of major crimes." No one quarrels with the Omnibus Act's prohibition of all bugging and tapping by private individuals. The current debate has to do only with bugging and tapping by police, and in that debate the issues are pretty much as they were stated in 1928 by Mr. Justice Brandeis, and in 1937 by Mr. Justice Sutherland, both of whom are quoted by Lewis.

Because all courts place one set of human values above another, all courts are likely to come under attack. The Supreme Court has been expressing value preferences since the day it was founded, and, probably because the word "supreme" is symbolic, it also has been the subject of severe criticism since the day it was founded. As Professor Westin observes, however, most earlier attacks centered on what was considered the Court's interference with business and economic affairs. One set of economic values was weighed against another. The direct beneficiaries of the Court's decisions were businessmen, especially big businessmen. Now the values being weighed by the Court involve liberty, equality, privacy, and dignity. The direct beneficiaries of the Court's criminal procedure decisions are not affluent businessmen. They are the powerless, unpopular, and offensive thieves, rapists, and murderers who, despite their crimes, are entitled to constitutional protections.

Is the Court
Handcuffing the Cops?

by James Vorenberg

IN MY VIEW, the contest between the police and the United States Supreme Court is grossly exaggerated. In any event, that contest, to the extent that it exists at all, has very little to do with crime. What the Supreme Court does has practically no effect on the amount of crime in this country, and what the police do has far less effect than is generally believed. The nation seems to have its attention riveted on a largely irrelevant, overdramatized confrontation between the police and the Court, and thus is impeded in doing anything constructive about crime—or even understanding it.

The controversy over confessions is probably the best example of how the effect of Supreme Court decisions on the volume of crime has been exaggerated. The principal target of those who attack the Court is the *Miranda* decision of 1966. *Miranda* held that once a suspect was in police custody he had to be given a warning of his rights, including an offer of counsel if he was too poor to provide his own counsel.

What is suggested is that this decision is in some way accountable for a very large rise in crime that has occurred since 1966.

But what are the facts? In the first place, the President's Commission on Law Enforcement and Administration of Justice, which is generally known as the Crime Commission, found that only something between one-tenth and one-third of the crimes committed are even reported to the police.

It's not very likely that a decision that deals only with people in custody is going to have much effect on crimes that are not even reported to the police.

We also found in one study that, of those crimes that are reported to the police, only one-quarter lead to arrest. And of those that do lead to arrest, only a small proportion are cases where a confession is crucial to solution. The others are cases where there is a witness or some piece of tangible evidence.

Already we are probably down to a maximum of 1 per cent or 2 per cent for cases in which *Miranda* could have a direct impact. Then we have to take account of the fact that, in many cases since *Miranda,* the suspect still confesses, and that, in many cases before *Miranda,* the suspect did not confess. The result is that the maximum direct statistical impact of this much-reviled decision is of the order of a fraction of 1 per cent.

But, it is said, there is more to it than that: *Miranda* in some way provides general encouragement to potential criminals. What that means is that, to get the encouragement *Miranda* is said to provide, before I set out to commit a crime I have to go through the following reasoning process: "If I commit this crime, and if I'm caught, and if I confess, that confession can be excluded if the police don't offer me counsel." I suggest that, in view of what little we do know about the people who are committing crimes, and the conditions under which those crimes take place, it is unlikely that that rather elaborate hypothetical reasoning process is going on.

Then it is said by the critics of *Miranda:* "It's not what *Miranda* actually says that has such a demoralizing effect on the police and encourages crime. It's what it is thought to mean, what the exaggerated view of it is." An obvious first step to remedying this effect of *Miranda* is for these very people to stop overstating the effect.

I am not a great champion of the *Miranda* decision. It is an unnecessarily confusing opinion for law-enforcement officers. It does not really make it clear whether confessions are or are not to be sought. I suspect it has had some demoralizing effect on law enforcement. But I strongly urge that it is not the culprit in any sense for the increase in crime, and I think the same is generally true of other Supreme Court decisions.

In one sense, it is true that Supreme Court decisions are responsible for some of the "crime problem." They are responsible for much of the improvement in police reporting of crime. For many years, it was the custom in our big cities for the police not to report all crimes because the figures were embarrassing. They might suggest the police were doing a poor job. Then, especially since *Miranda,* it became acceptable to report large crime increases in our cities because there was now an attractive scapegoat. So, in that sense, the Court probably is responsible for part of the reported increase.

But it is not just a reporting increase that we are facing. I am satisfied on all the evidence that enough of our cities are now reporting crimes sufficiently well so that what we see is not simply a paper increase. There is a significant increase in serious street crimes.

What is the explanation? The only honest answer is that we do not know, and as a nation we are doing very little to find out.

For example, in New York City between last year and this year, the number of reported robberies—which I think is in some ways the most important class of crime—increased from 36,000 to 54,000. That is a 50 per cent increase in one year, really an astonishing increase—particularly when you look at the gross numbers.

During that same period the number of robberies in Chicago as reported to the police stayed just about the same. That at least entitles one to ask the question: Why?

There are a number of possible theories. One is that the police in Chicago are better, that they're doing a better job in holding down crime. Those of us who watched the Democratic convention would be rather discouraged if that turned out to be the answer.

Another theory is that the Chicago police are much worse, that people don't report crimes to them because they don't have confidence in them. Take your pick.

Chicago and New York are not the only examples. Cleveland had no increase in robberies; Pittsburgh had a 70 per cent increase.

What I find striking is that virtually nothing significant is being spent in this country today to try to find out what is happening and why. Think what would happen in the medical field if there were an astronomical increase in cancer or polio cases in some cities, with no increase in other cities. Congress would be pouring money on medical researchers to try to find an answer.

If "curbing the Court" is not a constructive way of dealing with the nation's crime problem, what can be done? I would suggest three possible promising lines for change in dealing with the problems of crime.

First, we need to recognize that most defendants plead guilty, and thus, in the great majority of criminal cases, the crucial question is not whether the defendant committed a crime, but what should happen to him as a result of his conviction.

In spite of the fact that less than 1 per cent of the cases are tried by a jury, the general view of the criminal process is influenced by what might be called the Perry Mason syndrome. Too little attention and too few resources are devoted to the administrative process involved in accepting pleas of guilty and deciding on a sentence—as compared to the adjudicating process of the full criminal trial. The sentence often does not reflect a thoughtful and informed judgment as to what should be done with the defendant. It simply is a part of the process of keeping cases moving through the system in order to keep the traffic of criminal cases from grinding to a halt. Often there has been no real investigation as to what kind of treatment the defendant really needs.

We are thus losing our best opportunity to use the criminal system to reduce crime. We have identified somebody who is a potential future criminal (most crimes are committed by persons who have committed prior crimes), and in many cases we have identified him early in what may turn out to be a long and destructive criminal career. We have an opportunity to try to deal with him intelligently at that point, to devote some major resources to deciding what he needs. Does he really need to go to prison? Does he need some sort of medical or psychiatric treatment? Can he be released into some sort of job-training program?

There are some programs trying to deal with this problem. The Crime Commission proposed the establishment of Youth Service Bureaus which would take many nonserious juvenile cases out of the criminal system and offer the juvenile and his family helping services on a voluntary basis. In New York, the Manhattan Court Employment Project, run by the Vera Institute in cooperation with the court and the prosecutor's office, provides for the dismissal of a case after 90 days if the defendant is accepted in the program and is successfully placed in a job. This, I think, exemplifies the possibilities of private agencies taking over some of these nonadjudicatory cases.

The second major change we might consider is the way we deal with those who are convicted. Here we are presented with two polar theories. One is to be as tough as possible. The other extreme is the view of the therapist—lots of treatment in prison will lead to personal reformation.

On the hard-nosed view: We know very little about the deterrent effect of the possibility of a serious penalty. And since we are not really prepared to take every defendant out of circulation for the rest of his life, they are going to be released at some point. If we release them more dangerous than when they went into prison, we have not done much with the problem of public safety.

The therapist's view has not turned out to be much more promising. A recent California experiment took four groups of prisoners, 600 each. It offered three of these groups different kinds of intensive group counseling; the fourth group got the same prison treatment as the other three, except no group counseling. When they were all through, and had been followed up for five years, it turned out that there were no significant differences in the recidivism rates of the four groups.

Perhaps this suggests that maybe we should experiment with doing as little as possible in as many cases as possible. To the extent that any form of treatment takes away responsibility for handling one's life, it makes it harder to get back into society. Thus the use of half-way houses, probation, work release—anything that, in effect, permits the convicted person to begin living as soon as possible in the kind of world he's going to have to live in—may, in the end, turn out to be the most promising.

Finally, we have to recognize frankly the limits on what the criminal justice system can do for us in dealing with crime.

The first part of that is to recognize how overburdened the system is already, and to remove from it as many forms of conduct as possible that are not, and should not be, central areas of concern. The Crime Commission's proposal in 1967 that drunkeness should not be a crime has won increasing support. There are a variety of sex offenses, most of those between consenting adults, that should also be candidates for decriminalization, and a very hard look should be given to at least some of the drug crimes that are occupying more and more enforcement time.

More important than trying to take out of the system those cases that should not be there is to recognize how little the system itself can do in dealing with the problem of crime and to focus more on what broadly has been called prevention.

It is increasingly clear that the police, the courts, the prisons and the correctional services generally are engaged in what, at best, is a holding action. The most important finding of the Crime Commission is that any major reduction of the kind of predatory crime that is producing frustration and despair in the nation depends on ending the frustration and despair of the millions of Americans we have neglected for generations.

Simply put, this means that until we are willing to give poor people a stake in law and in order and in justice, we can expect crime to increase. The best hope of crime control lies not in better police, more convictions, longer sentences, better prisons. It lies in job training, jobs and the assurance of adequate income; schools that respond to the needs of their students; the resources and help to plan a family and hold it together; a decent place to live; and an opportunity to guide one's own life and to participate in guiding the life of the community.

Of course, these are things that a fair society does not only in the name of crime control but in the name of social justice.

Perhaps fear of crime will provide the added impetus that so far has been lacking in the nation's commitment to these programs. If not, and if there are new attempts to curb crime by new repressive measures, including possible constitutional changes, I think we can confidently predict that, 5, 10 or 25 years from now, crime will be an even more menacing part of the life of the nation than it is today.

The Criminal Gets
the Breaks

by Daniel Gutman

"UNDER OUR criminal procedure the accused has every advantage. While the prosecution is held rigidly to the charge, he need not disclose the barest outline of his defense. He is immune from question or comment on his silence; he cannot be convicted when there is the least fair doubt in the minds of any one of the twelve. . . . Our procedure has been always haunted by the ghost of the innocent man convicted. It is an unreal dream. What we need to fear is the archaic formalism and the watery sentiment that obstructs, delays and defeats the prosecution of crime."

So Judge Learned Hand wrote more than 40 years ago. Today, no one disputes that a mounting wave of criminal bestiality has become one of the nation's most serious problems. The streets, our parks, our homes and places of business—all are equally insecure against invasion, plunder and violence.

Every day in the week, criminals walk out of the courts, cockier and more brazen than ever, and looking for new prey. They "beat the rap"—a status achievement in the underworld. In many of such cases, the acquittal or dismissal has resulted not from lack of evidence, but from the fact that the evidence of crime was obtained by unapproved methods. A technicality has precluded its use.

Any discussion on how to handle the crime problem must consider the moral argument that it is better to permit the guilty to escape than for the innocent to be punished. Granted. Faced with a choice, most of us would certainly agree with this proposition. It must be remembered, however, that no reasonable rules of procedure can offer complete security against an occasional miscarriage of justice. The possibility of error will always be present until a means is devised for ascertaining truth with certainty. There is not much likelihood of such a development in the foreseeable future. In the meantime, let us not underestimate the potential danger that an unpunished guilty felon—one who "beat the rap"—represents to society.

It is regrettable that those who advocate measures that would enable us to deal more adequately with the repression of crime are accused, almost invariably, of being "opposed to due process." One need only suggest a study, the need for change, and he is open to a charge of taking short cuts with due process of law. Unsavory epithets are applied to those who take any position on this vital public question—"radical" or "reactionary," "leftist" or "Fascist," as the case may be. As a result, many intelligent citizens say nothing; they avoid the controversy, although they are disturbed by the growing rate of crime and the apparent inability of government to cope with it.

The structure of democratic government rests largely on the constitutional guarantee that no person shall be deprived of "life, liberty or property without due process of law." The function of our highest court is to enforce the requirements of law. This task it has done well. Controversy arises over cases in which the Supreme Court may have gone beyond the requirements of the constitutional mandate. The feeling that it may have does not justify the violent attacks that have been made on the Court, but does demand critical discussion of some decisions.

More serious, in their effect, are those procedural rules and some of our laws which circumscribe the determinations of the courts—and which must be changed, if at all, by the legislatures that promulgated them. A glance at some of the cases in which evidence pointing to guilt was held to have been improperly admitted will best serve to illustrate the problem.

Not long ago, in a United States District Court, a case collapsed for lack of evidence. Three times, the defendant, James W. Killough, had confessed to the murder of his wife. On one occasion, he had led the police to a dump upon which he had thrown his wife's body after the murder. Twice, he had been convicted of the slaying; twice, the convictions were reversed. And now the judge directed the jury to acquit, writing "finis" to the case. The principal evidence consisted of the confessions. But the confessions were ruled out, on appeal.

The reason was that the accused had been detained for some 26 hours after his arrest, in violation of a procedural rule that required his arraignment to take place "without unnecessary delay." Therefore, the confessions (although freely given) and *all evidence related to or growing out of them* were inadmissible.

"We know the man is guilty," said Federal Judge Hart, who presided at the trial, "but we sit here blind, deaf and dumb." Later, he added: "Felons will sleep better tonight."

Judge Hart's ruling was dictated by the oft-cited Mallory case. The defendant, suspected of a brutal raping, consented, after being questioned for an hour and a half, to submit to a lie-detector test. There was a delay of several hours before the test could be given. When confronted with the results, Mallory signed a full confession. By that time, seven hours had elapsed since his apprehension. It was then too late to arraign him in court, and that procedure was postponed until the following morning.

Despite the fact that there had been no coercion upon the suspect to take the lie-detector test or to admit the crime, the confession was held, on appeal to the Supreme Court, to be inadmissible. The Court decided that a rule requiring arraignment without unreasonable delay had been violated. "Unreasonable" is considered for practical purposes to require immediate arraignment. Mallory, who had been convicted by a jury, went free. He was never retried because, without the confession, there was not enough evidence to establish guilt.

Another landmark decision that enables many guilty felons to escape conviction was handed down in the case of *Mapp v. Ohio*.

A seizure of pornographic literature had been made, without a search warrant, and Dollree Mapp, who was convicted of possession of the material, appealed. The conviction was sustained until the case reached the Supreme Court. There it was held that evidence obtained by state officers in violation of constitutional requirements controlling search and seizure is inadmissible in any criminal action in state as well as Federal courts. Previously, this "exclusionary" rule had been held to apply only to prosecutions in courts of Federal jurisdiction.

The search in the Mapp case was illegal. Without question, it violated the defendant's constitutional rights, and the Supreme Court had no alternative but to rule out the evidence which brought about the conviction.

The impact of the Mapp decision lies in its retroactive effect. It will apply not only to future prosecutions, but will also nullify prior convictions in state courts, in cases where evidence that had been obtained improperly was admitted despite the fact that such evidence was previously admissible in all but Federal courts, in accordance with earlier rulings of the United States Supreme Court.

Then there is the Massiah case. Massiah, a seaman, was arrested and indicted on a charge of smuggling narcotics into this country. An accomplice, Colson, was indicted with him. By arrangement with Federal agents, Colson went for a ride with Massiah in an automobile that had been wired with radio equipment. The talk between Massiah and Colson was relayed to the agents, who were in another automobile. Massiah's statements were introduced in evidence. The conversation was incriminating. Massiah was convicted.

The United States Supreme Court set aside the conviction on the ground that Massiah did not have the benefit of counsel when the conversation in the automobile took place. The Sixth Amendment of the Constitution provides that: "In all criminal prosecutions, the accused shall enjoy the right . . . to have the assistance of counsel for his defense."

The full effect of the Massiah ruling may be to preclude any admission made by a person charged with crime in the absence of his lawyer. Justice Harlan, in a dissenting opinion in which he was joined by other justices of the Court, wrote: "The Massiahs can breathe much easier, secure in the knowledge that the Constitution furnishes an important measure of protection against faithless compatriots, guarantees sporting treatment for sporting peddlers of narcotics."

In the Escobedo case, the defendant, charged with the murder of his brother-in-law, was not permitted to consult his attorney, who tried to see him at the police station. Escobedo's admissions to the police officers who were interrogating him led to conviction.

The Supreme Court held that the refusal to permit the defendant to receive the advice of counsel was in violation of his constitutional rights. The following is an interesting excerpt from the dissenting opinion:

"The decision is thus another major step in the direction of the goal which the Court seemingly has in mind—to bar from evidence all admissions obtained from an individual suspected of crime, whether involuntarily made or not. It does of course put us one step 'ahead' of the English judges who have had the good sense to leave the matter a discretionary one with the trial court."

Whether or not constitutional privilege bars only compulsory incrimination, and does not preclude self-incrimination by voluntary statements, the far-reaching effect of the ruling in this case is readily discernible.

Discussing these rulings, a high-ranking Federal jurist commented not long ago: "It means that, from now on, a police officer about to arrest a suspect had better say to him: 'I have to arrest you. Would you mind waiting here for me while I go and get you a lawyer?' "

To be guilty of perpetrating a crime and to be proved guilty are two different things. A person accused of crime must be proven guilty beyond a reasonable doubt. The technical requirements for evidence cannot always be satisfied, and persons who are by no means innocent are permitted to go free.

One of the great loopholes for escape from conviction is found in the provisions regarding search and seizure. The strict application of these requirements is demonstrated in the case of Fahy against the State of Connecticut. The defendant admitted, before and at his trial, to painting swastikas on the exterior of a synagogue. But the paint and brush shown to have been used by him had been seized without warrant. Clearly, the seizure was illegal.

Fahy's position in court was that he had not violated the law and was not guilty of vandalism. The legality of the search and seizure was not questioned, and he was convicted.

On appeal, the high court of Connecticut upheld the conviction, and ruled that "harmless error" had been committed in receiving into evidence the articles that had been seized improperly. The United States Supreme Court reversed the conviction. The wrongful search and seizure was the underlying reason. Justices of the Court wrote, in a dissenting opinion, that the evidence of guilt was overwhelming, with or without the brush and paint.

The layman, as well as the lawyer, may find it difficult to understand the rationale that circumscribes action to be taken pursuant to a search warrant. The rule was laid down by the Supreme Court in the Marron case: "The requirement that warrants shall particularly describe the things to be seized makes general searches under them impossible and prevents the seizure of one thing under a warrant describing another. As to what is to be taken, nothing is left to the discretion of the officer executing the warrant."

Simply stated, this means that if law-enforcement officers, while making a lawful search pursuant to a search warrant, discover evidence of another crime the evidence of such other crime cannot be used against the possessor. As to such evidence, *or any information derived from it,* the search is of no effect.

A typical case, of frequent occurrence, is presented when police, searching pursuant to a warrant for evidence of violations of the gambling laws, find a quantity of narcotics. The latter evidence cannot be used even if its discovery is followed by a confession. The search for narcotics was not authorized, and confessions or other proof of commission of the crime that flow from or are developed by it are considered "fruits of the poisoned tree." The "poisoned tree" is evidence obtained in violation of statutory or constitutional rights, and anything that derives from or is discovered as a result of such evidence is characterized as its "fruits" and cannot be used to prove the crime.

No discussion of law enforcement would be complete without some reference to wire-tapping. By enactment in 1934 of Section 605 of the Federal Communications Act, the Congress banned "interception and divulgence" of telephone conversations for all purposes. Nonetheless, wire-tapping pursuant to a court order, on a showing that there are reasonable grounds to believe that evidence of crime could be obtained, is authorized by the laws of New York State.

In the Benanti case, the United States Supreme Court precluded the admission in the Federal courts of such evidence even when obtained by local or state officers acting under authority of a state law. It is likely that the use of such evidence in all courts will ultimately be prohibited. Some Justices of the New York State Supreme Court have announced that they will not sign orders permitting wire-tapping for evidence of a crime—even though the statutory requirements have been met. They reason that the decisions of the highest court render illegal such orders and all actions taken under them, under any circumstances.

The Congress for several years has been "studying" the wire-tapping problem, but no action has been taken to amend the Federal laws. In the meantime, the activities of narcotics rings and other groups of organized criminals continue unabated.

The cases of the guilty who are permitted to go free are legion. The reader must remember that we are not speaking of those cases where, after a trial, the jurors conclude that a reasonable doubt exists as to guilt. In such cases they should acquit. We speak of the criminals who are able to get away with their crimes, and to go free to commit further crimes. Nor do we disagree with the rules excluding a confession, or other evidence, that has been obtained by coercion of any type.

There is a reasonable case to be made for changing some of our technical requirements. We do not solve the problem of dealing with those who make crime their business by providing procedural methods of escape for the guilty, to the detriment of the law-abiding who are victimized by the lawless. Some changes can be made within the framework of the Constitution and the Bill of Rights.

These changes cannot be accomplished, however, without divesting ourselves of the currently fashionable practice of being oversolicitous of the criminal and indifferent to the rights of the citizenry at large. Treating with crime is a serious business. We, our children, our possessions are its targets. It is an enemy that recognizes no law but that which is spawned in its own corruption. It knows no moral code—it violates everything that is human and decent. It is not a theory—it is real, it is ugly—a deadly, ever-present enemy.

These steps can be taken—now:

(1) Enactment by Congress of legislation to permit wire-tapping, pursuant to court order, for evidence of major crimes.

(2) Recodification of procedural requirements for search and seizure, which are distinctive for ancient strictures no longer valid.

(3) Extension of the right to detain and interrogate, with proper safeguards against coercion or violation of constitutional rights.

(4) Clarification of the extent and application of the "right-to-counsel" concept.

(5) Relaxation of the rule excluding all evidence improperly obtained, so as to vest discretion as to admission in the trial judge.

(6) Convening in extraordinary session ranking members of the judicial, legislative and executive branches of the Federal Government for thorough consideration of the problems of law enforcement.

The challenge is to the bar, the public and the lawmakers. The executive and the judiciary must cooperate. This is everybody's responsibility.

Tangled Issue
of Wiretapping

by Anthony Lewis

FOR THREE DECADES, since the Supreme Court first dealt with the problem, wiretapping has been the subject of recurrent controversy in this country. Waves of public outrage at notorious uses of the dismal art have alternated with campaigns by law-enforcement officials to eliminate restraints on tapping.

At the moment the cycle seems to be in its second phase. Police and prosecutors, who consider wiretapping an essential weapon against crime, are concerned about what they believe is a movement in the courts to clamp down on tapping. "You can't hunt lions with a bean-shooter," Brooklyn's District Attorney Edward S. Silver explained to a group of Congressmen in urging them to support permissive wiretap legislation. Mr. Silver is president of the National District Attorneys Association, which shares his view.

Scientific developments have made wiretapping easy—and its detection extremely difficult. A cheap induction coil placed next to a telephone line will pick up a conversation without causing any tell-tale hum or interference. A device known as a pen register or dial recorder picks up the number dialed by the unsuspecting party and prints it in dots or dashes on ticker tape.

The legality of wiretapping is an intricate question that can be considered most simply if broken down into three parts—tapping by Federal agents, by state and local officers, and by private persons.

The Federal constitutionality of wiretapping was upheld by the Supreme Court in 1928. Over the dissent of Justices Brandeis, Butler and Stone—and Holmes on non-constitutional grounds—the Court ruled that tapping was not an "unreasonable search and seizure" of the kind prohibited by the Fourth Amendment, and that use of wiretap evidence at a trial did not violate the Fifth Amendment's guarantee against compulsory self-incrimination.

Then, in Section 605 of the Communications Act of 1934, Congress provided: "No person not being authorized by the sender shall intercept any communication and divulge . . . the contents." This cryptic language was given content by the Supreme Court in 1937. It held that the statute applied to Federal agents as well as private persons and prohibited the use of wiretap evidence in Federal courts.

Despite Section 605, the Federal Bureau of Investigation and other Federal agents continue to wiretap. The F.B.I. asserts that its tapping is legal because Section 605 makes it a crime only to "intercept *and* divulge"—both acts, not just the first—and because only *public* disclosure, not merely reporting to an official superior, counts as "divulging" under the statute. These somewhat fragile legal theories have never been passed upon by the Supreme Court, but successive Attorneys General have supported them.

At one time the director of the F.B.I., J. Edgar Hoover, opposed wiretapping on the ground that its benefits would be outweighed by the "discredit and suspicion" it would bring on law enforcement. But his views changed in the Nineteen Thirties, and in 1940 President Roosevelt officially authorized wiretapping by the F.B.I. provided that approval for each tap be obtained in advance from the Attorney General. That procedure is still followed. According to Mr. Hoover, the bureau uses taps only in internal security cases and where life is at stake, as in kidnapping and extortion. He testified last Feb. 8 that the F.B.I. then had seventy-eight wiretaps.

As for the states, only a few have restricted tapping. Illinois and Pennsylvania in 1957 enacted statutes flatly prohibiting all wiretapping, police taps included, and barring wiretap evidence. The courts of California and Florida have ruled out the use of wiretap evidence. In five states—New York, Massachusetts, Maryland, Oregon and Nevada—the police are permitted to tap if they first obtain a court order from a judge.

State and local officials are concerned now at the possible effects of the Federal law, Section 605, on their use of wiretap evidence. For in 1957 the Supreme Court said Section 605 applied to state officials and overrode any state laws purporting to authorize tapping. Since then a few judges in New York have refused to issue wiretap orders or have barred evidence obtained by tapping under other judges' orders. The Supreme Court said in 1952 that nothing in Section 605 compelled state courts to exclude wiretap evidence, but this principle is being challenged in a case which the Supreme Court will review next term.

Private wiretapping—by marital investigators, private eyes of all kinds and criminals—is illegal under Section 605 and under some state laws. Until recently there had been virtually no prosecutions, a fact sometimes said to result from government's embarrassment in punishing others for what its own agents do. But in the last half dozen years there has been significant action against private tappers. A tapping case in New York led to a legislative investigation and a general crackdown on tapping by private detectives. Other state prosecutions have been reported; and the Federal Government, which had obtained only one conviction in the first twenty years of Section 605, has chalked up six since 1954. (It lost the best-known case, against Teamster chief James Hoffa.)

In this legal wilderness, how much telephone tapping actually goes on? There are no reliable estimates, but undoubtedly there is a great deal. In 1955 a New York private detective, John Broady, was found in a room with access to 100,000 telephone lines, some of which he was busily tapping. The New York City police, probably the most active official tappers, obtain perhaps 1,000 court orders a year authorizing taps. A recent study by the Pennsylvania Bar Association estimated that the police in New York actually tap as many as 20,000 lines a year without bothering to obtain court orders in advance, but officials ridicule this figure.

The foremost legal analyst of the problem, Alan F. Westin of Columbia University, wrote in 1952: "Despite the statutes and judicial decisions which purport to regulate wiretapping, today this practice flourishes as a wide-open operation at the Federal, state, municipal and private levels." This year Professor Westin has expressed the belief that the amount of tapping is down somewhat since "the high tide of the early Nineteen Fifties."

Since no one has a good word to say for private wiretappers, the question of what to do about wiretapping centers on official tapping by law-enforcement agencies. What, then, are the arguments pro and con?

The basic argument for police wiretapping is that it works. Taps are said to be an essential weapon against crime—especially against a criminal element that is becoming better and better organized. As distinguished a liberal as the late Robert P. Patterson, judge and Secretary of War, endorsed official wiretapping as a necessary device to fight ever more resourceful and sophisticated criminals who do not hesitate to use any contrivance against the law-abiding.

A second argument of those who favor official wiretapping is that, under modern conditions, respect for privacy is an insufficient basis for policy. Society and the individual himself have interests aside from privacy, and one of them is protection against crime. If wiretapping is "dirty business," as Justice Holmes said, so is crime. When the Supreme Court in 1937 construed Section 605 to bar wiretap evidence, Justice Sutherland wrote in dissent:

"My abhorrence of the odious practices of the town gossip, the Peeping Tom and the private eavesdropper is quite as strong as that of any of my brethren. But to put the sworn officers of the law, engaged in the detection and apprehension of organized gangs of criminals, in the same category is to lose all sense of proportion. . . . The necessity of public protection against crime is being submerged by an overflow of sentimentality."

Wiretapping proponents argue that under the control of court orders tapping is no more reprehensible than many traditional police practices—the use of informants, for example, or searches under warrant. They argue that regulated wiretapping will not touch the law-abiding.

Some who oppose wiretapping doubt that it is really necessary to law enforcement. Senator Thomas C. Hennings Jr., whose Constitutional Rights subcommittee has made an exhaustive study of the subject, says the verdict as to need is "not proven." Others concede that wiretapping helps the police, but say the price is not worth paying. Thomas McBride, former Attorney General of Pennsylvania, told the Hennings subcommittee that tapping does not catch enough criminals to outweigh the loss of "the feeling of freedom that people have that they are not being listened to."

This threatened loss of privacy is, of course, the basic objection to wiretapping. The fear is that to put this weapon into the hands of Government agencies is to move toward totalitarian spying on individuals. The classic statement of the values at stake was that of Justice Brandeis, in his dissent from the 1928 decision upholding official wiretapping:

"The makers of our Constitution . . . recognized the significance of man's spiritual nature, of his feelings and his intellect. They knew that only a part of the pain, pleasure and satisfactions of life are to be found in material things. They sought to protect Americans in their beliefs, their thoughts, their emotions and their sensations. They conferred, as against the Government, the right to be let alone—the most comprehensive of rights and the right most valued by civilized men."

The right to be let alone—a phrase first used by Brandeis in an 1890 law-review article—sums up what lies behind the instinctive aversion to wiretapping. Opponents dispute the claim that tapping affects only the guilty or can be effectively regulated. A judicial order for a tap is not like a search warrant, limited to a particular time and place and object; it may go on indefinitely, without the notice that a search warrant gives the suspect. Conversations with innocent persons as well as conspirators are overheard.

Moreover, say the opponents, authorities may misuse supposedly limited wiretapping authority. A Brooklyn grand jury charged in 1950 that police were using taps to blackmail gamblers after attaching the taps without court approval, and that they were obtaining court orders wholesale on the basis of inadequate or false affidavits of need. The F.B.I. was said to have listened in on conversations between Judith Coplon, the alleged Soviet spy, and her lawyer.

In the present situation, one may conclude, there are elements that dissatisfy all sides. The police and others concerned with law enforcement see what they consider their necessary power to wiretap clouded by Section 605 of the Federal law. Opponents of official tapping think too much of it is going on. The citizen has no confidence that private tapping is effectively controlled. Worst of all is the impression that law-enforcement officers themselves are violating the law. That was the situation in the 1928 Supreme Court case: Prohibition agents had wiretapped in violation of a District of Columbia statute. Justice Brandeis, in the greatest passage of his great dissent, foresaw the consequences:

"In a government of laws, existence of the Government will be imperiled if it fails to observe the law scrupulously. Our Government is the potent, the omnipresent teacher. For good or for ill, it teaches the whole people by its example. Crime is contagious. If the Government becomes a law-breaker, it breeds contempt for law; it invites every man to become a law unto himself; it invites anarchy. To declare that in the administration of the criminal law the end justifies the means—to declare that the Government may commit crimes in order to secure the conviction of a private criminal—would bring terrible retribution."

The observer seeking a solution to the wiretapping dilemma may find the British example instructive. A country hardly insensitive to the claims of freedom and privacy, Great Britain nevertheless permits police wiretapping—under the strictest of controls. Each tap must be approved in advance by a high official of the Home Office. A 1957 report by a committee of Privy Councilors, approving the continuation of controlled wiretapping, said it was "an effective weapon" against crime and concluded:

"The interference with the privacy of the ordinary law-abiding citizen or with his individual liberty is infinitesimal, and only arises as an inevitable incident of intercepting the communications of some wrongdoer. It has produced no harmful consequences."

That conclusion of the Privy Councilors can be understood only against the background of the facts on wiretapping in Britain. Official taps in the entire United Kingdom have averaged fewer than 150 a year. The police invariably destroy all records of wiretaps, the Privy Councilors found; it was unthinkable that officials would use taps for private ends. Most astonishing to an American, the councilors found no evidence of the existence of any private wiretapping whatsoever.

The secret behind the generally accepted and satisfactory wiretapping situation in Britain, then, is public confidence—confidence that power given officials will not be misused, confidence that the privacy of the honest citizen's conversation is unlikely to be invaded by either private eavesdroppers or overzealous police.

The problem in this country is to create conditions giving rise to the same degree of confidence. Some argue that in a nation without Britain's tradition of official self-restraint, the only answer is absolute prohibition of all wiretapping. Others believe that there should be regulated wiretapping. Perhaps in part because complete prohibition is likely to be an unrealistic idea so long as crime remains as severe a problem as it is, the alternative of regulation seems to be gaining support among those concerned about wiretapping.

Professor Westin, who favors such limited tapping, notes that the vital element in any legislative plan to that end is control to insure against police excesses. The legislation must at the same time be sufficiently workable so that it will be obeyed and not avoided by law-enforcement officials. Because this is now overridingly a problem of Federal law, any meaningful resolution of the wiretapping conflict must come from Congress.

The legislation envisaged by Professor Westin and others would allow the states to wiretap—if they wished to at all—only under a court-order system rigorously defined by Congress. The state courts would be allowed to issue orders only upon a genuine, particularized showing of need. Orders would be good for a limited time, say a month. The wiretap authority might be limited to serious crimes and placed in the hands of District Attorneys rather than the police.

On the Federal level—where the need for legislation is certainly less urgent—the ideal statute would provide a clear legal basis for the kind of wiretapping now done by the F.B.I. Tapping authority might be limited to certain crimes, such as espionage and kidnapping, and certain Federal agencies, perhaps only the F.B.I. Some think a Federal court order should be required for each tap, while others think the Attorney General's personal approval, as at present, suffices.

Along with these permissive provisions, the legislation would include a flat and total prohibition on all other wiretapping—that is, on the tapping itself, without regard to fine points about "divulgence." There would be an assumption of strict enforcement by the Justice Department, including prosecution of officers who violate the law.

It would be foolhardy, in light of the record, to forecast early Congressional action. Dozens of bills have been introduced and dozens of hearings held in the last twenty years, and Congress has done nothing. But the pressures are rising now and they come from several directions—from law-enforcement officials worried about their legal position, from libertarians concerned about wiretapping in general, from those who see a gradual breakdown of legal controls in this area. Perhaps the time is approaching when Congress will have to settle this particular conflict between liberty and order.

When the Public
Judges the Court

by Alan F. Westin

IN THE PAST three years, the Supreme Court has been denounced
for "judicial misbehavior" by a wide assortment of critics, ranging from the American Bar Association and Southern officialdom
to state court judges and the Daughters of the American Revolution. Bills and constitutional amendments have been sponsored in
Congress to limit the Court's jurisdiction, and to make the justices think twice before extending their "offensive" doctrines.

To listen to many of the wisest commentators on our constitutional politics, this imbroglio is not strikingly different from situations which the Supreme Court has encountered ever since the
days of Chief Justice John Marshall and his self-declared archfoe,
Thomas Jefferson. But is it? In my opinion, this battle between
Court and critics is distinctively different from any other in our
history.

In each previous struggle over the proper role for the Federal
judiciary in our governmental system, a property issue has been at
the heart of the controversy. While the doctrines of the justices
have always been a matter of debate, there were five notable
periods when the Supreme Court became a leading political issue,

From the *New York Times Magazine,* May 31, 1959, copyright © 1959
by The New York Times Company.

and prompted campaigns by powerful blocs in Congress to alter the Court's personnel or its powers.

The years 1821–24 and 1831–33 saw protests against the Court's interference with state regulation of banks, land titles, companies and other parts of the mercantile establishment. Arguments during 1857–60 dealt with the Court's treatment of slavery as a property matter and the impact of the slave system upon the economies of the West, North and South. The years 1896–1912 were marked by protests against the Federal judiciary's insulation of corporate enterprise from both state and national measures aimed at monopoly, taxation and labor relations. Finally, 1934–37 centered on the Supreme Court's barriers to social welfare legislation and to national management of the national corporate economy. In all of these episodes, powerful economic interests were directly involved in defense of their privileges.

The current debate over the Court's role has no comparable economic basis. The reason for this lies in the character of the decisions that have precipitated protest. While the Supreme Court under Chief Justices Vinson and Warren has not been a "pro-business" Court, as in the days of Chief Justices Marshall or Taft, neither has it been "anti-business." In matters directly affecting business, as in labor relations, anti-trust and tax issues, the Warren Court has been simply an enunciator of the "social capitalist" *status quo* in American politics.

Instead of property issues, the present controversy deals with matters of liberty and equality. Where the outcome of disputed cases in the past decided what people could do with their property, free from Government restraint, the new cases decide what people can advocate and organize to promote, which people are consigned to be "more equal than others," and what procedures Government may follow in apprehending and prosecuting the non-propertied antisocial elements in our population.

Where the beneficiaries of the Court's rulings were once land speculators, planters, railroads and public utility holding companies, the new befriended are Negroes, syndicate leaders, Communists, balky college professors, rapists and Government employes accused of disloyalty.

Accompanying this shift in the issues has been an equally

fundamental shift in the groups who attack and defend the judiciary. Previously, it was the spokesmen for liberalism and majority rule—from Jeffersonians to New Dealers—who denounced the Supreme Court. They did so on the rational liberal theory that the Court was an insufferable restraint upon majority will. In a democratic society, they argued, judges with life tenure had no right to substitute their notions of good policy for the wishes of the people acting through their elected representatives—Congress, the President, and state governments.

Yet, in the Nineteen Fifties, liberal groups are defending the judiciary as a wise agency to check mass passions and to protect natural rights from invasion by the "political" branches of Government.

A similar reversal has taken place in the conservative camp. Previously, liberal critics were opposed by propertied groups who declared, in rational conservative doctrine, that the Supreme Court was a badly needed brake upon populist democracy. Yet, in the Nineteen Fifties, the critics of the Court are led by groups we ordinarily associate with conservatism—the American Legion, the D.A.R., the American Bar Association, state and local law-enforcement officers, Southerners, right-wing Republicans and Democrats in Congress, and the like. Their cry now is that the Supreme Court is tampering with the wise conclusions of the people's representatives, and they denounce the notion that any doctrine of higher right permits the judiciary to intervene.

Finally, this is the first conflict not to present basically a party-line division. Previously, Jefferson, Jackson, Lincoln, Bryan and Roosevelt led the bulk of their party faithful against the disputed judicial doctrines. The party dominated by property interests being protected by the Court defended the justices. Today, with property issues absent, there are no party positions. Eisenhower remains aloof. Stevenson supports the Court. Congressional Republicans and Democrats are divided. In this controversy, conservatives among the two parties face liberals from the two parties.

What do these changes import for the present controversy over judicial review? On this score, I think it may be wiser to ask questions and supply speculations than to issue firm conclusions.

First of all, why have liberal and conservative elements changed

positions? Have the ideological bases of these classic camps under-
gone a transformation in the Nineteen Fifties? I think the answer
is less spectacular than that. An overwhelming majority of liberals
now defend the Supreme Court and judicial review because the
justices are handing down rulings on liberty and equality issues
which accord with liberal beliefs. Conservatives are opposing
the Court because it has become "dangerously unsound" on these
matters.

It is clear that whether a group's ideological toe has been
pinched is the first determinant of whether the pinching institution
will be praised or damned. Since the five major crises over
judicial review in our past found the Court steadfastly devoted to
conservative positions, the simple explanation of the first liberal
switch toward judicial review is that liberals have had to wait
from 1790 until the Nineteen Fifties to find a set of justices to
whom they could attach their allegiance.

A second question is why a majority of justices came to make
this shift of positions possible. On this subject, since justices do
not allow themselves to be polled or given Rorschach tests, the
area of speculation is remarkably wide.

Perhaps, like nature, Supreme Court justices abhor a vacuum.
Since 1937, a majority of justices have been committed to the
concept of "judicial self-restraint" in matters of economic regulation by the elected branches of government. For two decades, not
a single Federal tax measure, regulation of commerce, national
welfare program or labor law has been declared unconstitutional.

While there was some talk within the Court between 1937 and
1953 of applying a different, more interventionist, standard of
review for liberty and equality cases, a majority of the Court
generally applied self-restraint across the board. Appointees who
looked forward to enunciating high constitutional principles must
have chafed under these self-imposed bonds.

By itself, I doubt whether this yearning for glory would have
precipitated the departures of 1953–59. The personal discomfort
coincided, though, with urging by powerful elements, including
the Eisenhower Administration, to advance from the "gradualist"
approach of the Vinson Court on equality matters and overturn
the whole separate-but-equal doctrine of racial segregation. Grow-

ing sentiment in condemnation of the Court's "ducking" of fundamental issues, rising anti-McCarthyite spirit in the nation after 1954, and the arrival on the Court's docket of liberty cases which represented the most excessive and least necessary aspects of the internal security programs—all these factors pressed in upon the Court.

However, the Supreme Court, or even a majority, is not something with a life of its own. Justices are distinctly individuals, with viscera and predilections inside them rather than gears or I.B.M. cards. Thus one has to consider personalities as well as "forces" to reach satisfactory explanations of judicial behavior.

Chief Justice Vinson and Justices Jackson, Reed, Minton and Burton were judges who either found the case for authority persuasive in most liberty cases or else felt that the Supreme Court ought to exercise self-restraint in these as well as property cases.

In place of these justices, the Eisenhower Administration has installed Chief Justice Warren and Justices Harlan, Brennan, Whittaker and Stewart. While there are important differences in constitutional philosophy among these men, ranging from the liberal interventionist credo of Warren and Brennan to the legal institutionalist focus of Harlan, the Eisenhower appointees as a group are different from the justices they replaced.

Trained in law school when legal realism was at its height, and free from personal involvement in the anti-Court, judicial self-restraint fight of the Nineteen Thirties, these men approach the post-1954 cases with a freer and less self-conscious perspective than their predecessors.

However, I think the earlier justices, had they still been on the Court when the outer limits of the internal security issue were reached, between 1954 and the present, would also have been impelled to take a more active position than they had previously. Justice Frankfurter, for example, has found a way to vote against Government action and for defendants far more after 1954 than he had before. Justice Jackson would very likely have done the same.

In support of this hypothesis, it is useful to remember that courts have a way of defending liberty after a crisis has passed its peak. A delay in constitutional showdowns occurs on the theory that only when the dangers of excess are demonstrable and hysteria has diminished will the public heed the justices' call to constitutional ideals.

It is also pertinent to note that the liberty and equality issues, while similar in being non-propertied, do not represent identical problems for the Supreme Court. This has led to two different configurations within the Court. On cases dealing with segregation and its implementation the justices have presented a 9-0 face to the nation. Here, liberal interventionism is the judicial credo.

In liberty matters the present Supreme Court has a four-man interventionist core made up of Chief Justice Warren and Justices Black, Douglas and Brennan. Justices Frankfurter, Harlan and Whittaker have joined the four-man liberal phalanx in many of the disputed liberty cases, but usually with opinions which adopted more limited grounds for the result in the cases. Justice Clark has been in dissent in virtually all liberty cases. This leaves Justice Stewart, who has not participated in enough cases as yet to indicate exactly what his position represents, but seems to lean to the Frankfurter-Harlan group. Thus, close divisions are destined to be the rule in the liberty cases, with a divided court mirroring nonsectional public divisions on these questions.

A third question to consider is what effect these changes in the fight over judicial review will have upon the Supreme Court's power position, or, put another way, whether the Court can find as powerful a constituency to support it today as in the past.

Most Americans are not used to thinking that the Supreme Court has a constituency, like Congressmen with their electoral districts or the President with the national electorate. Yet the Supreme Court, despite life tenure for its members and a tradition of judge-worship in the population, remains a highly vulnerable institution. Decrees from the high tribunal are realistically enforced only if the President and Congress acquiesce in them and public opinion supports—or is not actively opposed to—the basic trend of decision.

Who will support the Court today? It seems to me that business conservatives have been uncommitted so far in the present Court controversy and are likely to remain so as long as the Court does not add anti-business decisions to its disputed doctrines. To be sure, a few men associated with business organs, such as David Lawrence, have joined in the attack upon the justices, but I think it is more significant to note that corporate spokesmen and business associations, such as the N.A.M., have chosen to stay out of this campaign.

Can the Court depend upon liberals, plus residual Court-worship in the population, to defend it against the nonbusiness conservatives? As Congressional events in 1958 showed, the Court's critics are far from few. With the unending animus of the Southerners (and Southern political power in Congress) to lead the drive, the Court is faced with more than a temporary round of dissent.

On the other hand, it would be a mistake to underestimate the strength of the Court's defenders in the new political atmosphere of post–World War II America. With the importance of Negro voters constantly growing in urban politics outside the South, and with white groups such as Jews continuing to identify themselves strongly with the anti-segregation issue, the Court's equality decisions are likely to be supported not just by liberal groups but by the urban machine leaders of both our political parties.

I think the Court has a somewhat rockier road for its liberty decisions, and it would not be at all surprising to see Congress reverse several specific rulings such as those dealing with the Smith Act, passport policy or state sedition laws. Even on the liberty side, however, the Court is not altogether defenseless. Distaste for McCarthyism, a desire for more careful scrutiny of internal security measures and concern for fair procedure seem to be steadily increasing since 1954.

Indeed, the existing sense of moderation is indicated in the fact that many local bar associations have dissented from the American Bar Association's criticism of the Supreme Court, that the A.B.A.'s resolution was really rather mild and that the president of the A.B.A. has felt it wise to stress publicly that the A.B.A. had no intention to attack the Court but only to suggest stronger antisubversive machinery.

I do not mean to give the impression that a determinist tide rules the future of the present conflict over judicial review. Much will depend on how wisely and well the justices decide specific cases, when they choose to intervene and when to leave issues to the political branches of government, and whether the Court displays that basic craftsmanship in opinions without which a judge appears naked to those who do not agree with the results in cases.

The debate will also be affected by many factors not under the control of the justices at all, such as whether the nation can find a President who understands what the justices are saying and will place the prestige of the White House behind the Court's decisions.

At present the Court seems firmly fixed in its course. For the interventionist justices there are the lures of making high national policy and promoting liberal goals to spur them onward. For the justices who lean toward judicial self-restraint there are other compelling factors. Concerned with the prestige of the Court, they realize that the Court cannot draw back from its desegregation approach without compromising its basic position.

On the liberty side they realize that the arrival of radical anti-subversive measures, threatening the traditional values of fair procedure and ordered liberty, has impelled them to take the distinctly moderate stands inaccurately described by angry critics as sweeping doctrines. There is nothing which can stiffen a good judge's back more firmly than erroneous charges by groups which equate assumption of inescapable responsibility with a "treasonous" arrogation of power.

Whatever this examination of the history of American judicial review indicates about the present or the future, one thing seems clear. French proverbs to the contrary notwithstanding, the more things change, the less likely they are really to be the same. History may teach the justices that they are not the first to face fundamental attacks, but this Court will have to find its own path to success in dealing with "status" issues which have replaced property politics of past generations.

Part **3**

THE WHEELS
OF JUSTICE

NO ORGANIZATION works the way it is supposed to work. Bureaucratic rules are the essence of any organization, but administration of these rules always results in the invention of additional rules. These are not mentioned in manuals of standard operating procedures, or depicted on official organizational charts. Sometimes the rational system set up to achieve some goal or set of goals is too cumbersome for its purpose. Organization personnel do not then simply abandon ship. They change the formal rules, and they invent informal rules which enable them to bypass the formal system in order to get the job done. In other cases, organizational arrangements do not in fact provide for achievement of all the goals assigned to the organization, so the personnel unofficially invent systems for achieving unofficial goals. And sometimes the official rules of an organization do not allow for the personal and somewhat idiosyncratic needs of the participants. Unofficial systems of behavior then arise to meet those needs.

By and large, the authors in this section assume that everyone knows how police departments, prosecutors' offices, the United States Supreme Court, and prisons are *supposed to* work. Their objective is to give insights into how these agencies *really* work.

Saul Braun, a New York free-lance writer and novelist, dramatically shows that only a small part of a policeman's work involves "law enforcement." The principal part of Inspector Joe Fink's time is given over to keeping the peace and to furnishing services. Thus the inspector, like most other policemen, is engaged in administering justice rather than in enforcing criminal statutes. James Q. Wilson, professor of government at Harvard, shows in more detail that the police devote most of their energy to peace-keeping and rendering services ("crime prevention") rather than to detecting and apprehending criminals.

Professor Wilson also describes a crime-reduction experiment in which a New York neighborhood was saturated with police. The results were consistent with the Copenhagen and Montreal natural experiments, which suggested that withdrawal of the police from a community affects the rate of utilitarian crime, but not the rate of expressive crime. The New York experiment showed the obverse, namely that a heavy concentration of police serves to diminish the number of street crimes considerably, but has no effect on the murder rate.

The police engage in peace-keeping when they stop, question, and frisk people on the street. Professor Wilson, an expert on police organization and behavior, favors this practice, which the Supreme Court recently held to be constitutional. It is clear, however, that if the police are to prevent crime they must do something more positive than merely "show the flag." Yet there is no reason why preventive activity by the police should duplicate prevention programs conducted by public and private youth service agencies. In the first place, such attempts to forestall the commission of first crimes do not appear to be a proper police function. In the second place, such prevention programs have been notably unsuccessful. The police should concentrate on the prevention of recidivism and, in that way, join forces with probation, prison, and parole workers. Most criminals are repeaters. If first offenders could somehow be prevented from committing additional crimes, the crime rate—at least the rate for "street crimes"—would immediately decrease to less than half its current size.

Martin Mayer is the author of *The Lawyers* and other books.

His description of the work done in the office of the New York County District Attorney again reveals that unofficial arrangements have developed, and probably are essential, for administering criminal justice. One such arrangement, present in most court-houses and prosecutors' offices, is the system of so-called "plea bargaining." In this system a defendant, by pleading guilty to an offense calling for a penalty less than the one prescribed for the offense he is charged with, avoids the risk of conviction of the serious offense. As Mr. Mayer shows, however, most such arrangements for settling criminal cases cannot properly be characterized as "bargaining." In District Attorney Hogan's office, the defendant is rather bluntly told how strong the prosecution's case is. He can then intelligently decide whether he wishes to risk conviction by going to trial or to plead guilty to a lesser offense. This is not "bargaining" or "negotiating" for pleas of guilty. It is criminal justice administration.

The statistics presented by Mayer indicate that New York County prosecuting attorneys go to trial only if they are certain that the defendant is guilty. This finding may be generalized to the conclusion that prosecutors are not merely in the business of presenting cases to judges and juries for decisions as to guilt or innocence. On the contrary, the prosecutor, in collaboration with the defense attorney, in most cases makes the decision as to whether a defendant in fact did what he is accused of doing. The adversary character of the criminal justice system is thus mitigated to a considerable degree. While the facts of a case may be determined more effectively by administrative conferences between prosecution and defense than through "trial by combat," the administrative system of justice also has its faults. Among other things, the defendant's fate is decided in hurried conferences in corridors and men's rooms, not by means of the slow, deliberate, painstaking, and presumably impartial processes of law. Further, under the current system of court organization, administrative decisions about guilt or innocence are not subject to careful review.

Even the justices of the Supreme Court have developed informal procedures for getting their work done. Mr. Justice William J. Brennan, Jr., shows how the Court goes through the process of exercising its discretion to select the cases it will hear. Since the number of cases coming to the attention of the Court doubles every six to eight years, the Court's discretionary procedures are increasing in significance. Yet—despite Justice Brennan's "inside story"—lawyers, legal scholars, and plain citizens know very little about the details of the Court's decision-making processes. In recent years, lawyers and social scientists have begun to study the processes by which policemen decide to take one suspect, but not another, into custody. They should, by the same token, start studying the processes by which the Supreme Court selects for decision only about one out of every sixteen cases coming before it.

It may properly be concluded from the first four articles in this section that the hallmark of our criminal justice system is the discretionary character of the decisions made by all personnel, from arresting officers to court officials. Once a person has committed a crime, almost everything that happens to him—from arrest (or release) and trial (or dismissal) to imprisonment (or probation or parole)—depends on administrative decisions which are not readily subject to public scrutiny or, for that matter, to appeal. M. Arc, a former prisoner, tells how important it is, in this situation, that the decision-making personnel be intelligent men possessing wisdom, compassion, and a tempered sense of justice. In all criminal justice agencies, not just in prisons, the personnel must be able to take actions in the direction of abstract goals, such as rehabilitation, rather than in the direction of mere institutional functioning, such as manning the housekeeping and maintenance departments. When prison workers are unable to do more than "enforce the law" repressively, Mr. Arc reveals, prisoners respond with their own organizational arrangements for mitigating the conditions of the repression. As a consequence, the prison neither rehabilitates nor represses. Probably the same thing could be said about other criminal justice administrators. When the police, for example, can do no more than try to repress crime, perhaps the citizens simply respond with systems for avoiding the police altogether, thus increasing the crime rate.

The Cop as Social Scientist

by Saul Braun

THE NINTH PRECINCT runs from the East River west to Broadway and from 14th Street south to Houston Street. It comprises some of what was the classic Lower East Side of the great Jewish immigration, some of the Bowery and all of what is now known as the East Village. The Ninth is a high-crime precinct. In 1968, it was 13th from the top among the city's 78.

Because of the runaway microboppers and the hip street people with their drugs and piquant life styles, and the collision of their egotistical and self-abasing presence with the mired Puerto Ricans and the old-style, semipoor decent people, who neither like them nor understand them, the precinct is a dramatic and highly political one, with great visibility and much media attention focused on it. The commander of the precinct is Deputy Inspector Joseph Fink, who understands this perfectly well.

Normally, a captain commands a precinct. Inspector Fink remains in the Ninth, informed sources suggest, because he is too valuable where he is: without him, the lid on the precinct would very likely blow off, leaving the city open to the worst kind of police/community warfare. So, Fink is the key to peace in the

From the *New York Times Magazine,* August 24, 1969, copyright © 1969 by The New York Times Company.

Ninth, and the key to Fink's success is his recognition that in this day and age police authority must sometimes wear the mask of social science. As Fink himself puts it: "The policeman must make an effort to secure the cooperation and approbation of the people who make up the neighborhood." He has managed to win a lot of that approbation; a precinct resident says in all seriousness that if the inspector had been in charge, Chicago would not have happened. And his approach has won plaudits outside the Ninth, too—from police professionals and from politicians, who have a special stake in keeping the peace this year. Mayor Lindsay is said to have called him "my favorite hippie."

Joe Fink sits at his desk in the station house on East Fifth Street. The desk is crowded with paperwork, two telephones, in and out baskets, a shell-shaped ash tray, a "Give a Damn" button and a two-pen onyx desk set with shield number 19378 laid into it. He is a large man with sparse red hair, a Roman nose and a fleshy, ruddy face. His eyes are brown, his gaze more purposeful than it at first appears. In private conversation, his voice is resonant and well-modulated.

Now, he is talking comfortably and easily and with assurance, interrupting himself periodically to transact some business that has come to mind, to answer the phone or to walk to the door of his small office to pass some comment upon precinct matters, which he does in a booming "command" voice that loses subtlety and distinction as it takes on authority. On his right hip he wears a small Colt .38, the off-duty size, with the butt facing forward; he is left-handed.

He is not in uniform. He wears a sharkskin suit with a blue shirt and a blue-on-blue tie held with a gold tie clip. The shirt has cuff links and a white embroidered figure, a crown, on the breast pocket. He could just as easily be the biggest Pontiac dealer in a small upstate city, or its mayor.

A cop comes to the door and asks to have his shift changed. The inspector's glance darts back and forth between the man and some papers on his desk and he says, "Uh . . . er . . . did you check with whatyacallit?" and riffles the papers, " 'cause . . . uh . . . ," and the cop says he did and the inspector hems and haws, and it is as though he has put the cop on hold while he shuffles through his mind for all the factors that weigh on his decision and he says, finally, "Yeah, all right. Okay." The whole thing has a curious ritual quality. He is like a father who hates to say no but doesn't want to be too easy.

He shows me a statistical breakdown of crime in the precinct, which comes down from the Police Statistics and Records Bureau every month. "Here's murders, the first three months of '69. Eight homicides. We had one the other night where a fellow shot his brother-in-law. Statistics indicate that in many cases the victims and perpetrators are known to each other. Not only in murders but in assaults and frequently in rapes. In rapes roughly about half the people that commit rape are known to the victim."

He runs his finger down the report. ". . . Post 13, that's one short part of Avenue C . . . post 14 . . . then we have one on post 22 . . . post 39 . . . non-negligent manslaughter . . . paid informers . . . Hippie Squad . . . F.B.I. Crime Index. . . ." The verbal paraphernalia of law enforcement. He shows me an article he wrote for the Journal of Criminal Law, "Police in a Community—Improving a Deteriorated Image." The short bio preceding the piece says he "holds a Bachelor's Degree in Police Science and Sociology from the City University of New York and has received seven departmental citations for outstanding performance of duty."

He hands me a picture postcard. There are freckles on the back of his hand. "I got this card from Abby Hoffman." The picture is of the Montreal exhibition, "Man and His World," a vision of harmony, of man as he can live in a golden future. "In five years," writes Abby Hoffman, *provocateur* and revolutionary to his local police chief, "the Lower East Side will look like this. I'm leaving soon for Europe and Prague, Checkslovakia [sic], so if you don't see me by September 26 you'll know I'm in Siberia fighting the T.P.F."

This last is a reference to the Tactical Patrol Force, an autonomous police unit, which is feared and hated by many residents of the Ninth Precinct. They are not Fink's cops and, like all police who come from a distance to establish order, they are not overly concerned with securing "the approbation of the people who make up the neighborhood."

Inspector Fink hands me a clipping of Jimmy Breslin's column for Sept. 6, 1968: "You can with two or three jokes handle Abby Hoffman and turn him into an excellent straight man for your speech openers. Here, in New York, one cop, Inspector Fink, keeps Abby Hoffman in a whirl. One cop with a little sense."

I ask the inspector about this unusual relationship. He tells me of the time Abby Hoffman was passing by the station house and saw a dozen blacks inside and came in and said, Why did you arrest them?, and Fink said it was for loitering for the purpose of using eight marijuana cigarettes, and Abby said, That's crime and if you arrest them you have to arrest me. Fink said, Okay, hang around. Abby lay down in the station house doorway where it says *"Aquí Se Habla Español"* and two cops picked him up and put him in a back room. Inspector Fink booked the blacks and sent them home and said, Abby, why don't you go home, too?, and Abby said, No, you've got to arrest me, and then went over to the glass case where the precinct has its P.A.L. athletic trophies and gave it a kick and broke it.

It is said that this was the only time anybody heard of Joe Fink losing his temper. "So I says, 'All right, now you're under arrest for breaking property,'" Fink says. "So the next day he walks into the station house and he throws a $5 bill on my desk. And he says, 'Here's for the glass.' So I says, 'Abby, we can't take it. If you wanna, pay the judge, and he'll let you off with a charge of malicious mischief.'"

Fink does not recall the disposition of this case, but he has had to arrest Hoffman several times "personally," without breaking up their friendship. "You try not to get annoyed with individuals," he says. "People used to ask us, how do you treat hippies that you get along so well with them? I treat them equal, I treat them as individuals. If they are a cause of trouble, you gotta take whatever steps are necessary. I've locked up Abby a number of times, but that has no bearing on how we spoke to each other the next day."

Fink rises and puts on the jacket of the sharkskin suit. The hankie in the breast pocket matches his tie. "Come on," he says, "let's take a look and see if he's in."

We go out of the station house walking east along East Fifth and into a tenement basement where Abby Hoffman has an office. There is no answer. Fink goes to another apartment and knocks peremptorily, just the way you imagine cops do. He wears a big imposing ring with a blue stone. The ring is inscribed: "John Jay College of Criminal Justice. 1966."

A thin girl with a thin voice comes to the door and claims not to know where Hoffman is. The inspector thanks her politely and goes out.

"Let's walk along here," he says, "I want to check on something. There's going to be something in Tompkins Square today. I want to find out what's going on."

He walks along the street with the air of a feudal lord up out of the manor house taking a stroll into the village. His walk is mostly manly stride with just a touch of waddle. Often he is recognized and he will stop to chat, as he does with Marty Schlass, the owner of a health food restaurant called The Caldron, which is I Ching hexagram number 50.

They discuss the local labor market (Fink suggests he go to Mobilization for Youth to find workers), and they discuss *fellafel* and *kashe* and other mythic Jewish dishes. Fink is a Conservative Jew who was past president (when he was a sergeant) of Shomrim, the police society for Jewish cops. But he is not religious. He attends "on High Holy Days." The only thing "Jewish" about him is his voice, which has the thickened oatmeal texture and nasal aging of the typical New Yorker who grew up on the Lower East Side, as he did.

"Listen, I'll be back later and maybe we'll have a dinner," Fink says. "Very good," says Schlass, a tanned, muscular fellow who wears a sort of loosely woven fishnet shirt.

"I can admire and envy a guy like that who dresses freely and is productive," says Fink, now going east on East Sixth, "a guy who is doing something to make a living and producing some sort of goods and he's part of a society that means something. But I don't envy these kids that leave themselves open to all kinds of drug hangups and end on street corners and panhandle for everything and wind up in fights or off on trips that can, you know, kill them, and who are anxious to avoid responsibility."

Fink goes down a flight of stairs (the top of his head is freckled) and into a basement storefront marked Renaissance. There is a phone number and a bulletin board: Mail for Chester K, Billy Joe C, Betty B, Neil W, Judy K. . . . Am looking for people with the mark of Caine. Leave name and address. Bill. . . . If you are pregnant and can't keep your baby, my mother wants to adopt a baby. Call Mrs. Edwards collect.

The man who runs the place is 25-year-old Sam Andox (that, at least, is the name he gives) and it is a sort of switchboard for the community. Sam finds pads for runaways. His interests are social and political. Fink is here to negotiate. He hopes to find in Sam someone who can help the community get itself a little more cohesive and self-serving.

They walk around the room, circling, seemingly inattentive but very aware of each other's weights. Sam says, What about the roundup of runaways last Thursday? . . . and Fink says, There was no roundup of runaways last Thursday . . . and Sam says, I saw it with my own eyes . . . and Fink says:

"Let me tell you this. We don't have any special day for whatyacallit. The men are supposed to pick up visibly young kids all the time. A 14-, a 15- or a 16-year-old kid who is away from home without parental consent—uh—do you give them, can you say legally or morally they're entitled to do what they want even to their own detriment? Would you say—uh—uh—let 'em shoot drugs?"

Sam looks at him unblinkingly but says nothing. In this look are, at the same time, something grudging—a little like affection —and an abiding mistrust that will not be manipulated out of existence. Later, Sam will tell me that a friend on the Mayor's staff has told him that Fink has "a couple years of public relations courses" in his background and Sam doesn't doubt it.

A small Oriental girl comes in. Sam has started talking about an incident in which five or six cops manhandled a kid on St. Marks Place and Fink says, Is that the kid who was pushing junk? Sam snorts, finding Fink's response a thinly veiled evasion.

The inspector in the meantime has begun questioning the girl: Are you the little girl who was almost raped last night? *Yeah.* And they arrested the man? *Yeah, they arrested him.* How come you went out at 3 o'clock in the morning to buy something in the store? *I went out for apples.* At 3 o'clock in the morning? This is something I can't understand. What's your name? *Lee.* Did you go to court today? *No.* Why not? *Oh, listen, when he comes out he'll be more violent.* But by your not going you're subjecting somebody else to these frightening things happening to them.

The girl looks at him uncomprehendingly. He can no more understand why she doesn't want the police into it than he can relate to her when she commences a rhapsodic, impressionist account of a recent acid trip. There are a large number of these sexual assaults, and many go unreported. Blacks and Puerto Ricans prey on hippie chicks, who have a victim's mentality and anyway don't feel the cops can or will protect them.

Can I ask you something? says a long-haired boy who has wandered in. What's your attitude to pot? The inspector says, I have opinions but I can't take an attitude on something that's controversial from my point of view or from the point of view of the system that I'm working in. But there's enough research that shows that marijuana does do something to a person's perception, you know, reactions, and his emotional state.

All right, Fink says, raising his voice preparatory to departure. Sam, I'll talk to you more about this. I'd like to see if we could, you know, find some way of—uh—reaching . . . I don't know how good you are at talking to the Mother—— and the Crazies but—uh—let's see if we could get some sort of situation going where, when, you know, 11 o'clock comes and they sit down and relax and stop the music and—uh—cool it. He raises his voice until it is a hearty booming shout. All right?

Sam says, All right.

Outside, Fink says, "They're having a whatyacallit; a sympathy rally for the People's Park in Berkeley. Let's go over there."

On the way, heading east on Sixth he tells me about an incident involving the Mother—— and Crazies last February at Cooper Union, where he was making a speech on Crime and Fear in the City. The kids went in, maybe 80 or 100 of them; they banged on tom-toms, they danced, sang; one girl bared her breasts in front of the auditorium just below Fink's podium. "I had some policemen available on call," Fink says, "but I didn't want to make any arrests and take any police action so we just canceled the meeting. These Mother—— and Crazies wanted everybody to, whatyacallit, to know they think the police are responsible for all the crime and fear, not the people."

Other sources verify that Fink does not tend to take hasty police action. Kip Cohen, the manager of Fillmore East, tells of the Siege of the Fillmore by the Mother—— in November, 1968, when they tried to "liberate" the hall. "They knew we wouldn't call the cops," says Cohen. "We kept the police advised, but at our request they were not to come in. And it is our feeling that in any other precinct or in any other city this place would have been a bloodbath. I don't think Fink is necessarily more liberal, but I think he's smarter than most cops, more sane and sensible. He knows who these people are, who the leaders are. It's my personal feeling it's going to be quiet down here this summer."

Tompkins Square is full of the people of the hip community and also winos up from the Bowery who have rolled their pants legs up and think they can pass for hippies. As we walk along, the inspector is recognized. "Hey," someone says, "there's Fink." He waves.

A young mother has unbuttoned her blouse and is breast-feeding her infant, sitting crosslegged in the walkway. On the evidence, no girls in the East Village wear brassieres. What does Fink think of it? "I think it's fabulous," he says with a wide grin.

He stands off to one side and comments on the scene in transition. "In 1967 the hippie thing was in full bloom. You had the flower kids and the love generation, everything was sweetness and light and all were anxious to, you know, live and let live. And the sexual freedom. Then you had the people who came in and said, Hey, let's get a free piece. Then you had a rough element that got in and tried to squeeze all the goodness out of it for their own benefit. And, you know, there wasn't much left. People began to see that the hippie, you know, the Love Generation or the love concept wasn't a viable one in this world."

Post 64. Lafayette Street and Astor Place. Here there is a large black sculpture poised daringly, a cube balanced precariously on one point. It looks as though at any moment it will come crashing down upon the large number of kids who have made a more or less permanent encampment beneath it, sleeping, sitting around, strumming guitars, begging. This is the portal and gateway to the East Village. A girl of perhaps 13 holds up a metal rod with some Christmas tinsel pasted onto it. "Sir, you wanna buy this for $3.99?" A boy about her age says, "Sir, you have a safety pin?" Everybody not sleeping titters.

There is an Australian bush hat with a couple of buttons on it. One says, "Thirty-five Thousand GI's Died in Vain." I can't read the other. I ask about it. A boy with sullen eyes picks up the hat and puts it under his arm, hiding the button, and turns his back to me.

I walk along St. Marks Place and strike up a conversation with a fellow with thin brown hair to his shoulders and a long thin face that looks bruised, but not with respect to any particular blows. We go into a candy store and drink chocolate egg creams. He offers me a handsome variety of drugs, acid, pot, Mighty Quinn (whatever that is) at the same time warning me against any drugs offered me on the street. "They're selling this stuff and it's really hog tranquilizer. It's a trip, sure, but you know, man, I can't take it knowing it's hog tranquilizer."

"The drug scene?" says Fink later. "Well, let me say this, everybody seems to think the use of hard drugs and LSD is diminishing, reaching a plateau. There is no hard and fast information. Mafia figures have been involved in large-scale handling of narcotics, but in the precinct, mostly local people are dealing, to feed their habit or to make money."

"His way is to keep everybody happy," says Nettie Di Mauro, the secretary of the Church of the Nativity. "The population of the precinct is Italian, Jewish, Ukrainian—you have Maltese people, now even some Chinese. Not too big a Negro part. And you have these hippies or yippies or whatever you want to call them. But the Puerto Ricans I think would almost equal everybody else. And I've seen Fink's instructions to his men: 'Keep the place fluid. Be sensitive to the situation.' I really think he's trying to be very fair to everybody."

"He's a psychologist," says a precinct cop approvingly. "I have driven with this man, and if he has anything derogatory to say, he steps out of the car and takes the officer aside. And boy, that means a lot. You don't *know* what it means. Sometimes a cop needs a good dressing down, but it hurts when you're in that uniform, you know, it's very *embarrassing*. You feel about two inches tall. And I have never heard him criticize a cop in front of anybody.

"There's always a griper or two, but over-all I would say he's well liked. He's a very *fair* man. He never takes that overbearing I'm-the-boss attitude. You know he's the boss, don't get me wrong. But to me he's a good boss to work for."

"Fink is an interesting cop," says Allan Katzman, the publisher of the East Village Other. "He's a media cop dealing with a media situation. Basically, he's a good guy, a father figure, who understands what's happening, a political cop. His cops have not caused violence; most of it is caused by the T.P.F. With any other cop other than Joe Fink here there would be five times as much trouble."

Fink himself is fond of quoting Abby Hoffman, who says, "Joe Fink is like a Jewish mother. His solution for everything is to pour chicken soup over it."

Post 15. Avenue C at East Ninth Street. A sign on the corner building says "Re-elect City Councilman Saul S. Sharison. For district leaders Harold Gonzalez and Freida Provda." Across the street in a storefront is the Iglesia Apostolica Cristiano de Bethsaida, Inc. Bus number 21 rumbles by on the cobbled narrow street. Three kids in diapers sit in a dirty puddle of water, playing. Down the block firecrackers are going off. An ice vender beneath a green and white beach umbrella: he scrapes a chunk of ice, looks at his array of red, green and purple bottles, scoops a cup and pours flavoring on it and commences eating.

"I'm a product of the East Side of New York," says Fink. "I was born down here in June, 1915, just 10 blocks south of the precinct. My father Louis was a modest merchant, a tailor. He's dead 21 years now. My mother Augusta lives with me and with my sister Ruth in Florida. I have a son, Kenneth, who's 26. He's a salesman.

"How I got into police work? Someone I knew had become a policeman and he thought it was a terrific job. I was working as a salesman then. He said, You're crazy, you never know when your firm will fold up, you don't have any security. He convinced me to take the exam just to see if I could pass it. This was in 1938. You'd be surprised how much was expected then from a young man to whom $8 to $12 a week was being paid, and not a 5-day, 40-hour week either. I worked for a dress manufacturer, a sort of salesman–shipping clerk. There was also the head shipping clerk and another fellow. The three of us took the exam. I was the only one that passed. The other two, one went into the Army and got killed at Anzio or Salerno. The other guy became very wealthy in the dress business. You never know where you're going to wind up, right?"

He is in civvies, wearing a tie with the seal of the City of New York on it. Mayor Lindsay gave him the tie, so he is apparently a member in good standing of the city's liberal Mafia. He chomps down on four ounces of white meat turkey on rye, in Hymie's Delicatessen at the corner of Second and East Fifth. A man walks over to him and begins without preamble. "Listen, inspector, they failed my kid. And you know what he told me? He said, 'Dad, they want cops so desperately, how come they failed me?' " The inspector urges him to have the boy take the exam again, and the man seems to feel better about it.

He walks over to the La Mama where his friend Ellen Stewart is proprietor and guiding light. We enter the theater just as the play is about to end. A character is saying, "I don't like the police very much, they're always asking questions: Who are you? What are you doing here?" Fink turns and grins at me. After the play we chat with Ellen Stewart in her apartment above the theater. "Joe Fink's not a cop, he's my friend," she says with animation. "If they try to take him out of this precinct, we'll send a petition around."

"She's a great gal," says Fink later, "we've been friends for 10 years. I was a lieutenant in this precinct for six years, you know. My assignments have been mainly in deprived areas—South Bronx, Williamsburg, Greenpoint, Bedford-Stuyvesant, Brownsville, and then back again to the Lower East Side. In Brooklyn I was a shoofly for nine months, a supervisor of patrol. You fill in for other captains on their days off when you become a captain and then you become a shoofly for a period of time before they assign you a station house."

He looks out the window of his squad car and says to the driver, "Hold it, pull over here." An elderly lady is coming out of the park waving, screeching for the police. She is in a tattered dress, heavy dark stockings and black men's shoes with some cloth over her head. In the East Village they're called Yukies, for Ukrainians. "That's my kid," yells the Yukie, pointing to a defeated, disheveled man in his 40's, "and this guy here is going to hit him. Get him out of the park, please."

Out on the sidewalk, the son whines, "No matter where I go she follows me. SHE'S NUTS. SHE'S DRIVING ME CUCKOO."

"Don't yell," says Fink.

"Help me get away from her, please, she's driving me nuts."

"It's easy," says Fink. "Just walk away."

The son laughs bitterly, rubbing his day-old beard. "You think so? You just *try* it with her."

Fink says, "What does she want? She's your mother? Take her for a walk. Take her with you."

The man gives Fink a despairing look.

Back in the police car, Fink says, "Police work consists of three types of jobs. One is law enforcement. Another is keeping the peace. The third is furnishing services. I always, whatyacallit, felt that I never became a policeman to be a fighter. What I like to do is work with people, deal with people."

The driver pulls alongside a pair of kids who have been setting off firecrackers. "Hey, kids," the driver says, "don't shoot 'em off." The kids look frightened. Fink leans out the window. "Don't shoot firecrackers," he says, "you'll hurt yourself."

Inspector Fink is duty officer for Manhattan South this evening, which means he is responsible for half the borough's precincts. He is in his office removing the jacket of his iridescent, summer-weight, blue gray suit. I ask him if there is such a thing as police authoritarian personality. "Well, let me say this. You're in an organization whose cooperation you depend on and they depend on you. *Esprit de corps.* A cop's mentality, yes. You get to have certain concepts and certain ways of looking at the world and the people in it." He removes his trousers and puts on his uniform trousers and then his uniform hat. "Some people say that cops get authoritarian personalities, but I don't see this is true." He puts on his tie. "I don't think you can make a rule that all cops are going to fit into the same pattern." He puts on his uniform jacket then pulls out and inspects a nightstick. I can't imagine what he is inspecting it for but it makes me feel funny.

We get into his car and streak uptown, and the view from the back seat of a squad car is a new one for me. People look up as we pass by, and there is a special look that we get, something passes between them and us, something ineffable but real enough, and it is not at all unlike what developed in me as I saw Joe Fink transform himself into a Deputy Inspector with the major's gold leaf on his shoulders, into something a little more distant, a little . . . bit . . . alien.

"I'm always ready to talk to the people," says Fink, "but it's a problem. You're not going to get everybody to open up. And we ask our cops when they turn out to say hello to the people and smile so the people won't see them as enemies."

In an attempt to increase communication between the police and the community, Fink instituted a bi-lingual Ninth Precinct Newsletter which comes out sporadically, and he has brought in top cops like Commissioner Howard Leary to give human relations talks to the precinct cops: Who Is on Welfare and Why? A Capsule History of Immigrant Populations of the Lower East Side. Puerto Rican Customs and Culture.

Fink's cops have played basketball against the Tompkins Square Community Center kids, mostly black and Puerto Rican, and have taken on the staff of the Fillmore East at touch football. The cops lost 8-6 on a disputed safety they claimed was a touchback. They finally called Football Commissioner Pete Rozelle for the decision. "Both teams," says Fink, "complained how rough the other was. But it develops the feeling that everybody's human. On July 2 and 3 we're taking 30 kids away to Fort Totten in Queens. This is part of the Community Relations Bureau's program for a police-youth dialogue. Unofficially, also, we're running some sensitivity training for our cops. Get them together with a trained social worker to talk out their problems and get more familiar with their true feelings. We're experimenting with this. What we would like to do eventually is make, is bring people from the community in to interact with the cops in this thing. My big problem is how do you do all this and prevent crime at the same time?"

There is an antiwar demonstration this evening at the Coliseum —Youth Against War and Fascism.

At the Coliseum as we pull up, a dozen squad cars are parked side by side and the T.P.F. are out, patrolling and circumscribing —*keep moving*—pressure and force and grim pleasure in their alert, tense bodies, demonstrators scattering, an earnest young girl saying quietly, "There's a law of the right of assembly in the United States and the right of peaceful protest. Now look. Now look at this." And a bystander saying, "What's this—the Communists or the beatniks? See how they like it in Moscow." And Inspector Fink surveying the scene, hands clasped behind his back: "Evidently we're going to make some arrests and move some people out of here."

A tall, white-haired top cop is here. Assistant Chief Inspector Michael Codd. He and Fink and a uniformed captain look on as a jaunty, bouncy guy like a young James Cagney, in civvies, orchestrates the T.P.F. movement. This is Deputy Inspector James T. Sullivan of the T.P.F. He strides around and raises his arm and gestures and suddenly there is a swirl of activity, a sudden shocking burst of animal energy as the T.P.F. wheels down along Broadway to 59th Street, unleashed, plunging into the scattering throng and coming up with a struggling fish, transfixed, tight in the embrace of arms and clubs with eyes bulging, sullen and helpless, shoved into the car with the blinking light.

Inspector Fink stands with his hands clasped behind his back and observes the scene with professional interest and involvement, an imposing figure, the very model of the successful new cop. Later, in the squad car, I asked him about protest.

"Well, anybody has a right to protest and I feel the Constitution guarantees people's right to, you know, express themselves, whether it's a popular idea or an unpopular idea. I think we are in a time of great social change, but I don't accept the concept that you have to do violence to accomplish these changes. Notre Dame has made a lot of changes, even though Father Hesburgh laid down a pretty hard line. I think there's a point where some sort of order has to be maintained. Not at the price of using police as an absolute blanket, but the point at which legal action should be taken."

Police Work

by James Q. Wilson

I WOULD LIKE to speak specifically about two possible roles that the police can play in dealing with crime: first of all, the police as an agency of crime prevention and, second, the police role in the detection and apprehension of criminals who are believed already to have committed a crime.

I am confining my remarks to street crime because I regard robberies, muggings, holdups and the like as the most serious kind of crime. I want to distinguish street crimes from consensual crimes—gambling, the narcotics trade, sexual crimes of various sorts—and from crimes of stealth—burglaries and larcenies that are committed when no victim is physically endangered—and even from private crime. Most assaults, most murders—perhaps most rapes—involve persons known or related to each other. They are crimes among friends, so to speak.

I think street crime is the most important crime. What is striking to me is that there have been so few serious, carefully evaluated experiments as to how the police can best be deployed to reduce street crimes in high-crime-rate areas. One important experiment did take place in 1954 in New York. In the 25th Precinct of Manhattan, an area about equally divided among whites, blacks and Puerto Ricans and with a high crime rate,

From the *New York Times Magazine,* May 1, 1969, copyright © 1969 by The New York Times Company.

the entire graduating class of the Police Academy was assigned as supplementary patrolmen with the result that the patrol force, largely on foot in that precinct, was doubled or tripled for a four-month period. In addition, detectives, juvenile, narcotics and other specialized officers were assigned to the area.

The results were striking. The murder rate did not go down. Those private crimes continued unabated behind drawn shades of apartments and hotel rooms. But street robberies in this four-month experimental period compared with the four similar months in the preceding year, fell from 69 to 7; auto thefts from 78 to 24; disorderly-conduct arrests from 177 to 77; other robberies, not street robberies but store-front, liquor-store, gas-station robberies and the like, declined from 97 to 43. And of those crimes that were committed, a substantially higher percentage were solved by the arrest of the person involved, usually by a foot patrolman who was near the scene of the crime.

Yet this experiment, dramatic as it was, did not answer all the questions one might ask of how the police might prevent crime. We do not know, for example, how many of the criminals in Precinct 25 went next door to the adjacent precinct to practice their enterprises there, or perhaps even to an adjoining borough. We do not know what would have happened if the experiment had been carried on for a year or two. Some people can get used to anything, even the presence of a police officer on every street corner, and it might have occurred to somebody to enter those buildings from the rear rather than the front. We do not know how the citizens felt about it—whether they felt they were being subjected to unnecessary police surveillance or whether they felt relieved that the streets were safer.

What disturbs me is that no one has tried to duplicate this experiment to see if similar results can be produced elsewhere under other circumstances. All that energy that was devoted to this project, which on the surface had promising results, has been dissipated elsewhere, perhaps in attacks on the Supreme Court.

The role of court restrictions on the use of the police as a device for deterring, though surely not eliminating, street crime has to do with the point at which the police officer ceases to deter crime simply by his presence or discourage criminals by his questioning but instead begins to set in motion the train of events that will lead to a person's being arrested and charged.

The *Miranda* decision holds that once a person is in custody, he must be warned of his rights, and I believe, for one, that it is entirely proper that he be warned of his rights. But at what point does custody begin? At what point does a casual questioning on the street of a suspicious person, asking him to identify himself and to give an account of his intentions and his activities—when does that end and when does an arrest begin?

I think it is extremely important for the police to have, under a carefully drawn statute, the right to stop and question citizens about their activities and their place of residence. I believe this is one way the police, without seriously infringing on our right of free movement, can help make the streets safer for all of us.

What concerns me is that the tendency of some lower courts may be to discourage the exercise of this police right, leading not to the ending of street stops by police officers, but leading to their becoming covert activities. Most police officers, if they take their responsibilities seriously, will stop and question persons they regard, on the basis of their experience, rightly or wrongly, as suspicious. But in many states it is not clearly legal for a police officer to do this. Consequently, a local police administrator, wishing not to court the disfavor of higher opinion, will ignore the problem, not lay down any policies for his officers, not train them on how to carry out this function responsibly, and allow his officers to carry it out, so to speak, covertly.

The question of frisks is a more complicated one. Under what circumstances should an officer be allowed to pat down a suspect, a person he meets on the street? Generally the courts are of the view that if it is necessary for the protection of the officer— that is, if he believes a person is likely to be carrying a concealed weapon—they will be tolerant of it. But, again, it is a controversial area of the law, and as long as it is controversial, police administrators will be derelict in their duty to define policies and to train officers in the proper exercise of those policies.

One study done for the Crime Commission indicated that one

out of every 10 street frisks produced a concealed weapon. I believe this is enough of a gain to society to warrant giving police the right to stop and frisk persons on the street. What is needed is a very carefully drawn statute defining the right.

Let me turn now to the problem of the detection and apprehension of persons alleged already to have committed a crime. There have been a number of studies to see if the police were being inhibited by the rules of evidence that were being laid down by the Supreme Court. These studies are not clearcut in their findings, but I think it is fair to say that on the whole they do not show any substantial loss in convictions as the result of the police being instructed to warn the suspect of his rights—the right to an attorney, the right to a court-appointed attorney if he cannot afford one, the right to remain silent, and the like.

One reason for this is that in many cases the warning is made in a perfunctory way, or perhaps not made at all, and the person is not adequately appraised of his rights. But there is also a large number of cases in which the warning is made in a serious way and the suspect chooses knowingly to waive his rights.

A study published in The Yale Law Journal suggests that in the case of the New Haven Police Department neither the investigating detectives nor the law-school observers were of the opinion, after examining a large number of cases, that the warnings had inhibited the giving of confessions, or that the confessions had been necessary for conviction.

It is important when talking about the role of confessions in convictions to distinguish among kinds of crimes. I think that the role of confession may be extremely important in solving burglaries and other crimes of stealth where there is no witness to the crime. Confessions may be especially important in implicating accomplices. Confessions may be important in crimes of a consensual nature, where, of course, there is no complaining witness. But in street crimes there usually is a witness, a victim who was confronted face-to-face—or sometimes back-to-front.

Here the problem is usually first getting the witness or victim to report the crime to the police. Even with robberies, half are not reported to the police at all. The second problem, after the person reports the crime, is getting his cooperation in making an identification of such suspects as the police may turn up. This again is not an easy task.

I think the chief difficulty in making good cases against persons committing street crimes lies with us, the citizens, in not reporting crimes, or, when the crime is reported and a suspect is identified, in telling the police that we don't want to get involved and that we hope they'll understand if we don't come down there. That kind of citizen noncooperation with the police seems to me a far more serious impediment to law enforcement than most appellate court decisions in this area.

Beyond the question of getting a confession in a particular case is the question of the task the police are being asked to perform in the first place. The police, in effect, are being asked to add their energies to spinning a revolving door through which pass the people they have arrested before. Eighty-five per cent of persons arrested, according to a Crime Commission estimate, for something more serious than a traffic offense have been arrested before. The average man who is arrested once will be arrested seven times. In California, which keeps especially careful records on these matters, 38 per cent of those persons imprisoned for armed robbery are reimprisoned for the same crime within two years.

Recidivism is the real crime—about which we are doing so little. If arrest has no deterrent value, then pouring additional resources into the detective function of the police—finding persons and getting statements and witnesses and trying to lock the person up—will have far less value than we would like, and perhaps far less value than equivalent resources put into trying to devise sentencing procedures and correctional programs that could make some difference in this revolving door.

There is evidence that if we attempt to classify first offenders carefully; if we try to assign them to community treatment centers where they will be employed or in school during the day and reporting to the centers in the evening and on weekends for close supervision; if we take people who are nominally on probation off the street, where they are unsupervised, and place them in institutions where they are both supervised and near their own communities—there is evidence that we can make real gains in recidivism. California, by dealing with youthful offenders through community treatment centers, has found it possible, at least in some circumstances, to cut the recidivism rate nearly in half— and at a lower cost per offender than for locking up the same persons in conventional prisons and reformatories.

The gains we would make might do no more than slow down the present increase in crime. But I for one think any gain is worth it. And yet we do not try these experiments. Correction is an uninteresting subject for most people when they deal with law enforcement. They think it is wholly a police problem.

I know that a lot of crime will occur no matter what we do. But I also know we cannot hold the police—or the courts— responsible for the fact that the crime that does occur is committed by people who have committed similar crimes in the past. I hold us responsible for that. I hold us responsible for not asking our state legislators to take their correctional programs more seriously. I hold us responsible for backing law and order with bumper stickers but not money. I hold us responsible for insisting that the only way to deal with offenders is to lock them up in some bucolic retreat behind high walls in the countryside, not recognizing that if we isolate them from the community their attitude toward the community will wreak a terrible price on us when, as they will be eventually, they are released.

"Hogan's Office": A Kind of Ministry of Justice

by Martin Mayer

NOBODY IN the history of New York City has held a single elective office so long as Frank Smithwick Hogan, the tall, deliberate, pipe-smoking organizer and administrator who is now in his 26th year as District Attorney of New York County. Though he likes to say that everything he has done as D.A. has been merely an attempt to carry forward the policies of his predecessor Thomas E. Dewey—and though men first appointed during the Dewey regime still make up the majority of his bureau chiefs—lawyers who live in and off the criminal courts and who speak of "the Bronx D.A." and "the Queens D.A." will, when they speak of Manhattan, say simply "Hogan's office." It is a unique institution, thoroughly professional, truly nonpolitical, and very nearly non-controversial. The people who burn about the infrequent mistakes the office does make are usually law school professors and professional libertarians, whose contact with the criminal courts is remote. Defense lawyers, who can daily compare performance in Manhattan with performance in the other boroughs and the sub-

From the *New York Times Magazine,* July 23, 1967, copyright © 1967 by The New York Times Company.

urban counties, are uniformly enthusiastic about the great majority of Hogan's assistants and their schooling in his office. Other boroughs have contests for D.A., but Hogan has been unopposed since Dewey and Judge John A. Mullen (or maybe Tammany leader Christy Sullivan) jointly arranged his nomination by all parties in 1941.

In theory, the function of the District Attorney is to prosecute in the courts people charged with committing felonies and misdemeanors. In fact, so far as serious crimes are concerned, Hogan's office determines whether accused people are guilty or not. Once the New York D.A. decides you are guilty of a felony, you are. As of June 23, the office had prosecuted to a conclusion this year 2,182 people accused of a felony. Seven of them—one-third of 1 per cent—had been acquitted. Seventy-two had been convicted by juries, and 2,103 had entered a plea of guilty to something (not necessarily the full original indictment). "Our record of convictions," Hogan says, "does not show greater proficiency in the courtroom, but a better screening process. I ask a question whenever there's an acquittal, because it means the jury thinks we brought an innocent man to trial, and I think a jury is usually right."

Defendants plead guilty in New York County because their lawyers can demonstrate to them that they have no earthly hope of winning in court. Though Hogan has no firm policy on disclosing the prosecution's case, and an Assistant District Attorney who feels the defense lawyer is a crook is empowered to give him no more than the law demands, standard operating procedure is to lay out the people's evidence in a conference with the defendant's lawyer and then begin to negotiate about the severity of the charge to which the defendant should plead.

"Other jurisdictions have a lot of problems we don't have in New York," says Anthony F. Marra, chief of the criminal division of the New York Legal Aid Society, which represents about 70 per cent of all the defendants in Manhattan. "Elsewhere everything is done on motion—if you want information about the people's case you have to demand a bill of particulars. Here you just ask the D.A.—they'll make full disclosure. That saves us a lot of paper work. Then you can go to your client and say, 'Here's what the People have on you.' And that saves defendants a lot of time they'd serve if they went to trial and got convicted on the top count."

Even more remarkable, the defense lawyers in these conferences will usually reveal whatever evidence they may have. Except perhaps in the rackets and organized crime area, where the office retains a crusading zeal which also stems from the Dewey days, a defendant with a case stands a much better chance of persuading Hogan's assistant to dismiss than of persuading a jury to acquit. As against seven acquittals prior to June 23, there were 85 felony cases where, after indictment and assignment of the case to a court for trial, the Hogan office either dismissed the matter or discharged the defendant.

In other jurisdictions an indication that a witness is not trustworthy may provoke from an Assistant D.A. a comment such as, "Well, that's for the jury to say"—and then the prosecution prepares to counter the defendant's arguments at trial. In New York, because Hogan does not like acquittals, an assistant is more likely to get in trouble by proceeding with a shaky case than he is by recommending that a case be dropped. "You can disclose," says Gil Rosenthal, one of the city's more belligerent defense lawyers, "without worrying that they'll take unfair advantage." At a defendant's request, the D.A. may give him a lie-detector test on a risk-free basis. If the polygraph says the fellow is lying, everybody forgets about it; if the machine says he is telling the truth, says Marra, "ninety-nine times out of a hundred Hogan will drop the case."

Our legal theory and textbooks, our Supreme Court, our newspapers and magazines all discuss an "adversary system" of criminal justice, in which witnesses are examined and cross-examined in open court and a jury votes that it has or has not heard proof beyond a reasonable doubt. But in New York County—and to only somewhat lesser degree in other jurisdictions —what we really have is an administrative system of criminal justice, where the evidence is weighed and the important decisions are taken in the prosecutor's office. In Manhattan the primacy of administrative process is so thoroughly recognized that cases are assigned for trial not to a judge but to an Assistant D.A., and do not go onto a judge's calendar until the D.A. puts them there.

The classic (or Jim Garrison) image of the fighting D.A. is today an intolerable anachronism. If our system of criminal law is to be even minimally fair, the D.A.'s office must become, county by county, a ministry of justice. Hogan likes to say that his office is "ever-mindful of its quasi-judicial function."

The offices of the New York District Attorney occupy most of the sixth through ninth floors of the block-long, 17-story, Rockefeller-Center-style Criminal Courts Building on Centre Street in lower Manhattan. Like most New York public offices built in this century, they are stark and uncomfortable, inadequately lighted, with dirty plaster walls, bare wood chairs and old wood desks. The decorations on the walls are framed diplomas and certificates of appointment and photographs of ceremonial occasions. Only the bureau chiefs enjoy the luxury of air-conditioning, and not even all of them have carpets on the floor.

The legal work of the office is broken into eight bureaus—complaint, indictment, criminal courts (for trying misdemeanors), Supreme Court (for trying felonies), homicide, rackets, frauds and appeals. As the names indicate, the complaint bureau processes the problems of aggrieved citizens who want the People to take up their cause, and the appeals bureau defends the D.A.'s convictions against challenge in the higher courts. (To the great annoyance of the office, however, the appeals bureau does not defend post-conviction habeas corpus challenges in the Federal courts: such proceedings are brought against the warden of the prison, who is a state official, and Attorney General Louis Lefkowitz insists that only his men may defend state officials.) The rackets and frauds bureaus, introduced by Dewey, run investigations and "make cases," often with the help of grand juries, at least four of which are in session in the building every day. The other bureaus are involved in disposing of the business which the police department supplies in great quantities —about 60,000 cases a year, roughly one-third of the entire criminal case-load in New York State.

Mayor Lindsay's 1967–68 budget allocates $2.3-million and 260 positions to the District Attorney of New York County, 102 of the positions to be filled by lawyers, at salaries ranging from $6,750 for the newcomers to $37,000 for Hogan. A separate "D.A.'s Squad" of 75 detectives, permanently assigned to the office, though paid by the Police Department, does most of the investigative legwork, but the office also maintains its own staff of about 10 to look into situations out of town where there is some reason to distrust the local police (who would necessarily—*noblesse oblige*—be the main source of contacts and information for a visiting New York detective) or situations close to home where the subject of the inquiry is one or more of New York's Finest. Another D.A.'s squad of six or seven accountants checks out cases for the frauds bureau and for the rackets bureau. "Many crimes," says Jerome Kidder, the tall, rather sorrowful chief of the frauds bureau, "are concealed in the books." The office also has its own photographer, pathologist and engineer.

Every lawyer enters the Hogan office at the bottom, whether he comes fresh out of law school or from several years in practice. Despite the low salaries, there are 250 to 300 applicants a year, of whom about 100 pass through interviews with at least two bureau chiefs to the office of David S. Worgan, Hogan's executive assistant. About 50 reach Hogan himself. Ten to fifteen are chosen. The ideal candidate is a boy with a pleasing manner who grew up on the streets of New York and worked his way through Harvard, Yale, Columbia, Cornell or Pennsylvania Law School and made the law review. Any one of these requirements can be waived, but probably not two of them.

Everybody starts in the complaint bureau, where Melvin D. Glass, the youngest of the bureau chiefs (nine years out of Pennsylvania Law School) offers "a seminar in advanced criminal procedure." In the first week the neophyte learns how to fill out a complaint card, "what to say on the phone and what not to say on the phone," how to tell people that even if what they say is true they have a civil lawsuit rather than a criminal charge against the storekeeper or the landlord or the neighbor or the bigamous husband (bigamy is a crime in New York only if the *second* marriage was performed in the state). Then there are two weeks of following in great detail a hypothetical robbery case, from the policeman at the scene to the decision on appeal.

"We introduce them," Glass says, "to police forms, court forms, our forms. They hear lectures from experts on gypsies and con games, burglary, homicide, larceny; visit the prison; observe the summons procedure; watch a full trial; do a moot court on a gambling case."

The new men now begin to meet the public. About 2,000 complainants a year visit the D.A.'s office, and Hogan insists that everybody must be treated courteously. ("It is not our function," the manual for the complaint bureau explains, "to advise any person that he needs psychiatric treatment.") Generally, if the matter is one that should be handled by a private lawyer, the visitor will be referred to the bar association or Legal Aid. (There are exceptions: as a courtesy to the tourist industry, for example, the D.A. will call a local store accused, by letter, of failure to deliver the merchandise.)

Only about 35 complaints a year lead to arrests (an assistant must check with Glass before authorizing an arrest), but during the course of processing the bulk of noncriminal or self-serving complaints the new Assistant D.A. learns a great deal that law school never taught him about interviewing members of the general public to get their stories out of them. The lawyers of the complaint bureau also take calls from policemen who want advice about how to handle a situation, and toward the end of their six months or so in the bureau they get to try a few cases, if that is the right phrase for it, in the gamblers' court, where a ritualized ballet is played out by the police and the old men who have become the city's policy runners since the Legislature made prison sentences mandatory for gambling.

Next in the training program comes half a year in the indictment bureau, where the assistant learns to check out felony cases prepared by the police, and to present witnesses before the sympathetic audience of the grand jury. Older members of the 11-man indictment bureau run Part 1-A, the courtroom where prisoners are brought by the police for a judge to determine whether or not there is enough evidence that they committed a crime to justify holding them. Since January, under a new dispensation, Part 1-A operates around the clock, and over the course of the year half the whole office will take a turn presenting to a judge a policeman's reasons for wanting the person he has just arrested to be placed in the pipeline of criminal process. Until recently, that was the full extent of the assistant's duties in 1-A; now there is a complaint room where the assistant can talk over the arrest with the officer and the complainant and throw out before it ever reaches the court a case where no actual crime occurred or the evidence is already tainted or the policeman seems to have made a mistake.

The D.A.'s first tight sieve, however, is operated between arraignment in 1-A and indictment. "We want to see if these are proper cases," says Karl Grebow, chief of the bureau, who next January will celebrate his 30th anniversary with the New York District Attorney's office. "If they're not proper cases we want to get rid of them."

For each case which is to be presented to the 23-man grand jury (a majority indicts), an assistant makes up a fact sheet consisting of the crime and its circumstances and the evidence available for prosecution. Witnesses are called in rapid-fire order to give the bones of their story to the grand jury (in a proceeding from which defense lawyers are barred); the defendant may testify if he wishes, but of course waives his immunity to self-incrimination if he does so. About 6,000 indictments a year are sought by the New York D.A.'s office, and disposition of the average request takes a grand jury about 15 minutes.

The assistant in the indictment bureau has some authority to dismiss or reduce a charge on his own—"in an obvious situation," Grebow explains, "a rape without corroboration, when a man knows there's no case." Normally, however, it is simpler to let the grand jury make this decision itself, and over the course of the year, usually but not always following a hint from the assistant, the grand jury will dismiss about 13 per cent of the indictments and reduce 12 per cent to charges of misdemeanor. The work of the assistants is tightly supervised: either Grebow or his deputy Sal Pino reads every fact sheet and every indictment.

The final phase of the training program is a term, usually a year, in the criminal courts bureau, trying the misdemeanor cases that flood in from the police—shoplifting, unarmed assault, purse-snatching, simple theft, "resisting arrest," complicated disorderly conduct. (Traffic offenses, prostitution and drunk cases are processed directly by the police and not through the D.A.'s office.) Trials are considerably more common in this area. Of 8,202 cases pressed to a conclusion in the first four months of the year, 6,327 produced guilty pleas, 971 resulted in convictions after trial and 904 yielded acquittals. This huge volume was handled by a staff of only 18 men, headed by bureau chief Joseph Stone. The courts in which this activity occurs are monkey-houses, complete to official proceedings in corridors and cloakrooms; and everyone professionally involved—judges, prosecutors, defense lawyers, police—is under the most intense imaginable pressure to keep the business moving.

After a man has been two years in the office, one of them in the criminal courts bureau, he is eligible for more or less permanent assignment to the less frenetic trial work of more serious crimes in Supreme Court, the more profound responsibilities of the homicide bureau (which supervises investigations as well as trying cases), the mostly investigative labors of the rackets or frauds bureaus (which also, however, try their own cases when there are cases to be tried), or the intellectual labors of the appeals bureau.

Promotions within the bureaus are by seniority, to guarantee against any return to the pre-Dewey days when jobs in the D.A.'s office at all levels were the property of district leaders, who could give them as rewards to deserving followers or their children. Everybody hired into the Hogan office promises to stay at least four years; but when the four years are up a man is likely to look around, note that he is still making less than the $9,200 the Wall Street law firms pay their new recruits, and begin counting how many years must pass before death or retirement will give him a crack at the better jobs in the office.

The resulting turnover of 12 to 15 men a year has meant that apprentices have to be hustled through Hogan's training program faster than the book says they should move—some have even skipped the criminal courts year entirely. Not everybody feels, though, that the turnover is bad: "You hate to lose a man who's good and useful and grown up," says a lawyer now in private practice who ran a prosecutor's office, "but that's just when you ought to lose him. A long-range career at the D.A.'s office tends to warp a mind; a man doesn't have a full professional life just on that side of the bar." Hogan of course disagrees with that judgment. He has a remarkably developed sense of loyalty and about the best thing he can say about a man is that "he's been here a *long* time."

The turnover has put what is probably a wholesome pressure on the policy of promotion by seniority. Though six of the eight bureau chiefs are men who have been with the office more than 20 years, and their deputies have almost equivalent service records, rapid advance has become a possibility for a really extraordinary man. H. Richard Uviller, a patiently ironic Yale Law graduate (and amateur painter whose abstractions are about the only art in the office), became chief of the appeals bureau after only seven years; and the eager and earnest Melvin Glass was appointed chief of the complaint bureau after only eight years, partly as a reward for his work in demonstrating that the police had not solved the Janice Wylie murders when they drew a confession out of George Whitmore Jr.

Hogan runs this establishment from a very high eminence. He has not himself tried a case since 1945: "To be away from administrative work for four or five weeks is not a wise thing to do," he says, "even though it may be more satisfying personally." He speaks every day with his bureau chiefs, usually on the telephone—only executive assistant Worgan is a frequent visitor to his large office—and he receives a daily written report on work done before the grand jury and in the Supreme Court bureau.

Apart from the men in the rackets bureau, where Hogan maintains continuing personal interest, assistants below the senior level are likely to see him only at occasional office social functions—especially at the softball games. Until a few years ago, Hogan played third base for the office team, who wear shirts identifying them as Hogan's Hooligans; and he threatens to return to action next year.

Hogan has his own way of keeping up with his office. He reads the mail—"Everything," he says, "that comes into the office. Every morning the mail room brings me two big folders.

The smaller one is my own mail; the larger one is the mail for everybody else in the office. It doesn't take me that much time to read it all, because I've been doing it so long." Letters that indicate possible trouble get passed on to the man to whom they were originally sent with a copy of Form 38-2M-800230 (61), on which Hogan can check one of ten boxes—"See me about this," or "Let me see proposed reply," or "Telephone me," etc.

Part of the purpose of reading the mail is simply to enforce Hogan's rules of courtesy. A ceramic plaque with gold Gothic lettering stands on the table beside his desk: "Courtesy is the Golden Key that unlocks all the doors." Joseph Stone says, "We all know one thing Hogan won't stand for is being late with appointments or not answering letters. Around here you've got to handle people with plenty of Tender Loving Care." But the letters also keep Hogan informed about what defense lawyers are asking from his assistants, and tip him off to any situations which seem to be developing badly. New bureau chiefs quickly learn that when they call Hogan to talk over a problem he usually knows about it already.

Hogan reads the mail rather than discussing things with juniors because he is at bottom rather shy. He puffs his pipe and looks away when he talks with you. Dewey at the time of Hogan's nomination called him "the most sweetly honorable man I've ever known," which is an interesting description. (Hogan doesn't think much of it.) "He's formal with people," says appeals chief Uviller. "Gallant with ladies. He believes assistants should wear coats when ladies are in the room. He dislikes profanity, and believes in old-fashioned virtues, loyalty and courtesy. But he's a remarkably astute judge of the capabilities of the staff. He knows strengths, weaknesses and proclivities quite far down the line—knows who gets hot-headed, who takes trivia too seriously, who's a fighter, who's a scholar and how to use them. He has a remarkable ability to judge and respond to people." He can also be quietly funny, with the faintly acrid wit of a man who is successfully controlling a considerable temper.

The one major outside interest in Hogan's life is Columbia University, which he serves as a life trustee and, currently, as co-chairman of the giant new fund-raising drive. He and his wife

Mary, whom he married in 1936, live as they always have near Columbia at 404 Riverside Drive. They entertain modestly: Hogan is no part of a politician, as his dull race for the Senate in 1958 conclusively demonstrated. When Dewey listed Hogan as one of the four men on his staff whom he would be prepared to support as his successor, nobody had ever heard of him. Though he had helped Dewey on a couple of cases and had tried some cases himself, his job had been essentially that of his title, "administrative assistant." A few days after Tammany had announced that it would accept Hogan (the only Democrat on Dewey's list), and Dewey had, over La Guardia's protests, forced the Republicans to go along, the new D.A. made ritual visits to the headquarters of all the parties to meet the leaders, none of whom he had ever met before.

Frank S. Hogan was born 65 years ago in Waterbury, Conn., where "my people had a grocery store." He got his first job in the plating room of the New England Watch Company while he was a freshman in high school (the high school was on double-session, which gave him pretty much a full day's work), and he has held one job or another ever since. Some of them were pretty exotic. One summer he was an installment plan collector for a clothing store which sold suits for $1 a week; his salary was $20 a week plus 3 per cent commission. Another year he sold the People's Home Library—"Not a book, Mrs. Jones, but a complete library: medical book, cookbook, stock book." While he was a student at Columbia, he waited on table and played on the football team. ("In those youthful days," he told an alumni meeting in 1954, "I regret to say that a varsity 'C' was just a little more important to me than a degree. More deplorable, it still is.") In the summers he worked as a Pullman conductor all over the Northeast and once as a steward on the Leviathan.

On graduation from college, Hogan took a job as "organizing secretary" for a Russian baron who had discovered "the science of being," and who gave free large lectures to ladies' groups, followed by courses of small-group lectures at $50 a head for 10 meetings. "After four or five months," he recalls, "we didn't get along. I was beginning to feel like a con man." Leaving the baron, Hogan went to Guatemala as tutor to the sons of the superintendent of a gold mine, "moonlighting as an accountant for the company." Then he returned to Columbia for law school. One summer he worked as a steamfitter's helper on the construction of the Columbia-Presbyterian Medical Center; and then he got a steady year-round job, five in the afternoon to midnight, in the showroom of the New York Edison Company on 42nd Street between Fifth and Sixth Avenues. This paid $25 a week, and gave him a feeling of affluence.

On graduation from law school, Hogan worked two years as a junior associate in a downtown firm, then became half of one of the many struggling two-man partnerships in New York in the depression. He was still trying to put together a practice in 1935 when he read in the newspapers that Governor Herbert H. Lehman had appointed Thomas E. Dewey, from the U.S. Attorney's office, to run a special investigation of rackets in the city, and he wrote a letter of application. Hogan believes he was accepted strictly on the basis of the letter, but he was a classmate and fraternity brother of Paul E. Lockwood, who was to be Dewey's deputy, and Lockwood put in the necessary good word. In any event, Hogan was one of the original group of seven sworn in with Dewey on July 29, 1935, and he moved over to the D.A.'s office with the rest of Dewey's staff of special assistants when the future Governor won his first election in 1937.

The most publicized feature of both Dewey's and Hogan's administration of the office has been the separate rackets bureau, now headed by Alfred J. Scotti (another bureau chief who started with the original Dewey team), and staffed by a dozen to 15 lawyers, plus most of the D.A.'s squad. A highly persistent little man with extra supplies of bouncing energy, Scotti enjoys thinking up theories by which wrongdoing not explicitly covered by the penal code can be brought into the crime category, and his bureau does not qualify for the general encomium given to the Hogan office by defense lawyers. "He sees everything in black and white," one of them says, "and the world is full of grays."

Of all that happens in his office, Hogan is proudest of the self-starting pressure the rackets bureau applies impartially to government, business and labor, and of the "hundreds of convictions" for corruption, extortion and fraud which the D.A.'s own investigators have uncovered. The cases have included the basketball fixes; the TV quiz scandal; bribery in the State Liquor Authority (for which former Republican State Chairman L. Judson Morhouse went to jail); hanky-panky with labor welfare funds (resulting in the incarceration of George Scalise); the conviction of gamblers Frank Costello and Frank Ericson (and the accompanying disclosure of Costello's influence on judicial nominations); the revelation of waterfront racketeering, black market baby rings and a series of extortions by the city Fire and Building Departments which, among other results, led to a permanent residence in Mexico of former Mayor William O'Dwyer.

It is in defense of the work of this bureau that Hogan has spoken up for wiretapping and eavesdropping. Thus the other day, in an appeal to a Senate subcommittee to authorize new legislation on the subject, he called wiretapping "the single most valuable and effective weapon" in law enforcement.

"Without wiretapping," Scotti says, "we'd be in the dark—who's going to come in and tell us about these things?" Among the tasks Hogan accepted for himself as D.A. was the personal processing of applications for court-approved taps, bugs and extensions. "There weren't so many of them," he says. "About 125 a year."

Like most prosecutors, Hogan is less than enchanted with several recent Supreme Court decisions. "In the old days we had more leeway," he says. "You didn't have motions to suppress evidence, confessions were more . . . simplistic, you could use wiretaps without any court order. Now the delay is unconscionable, it's extremely difficult to move cases."

To Hogan's office the most troublesome of the decisions is the limitation on the use of confessions. In his recent appeal to the subcommittee, he declared that such decisions had "significantly increased the chances that a criminal will escape judgment." The homicide bureau has been particularly disturbed, partly because the absence of confessions makes convictions slightly more difficult to obtain (although two out of three accused killers still waive their right to counsel and make statements), partly because the assistant in charge of the case, who comes in at the beginning (the New York police make arrests for homicide only on the advice of the D.A.'s office), finds it more difficult to convince himself.

"If you have a case with four independent eyewitnesses and the guy confesses," says bureau chief Vincent J. Dermody, "you can sleep easy. But a case where you have one witness—he was passing by, he heard a shot, a man came running out with a revolver, he never saw him before . . . and a month later he picks him out of the lineup—then you've got a hot potato.

"You go into the whole background of the witness, what sort of job does he have, what sort of person is he, how good is his eyesight, what was the wattage of the bulb, when was the globe cleaned last, are we dealing with a nut or a guy who wants to be in the limelight or, worst of all, a guy who is honestly mistaken?"

Evidence other than the testimony of witnesses, or a confession, is unusual. (Fingerprints, Dermody says, are "a real rarity—maybe once in a thousand times.") Deprived of the chance to question and size up the prospective defendant, the Assistant District Attorney worries that ("God forbid") he may be prosecuting an innocent man. The worry is compounded by his knowledge that he will very probably get his conviction from the jury whether the man is innocent or not.

"A lot of people in the office believe," Uviller says, "that the courts are working against us." Still, nobody is crying, and Hogan has not noted any crime wave. "There hasn't been much change in 10 years," he says, "in the number of cases in the felony parts." One observer feels that Hogan, who reads appellate decisions (and The Congressional Record) with considerable care, has come out of the experiences of the last few years a better and wiser lawyer: "He never used to think much about criminal law, just about doing his own job. Now he sits on a lot of committees that wouldn't have interested him at all in the beginning."

Richard A. Green, director of the American Bar Association study on Minimum Standards of Effective Criminal Justice, believes that the uncertainties attendant on the Supreme Court decisions may have improved the performance of the office. "There's always a danger," Green says, "that you consider yourself so objective you're *sure* you can't possibly be prosecuting an innocent man. And you can be." Dissenting judges on the Court of Appeals and a Federal district judge have recently criticized Hogan's office for failure to make available to the defense derogatory information about prosecution witnesses. Behind this failure, obviously, was the attitude that the office had investigated these people and decided they were telling the truth, so why waste time going over it again. But even a ministry of justice must not have the right to suppress.

Hogan worries about the trial court judges—especially those who since court consolidation have been sitting on criminal cases for the first time in their lives. "They're not conversant with the criminal law," he says. "They don't like the work and have no hesitancy about saying it." He wishes the Mayor would look more often in the direction of his bureau chiefs when choosing judges, and likes to point out that Mayor Hylan appointed to the bench 30 assistants of Joab Banton, who held the office from 1921 to 1929 and is one of the few D.A.'s before Dewey whom Hogan respects. "It would be wonderful for morale," he says rather wistfully. "But La Guardia never did it, and Lindsay's taken only one. It's the penalty we pay for being a nonpolitical office."

Hogan's greatest concern is about the office's future pulling power on the new law school graduates. The alumni roster is distinguished—it includes, for example, Chief Judge Stanley H. Fuld and Associate Judge Charles D. Breitel of the Court of Appeals, former Attorney General William Rogers and Charles Tillinghast, president of T.W.A. Nobody is confident that men of this potential are coming to the D.A.'s office today.

Others at the office are concerned about what may happen, both to the office and to themselves, when Hogan leaves. Most of his bureau chiefs are his age or near it; and none of them seems a likely candidate to capture the nomination of all parties. Return to the political maelstrom would be a tragedy for the office and for the city, but civic tragedy is commonplace in New York.

Hogan's criminal courts bureau doubtless passes by some stones it should turn, not every assistant is the model of fairness Hogan thinks his men should be, and the operation of the seniority system has moved into high positions some men whose capacity does not greatly impress students of the office. But lawyers who work in other counties of the city—and in other cities around the country—envy Manhattan its D.A. and his office. "There are no hacks," says a defense lawyer. "Some bureau chiefs may be mediocre, but they're professionals. They're concerned about their cases." Practicing before a bench where many judges are disgracefully weak, pinched by a budget which allots less than $40 per case for the volume of work that passes through the building, Hogan has indeed made his office a functioning ministry of justice. He has had few imitators anywhere, but among the rather wistful hopes of the President's National Crime Commission is that more D.A.'s will try to be like Hogan. If Washington's current interest in the problems of criminal justice should persist, Hogan's accomplishment may have national significance.

Inside View of
the High Court

by William J. Brennan, Jr.

THROUGHOUT ITS history the Supreme Court has been called
upon to face many of the dominant social, political, economic and
even philosophical issues that confront the nation. But Solicitor
General Cox only recently reminded us that this does not mean
that the Court is charged with making social, political, economic
or philosophical decisions. Quite the contrary. The Court is not
a council of Platonic guardians for deciding our most difficult
and emotional questions according to the Justices' own notions
of what is just or wise or politic. To the extent that this is a governmental function at all, it is the function of the people's elected
representatives.

The Justices are charged with deciding according to law. Because the issues arise in the framework of concrete litigation they
must be decided on facts embalmed in a record made by some
lower court or administrative agency. And while the Justices
may and do consult history and the other disciplines as aids to
constitutional decision, the text of the Constitution and relevant
precedents dealing with that text are their primary tools.

It is indeed true, as Judge Learned Hand once said, that the judge's authority "depends upon the assumption that he speaks with the mouth of others: the momentum of his utterances must be greater than any which his personal reputation and character can command; if it is to do the work assigned to it—if it is to stand against the passionate resentments arising out of the interests he must frustrate—he must preserve his authority by cloaking himself in the majesty of an overshadowing past, but he must discover some composition with the dominant trends of his times."

However, we must keep in mind that, while the words of the Constitution are binding, their application to specific problems is not often easy. The Founding Fathers knew better than to pin down their descendants too closely. Enduring principles rather than petty details were what they sought. Thus the Constitution does not take the form of a litany of specifics. There are, therefore, very few cases where the constitutional answers are clear, all one way or all the other, and this is also true of the current cases raising conflicts between the individual and governmental power—an area increasingly requiring the Court's attention.

Ultimately, of course, the Court must resolve the conflicts of competing interests in these cases, but all Americans should keep in mind how intense and troubling these conflicts can be. Where one man claims a right to speak and the other man claims the right to be protected from abusive or dangerously provocative remarks the conflict is inescapable. Where the police have ample external evidence of a man's guilt, but to be sure of their case put into evidence a confession obtained through coercion, the conflict arises between his right to a fair prosecution and society's right to protection against his depravity. Where the orthodox Jew wishes to open his shop and do business on the day which non-Jews have chosen, and the Legislature has sanctioned, as a day of rest, the Court cannot escape a difficult problem of reconciling opposed interests. Finally, the claims of the Negro citizen, to borrow Solicitor General Cox's words, present a "conflict between the ideal of liberty and equality expressed in the Declaration of Independence, on the one hand, and, on the other hand, a way of life rooted in the customs of many of our people."

If all segments of our society can be made to appreciate that there are such conflicts, and that cases which involve constitutional rights often require difficult choices, if this alone is accomplished, we will have immeasurably enriched our common understanding of the meaning and significance of our freedoms. And we will have better appreciation of the Court's function and its difficulties.

How conflicts such as these ought to be resolved constantly troubles our whole society. There should be no surprise, then, that how properly to resolve them often produces sharp division within the Court itself. When problems are so fundamental, the claims of the competing interests are often nicely balanced, and close divisions are almost inevitable.

Supreme Court cases are usually one of three kinds: the "original" action brought directly in the Court by one state against another state or states, or between a state or states and the Federal Government. Only a handful of such cases arise each year, but they are an important handful. A recent example was the contest between Arizona and California over the waters of the lower basin of the Colorado River. Another was the contest between the Federal Government and the newest state of Hawaii over the ownership of lands in Hawaii.

The second kind of case seeks review of the decisions of a Federal Court of Appeals—there are 11 such courts—or of a decision of a Federal District Court—there is a Federal District Court in each of the 50 states.

The third kind of case comes from a state court—the Court may review a state court judgment by the highest court of any of the 50 states, if the judgment rests on the decision of a Federal question.

When I came to the Court seven years ago the aggregate of the cases in the three classes was 1,600. In the term just completed there were 2,800, an increase of 75 per cent in seven years. Obviously, the volume will have doubled before I complete 10 years of service. How is it possible to manage such a huge volume of cases? The answer is that we have the authority to screen them and select for argument and decision only those which, in our judgment, guided by pertinent criteria, raise the most important and far-reaching questions. By that device we select annually around 6 per cent—between 150 and 170 cases —for decision. That screening process works like this: When nine Justices sit, it takes five to decide a case on the merits. But it takes only the votes of four of the nine to put a case on the argument calendar for argument and decision. Those four votes are hard to come by—only an exceptional case raising a significant Federal question commands them.

Each application for review is usually in the form of a short petition, attached to which are any opinions of the lower courts in the case. The adversary may file a response—also, in practice, usually short. Both the petition and response identify the Federal questions allegedly involved, argue their substantiality, and whether they were properly raised in the lower courts. Each Justice receives copies of the petition and response and such parts of the record as the parties may submit. Each Justice then, without any consultation at this stage with the others, reaches his own tentative conclusion whether the application should be granted or denied.

The first consultation about the case comes at the Court conference at which the case is listed on the agenda for discussion. We sit in conference almost every Friday during the term. Conferences begin at 10 in the morning and often continue until 6, except for a half-hour recess for lunch. Only the Justices are present. There are no law clerks, no stenographers, no secretaries, no pages—just the nine of us. The junior Justice acts as guardian of the door, receiving and delivering any messages that come in or go from the conference.

The conference room is a beautifully oak-paneled chamber with one side lined with books from floor to ceiling. Over the mantel of the exquisite marble fireplace at one end hangs the only adornment in the chamber—a portrait of Chief Justice John Marshall. In the middle of the room stands a rectangular table, not too large but large enough for the nine of us comfortably to gather around it. The Chief Justice sits at the south end and Mr. Justice Black, the senior Associate Justice, at the north end.

Along the side to the left of the Chief Justice sit Justices Stewart, Goldberg, White and Harlan. On the right side sit Justice Clark, myself and Justice Douglas in that order.

We are summoned to conference by a buzzer which rings in our several chambers five minutes before the hour. Upon entering the conference room each of us shakes hands with his colleagues. The handshake tradition originated when Chief Justice Fuller presided many decades ago. It is a symbol that harmony of aims if not of views is the Court's guiding principle.

Each of us has his copy of the agenda of the day's cases before him. The agenda lists the cases applying for review. Each of us before coming to the conference has noted on his copy his tentative view whether or not review should be granted in each case.

The Chief Justice begins the discussion of each case. He then yields to the senior Associate Justice and discussion proceeds down the line in order of seniority until each Justice has spoken. Voting goes the other way. The junior Justice votes first and voting then proceeds up the line to the Chief Justice who votes last. Each of us has a docket containing a sheet for each case with appropriate places for recording the votes. When any case receives four votes for review, that case is transferred to the oral argument list. Applications in which none of us sees merit may be passed over without discussion.

Now how do we process the decisions we agree to review? There are rare occasions when the question is so clearly controlled by an earlier decision of the Court that a reversal of the lower court judgment is inevitable. In these rare instances we may summarily reverse without oral argument. The case must very clearly justify summary disposition, however, because our ordinary practice is not to reverse a decision without oral argument. Indeed, oral argument of cases taken for review, whether from the state or Federal courts, is the usual practice. We rarely accept submissions of cases on briefs.

Oral argument ordinarily occurs about four months after the application for review is granted. Each party is usually allowed one hour, but in recent years we have limited oral argument to a half-hour in cases thought to involve issues not requiring longer argument. Counsel submit their briefs and record in sufficient time for the distribution of one set to each Justice two or three weeks before the oral argument. Most of the members of the present Court follow the practice of reading the briefs before the argument. Some of us often have a bench memorandum prepared before the argument. This memorandum digests the facts and the arguments of both sides, highlighting the matters about which we may want to question counsel at the argument. Often I have independent research done in advance of argument and incorporate the results in the bench memorandum.

We follow a schedule of two weeks of argument from Monday through Thursday, followed by two weeks of recess for opinion writing and the study of petitions for review. The argued cases are listed on the conference agenda on the Friday following argument. Conference discussion follows the same procedure I have described for the discussion of certiorari petitions. Of course, it is much more extended. Not infrequently discussion of particular cases may be spread over two or more conferences.

Not until the discussion is completed and a vote taken is the opinion assigned. The assignment is not made at the conference but formally in writing some few days after the conference. The Chief Justice assigns the opinions in those cases in which he has voted with the majority. The senior Associate Justice voting with the majority assigns the opinions in the other cases. The dissenters agree among themselves who shall write the dissenting opinion. Of course, each Justice is free to write his own opinion, concurring or dissenting.

The writing of an opinion always takes weeks and sometimes months. The most painstaking research and care are involved. Research, of course, concentrates on relevant legal materials— precedents particularly. But Supreme Court cases often require some familiarity with history, economics, the social and other sciences, and authorities in these areas, too, are consulted when necessary.

When the author of an opinion feels he has an unanswerable document he sends it to a print shop, which we maintain in our building. The printed draft may be revised several times before his proposed opinion is circulated among the other Justices.

Copies are sent to each member of the Court, those in the dissent as well as those in the majority.

Now the author often discovers that his work has only begun. He receives a return, ordinarily in writing, from each Justice who voted with him and sometimes also from the Justices who voted the other way. He learns who will write the dissent if one is to be written. But his particular concern is whether those who voted with him are still of his view and what they have to say about his proposed opinion. Often some who voted with him at conference will advise that they reserve final judgment pending the circulation of the dissent. It is a common experience that dissents change votes, even enough votes to become the majority. I have had to convert more than one of my proposed majority opinions into a dissent before the final decision was announced. I have also, however, had the more satisfying experience of rewriting a dissent as a majority opinion for the Court.

Before everyone has finally made up his mind a constant interchange by memoranda, by telephone, at the lunch table, continues while we hammer out the final form of the opinion. I had one case during the past term in which I circulated 10 printed drafts before one was approved as the Court opinion.

The point of this procedure is that each Justice, unless he disqualifies himself in a particular case, passes on every piece of business coming to the Court. The Court does not function by means of committees or panels. Each Justice passes on each petition, each item, no matter how drawn, in longhand, by typewriter, or on a press. Our Constitution vests the judicial power in only one Supreme Court. This does not permit Supreme Court action by committees, panels, or sections.

The method that the Justices use in meeting an enormous caseload varies. There is one uniform rule: Judging is not delegated. Each Justice studies each case in sufficient detail to resolve the question for himself. In a very real sense, each decision is an individual decision of every Justice. The process can be a lonely, troubling experience for fallible human beings conscious that their best may not be adequate to the challenge. "We are not unaware," the late Justice Jackson said, "that we are not final because we are infallible; we know that we are infallible only because we are final." One does not forget how much may depend on his decision. He knows that usually more than the litigants may be affected, that the course of vital social, economic and political currents may be directed.

This then is the decisional process in the Supreme Court. It is not without its tensions, of course—indeed, quite agonizing tensions at times. I would particularly emphasize that, unlike the case of a Congressional or White House decision, Americans demand of their Supreme Court judges that they produce a written opinion, the collective expression of the judges subscribing to it, setting forth the reasons which led them to the decision. These opinions are the exposition, not just to lawyers, legal scholars and other judges, but to our whole society, of the bases upon which a particular result rests—why a problem, looked at as disinterestedly and dispassionately as nine human beings trained in a tradition of the disinterested and dispassionate approach can look at it, is answered as it is.

It is inevitable, however, that Supreme Court decisions—and the Justices themselves—should be caught up in public debate and be the subjects of bitter controversy. An editorial in The Washington Post did not miss the mark by much in saying that this was so because "one of the primary functions of the Supreme Court is to keep the people of the country from doing what they would like to do—at times when what they would like to do runs counter to the Constitution . . . . The function of the Supreme Court is not to count constituents; it is to interpret a fundamental charter which imposes restraints on constituents. Independence and integrity, not popularity, must be its standards."

Certainly controversy over its work has attended the Court throughout its history. As Professor Paul A. Freund of Harvard remarked, this has been true almost since the Court's first decision:

"When the Court held, in 1793, that the State of Georgia could be sued on a contract in the Federal courts, the outraged Assembly of that state passed a bill declaring that any Federal marshal who should try to collect the judgment would be guilty of a felony and would suffer death, without benefit of clergy, by being hanged. When the Court decided that state criminal convictions could be reviewed in the Supreme Court, Chief Justice Roane of Virginia exploded, calling it a 'most monstrous and unexampled decision. It can only be accounted for by that love of power which history informs us infects and corrupts all who possess it, and from which even the eminent and upright judges are not exempt.' "

But public understanding has not always been lacking in the past. Perhaps it exists today. But surely a more informed knowledge of the decisional process should aid a better understanding.

It is not agreement with the Court's decisions that I urge. Our law is the richer and the wiser because academic and informed lay criticism is part of the stream of development. It is only a greater awareness of the nature and limits of the Supreme Court's function that I seek. I agree fully with the Solicitor General: It is essential, just because the public questions which the Court faces are pressing and divisive, that they be thoroughly canvassed in public, each step at a time, while the Court is evolving new principles. The ultimate resolution of questions fundamental to the whole community must be based on a common consensus of understanding of the unique responsibility assigned to the Supreme Court in our society.

The lack of that understanding led Mr. Justice Holmes to say 50 years ago:

"We are very quiet there, but it is the quiet of a storm center, as we all know. Science has taught the world skepticism and has made it legitimate to put everything to the test of proof. Many beautiful and noble reverences are impaired, but in these days no one can complain if any institution, system, or belief is called on to justify its continuance in life. Of course we are not excepted and have not escaped. Doubts are expressed that go to our very being. Not only are we told that when Marshall pronounced an Act of Congress unconstitutional he usurped a power that the Constitution did not give, but we are told that we are the representatives of a class—a tool of the money power. I get letters, not always anonymous, intimating that we are corrupt. Well, gentlemen, I admit that it makes my heart ache. It is very painful, when one spends all the energies of one's soul in trying to do good work, with no thought but that of solving a problem according to the rules by which one is bound, to know that many see sinister motives and would be glad of evidence that one was consciously bad. But we must take such things philosophically and try to see what we can learn from hatred and distrust and whether behind them there may not be a germ of inarticulate truth.

"The attacks upon the Court are merely an expression of the unrest that seems to wonder vaguely whether law and order pay. When the ignorant are taught to doubt they do not know what they safely may believe. And it seems to me that at this time we need education in the obvious more than investigation of the obscure."

The Prison "Culture" —From the Inside

by M. Arc

FOR 23 MONTHS I was a prisoner in a Federal Correctional Institution. Along with 650 other men, I wore a blue uniform, worked at a prison job (in the kitchen office), dreamed of freedom. I shared the prisoners' myths and rituals, learned their language and found my place in an intricate social maze.

But, unlike the others, I took part in prison life with some objectivity. I am an anthropologist (convicted in a security matter), and as far as I know the first member of my profession to study a prison culture from the inside. My scientific colleagues would call me a "participant-observer." The United States Bureau of Prisons called me an inmate. I served in both capacities, of course, on an involuntary field trip among an isolated tribe of fellow human beings.

My habitat was one of the more progressive institutions in our prison system, located a few miles from a small town in the East. This was no Hollywood Big House with towering gray walls and searchlights that pierced the night. Trees and flower beds brightened the yard. The windows were not barred, but had unobtrusive steel frames. Instead of numbered cell blocks, we lived

From the *New York Times Magazine*, February 28, 1965, copyright © 1965 by The New York Times Company.

in "houses" named after a city or state in the East. Individual cells were "private rooms," and as residents in a minimum security prison our doors were usually unlocked except during a routine head count or at night. There was a reasonably well-stocked library, a school that offered courses leading to a high school diploma, and a cafeteria with piped-in music.

The adequate living conditions reflected more than the humane approach of the Prison Bureau. Our institution was "correctional," not "penal," a distinction that emphasized the goal of rehabilitating the criminal offender, not merely punishing him. The physical setting was intended to nurture self-respect, social responsibility and hope. Guided by a psychologically skilled and tolerant prison administration, the inmate would be prepared for his ultimate return to society as a "respectable citizen."

An excellent theory, but it did not work. Most of the prison personnel go through the motions of accepting the concept of rehabilitation because it is the professed policy of Federal experts, but in daily practice they act on the stereotype of the cunning, lying, thieving "habitual criminal." On the whole, they think of prison jobs as a means of punishment and a source of cheap labor, not as a way to develop vocational skills and good work habits.

For example, a key element in the rehabilitation process is the Classification Committee, which is supposed to assign living quarters and jobs according to the prisoner's social and economic needs, his talents and interests. In reality, the committee considers simply the current manpower shortage in a particular department, and how much hardship the prisoner deserves in view of his attitudes toward authority. Accordingly, aged Dr. S., in the terminal stage of a chronic disease, was assigned to sorting dirty socks in the laundry. Little Joe, an expert in passing checks and a drug addict, was given a job in the hospital. The Professor applied his educational experience in the kitchen while former bookmakers worked in the library and the Department of Education.

By scarcely concealing their distrust and contempt for inmates, prison guards and administrators soon erase any reforms that the system might produce. The officials are expected to develop a relationship with inmates based on trust and respect, without endangering discipline and order, but since the staff does not really believe in rehabilitation the inmates react with understandable cynicism. Thus do the enemy camps coexist in an atmosphere of mutual fear and hostility.

The climate spawns two characteristics of prison culture that often confuse an outsider: the appearance of conformity within the official system, and an underground pattern of nonconformity by which the individual inmate tries to live by his own code, preserving as best he can his personal preferences and habits. This response to rules and regulations is another example of human ability to adapt to a new environment and transform oppressive circumstances into a tolerable existence.

The newcomer's introduction to prison life goes on for several weeks during an orientation period. He lives in isolation from the prison population and hears lectures by various members of the administration, from the warden to the kitchen steward. He learns the rules of prison conduct and the penalties for transgressing them (such as being deprived of watching television, or reduction in time off from his sentence). He learns that anything except food and shelter is a privilege which can be taken away for misconduct or lack of cooperation. Finally, he learns the Golden Rule of prison—"doing your own time"— complete dissociation from other inmates' problems, needs and interests.

Thus prepared, the initiate is released among the inmates; slowly and cautiously he discovers the fact and fiction of what he has been told.

The myth of equality is among the first to be shattered. Just as in the outside world, the society of prisoners is composed of rich and poor, leaders and followers, "better men" and "bums," black and white, Jews, Italians, Irish and other ethnic groups— all participants in a complex web of prejudices and hostilities, friendships and alliances.

Though we were all identically dressed in blue uniforms, some of us had well-fitted coats, clean shirts and pressed pants, while others wore discolored and baggy garb, coats with missing buttons and torn pockets, footwear which had seen better days.

In the dormitories some beds had thicker mattresses, ironed sheets and cleaner blankets. Although newspapers, books and magazines were available to everyone, some inmates managed to have the most recent best sellers and the latest periodicals.

What makes some prisoners more equal than others? How do some inmates acquire "luxuries," while others receive only the scant necessities? The key to the puzzle is the "connection," a magic substance that can be as intangible as having status, or as real as a package of cigarettes.

Among the ways to be a "somebody," recognized occasionally even by the prison staff, is reputation. Big Joe has prestige simply because he has a venerable career as a law-breaker. Murph the Bookie is a millionaire. Max is a "real lawyer who got into trouble." Fat Leo has status by association; he knows "the right people," including Big Joe, Murph and Max. Many reputations were established by the news media. To have made the newspapers or television is a mark of distinction that convicts share with politicians and performing artists.

Occasionally, a reputation can be a nuisance. When a guard discovered a crudely jimmied lock on the warehouse door, the obvious suspect was Franks and Beans, a former safecracker. The fellow was indignant. "It's a sloppy, non-professional job," he said. "I could open any lock in the joint without a trace just by using a nail clipper." Thereupon Franks and Beans demonstrated his skill and—he thought—his innocence, by effortlessly opening several locks in the presence of the lieutenant and captain of the guards and the embarrassed prison locksmith. Nevertheless, he suffered the usual consequences of being a suspect. He was sentenced to two weeks in "segregation," a locked, completely isolated cell with minimum physical comforts.

But the troubles of Franks and Beans were not over. A few weeks later, after all the locks had been replaced with an improved design, the kitchen steward called upon his expert talent to open the lock on the bakery door, which the new key did not fit. Against his better judgment, Franks and Beans helped out the steward and used his nail clipper to open the door. Word of the "crime" filtered back to the guards, and the good Samaritan got another stretch in segregation.

Another avenue to status is a prison job that offers access to things ordinarily beyond the reach of the average inmate. The Old Greek works in the hospital and can provide his friends with extra vitamins, aspirin or sleeping pills. Johnny, the kitchen clerk, knows the cafeteria menus 10 days in advance, an eagerly sought piece of news because, in the monotony of prison, food assumes a vital importance. The library clerk can save the latest novel or magazine, and a mailroom worker knows whether your letter was withheld by the prison censor.

Such favors are exchanged as simple expressions of friendship or as signs of respect toward men with status. In either case it is considered poor taste to expect compensation for a favor; feelings of gratitude and obligation are sufficient. The same services, however, if they are not offered as favors, have a specific market value in the unique "cigarette economy" of prison life.

Prisoners are allowed to spend up to $15 a month, which some of them may earn by their work. But the money is credited to a commissary account and actual cash never changes hands. The unit of underground currency is the cigarette, the most desirable commodity in prison, which determines poverty and wealth. Everyone is entitled to buy two cartons a week, but there are enough nonsmokers or light smokers who use their weekly ration for various transactions with heavy smokers. Two packs of cigarettes will buy a shoe shine or a pressing for a pair of pants; for four or five packages a week the bed will be made every morning. A carton is the price of a new peajacket from the clothing room.

Doing favors for free or for cigarettes is strictly prohibited and the penalties are severe. I never heard of a guard being bribed. When the offender is caught the prison code dictates that he take his punishment "like a man" and keep his mouth shut, even when wrongly accused.

Albie, the prison butcher, had an almost neurotic compulsion for storing food and feeding people, a weakness he attributed to his hungry childhood during the Depression. One day Albie decided to feed the inmates chicken salad sandwiches instead of the usual leftovers of luncheon meat. He hid a package of boiled chicken in a filing cabinet, assuming that during the routine "shakedown" search the custodial officer would not examine the cabinet. Unfortunately, the package was discovered by a department head who happened to be looking for a file of papers.

Albie was not suspected. Instead, officials accused the office clerk, a young man with a history of getting into trouble, and brought him to trial before the "captain's court."

One of the peculiar characteristics of this court (euphemistically called "the adjustment council" in official language) is that the accused inmate hardly has a chance of winning his case. If he denies the charge, he is automatically punished for implying that the accusing officer is not telling the truth ("officers never lie, inmates always do"); if he admits guilt he is punished for breaking the prison laws.

The "court" found the clerk guilty and placed him in segregation. Albie was disturbed by the miscarriage of justice and confessed. But the guard lieutenant at first refused to accept the confession, suspecting some "dirty deal." Finally, the officer acted with Solomon's wisdom: Albie was clapped in segregation but the clerk was not released. Since the lieutenant was not certain who actually stole the chicken, it was better to punish both men rather than free the guilty one. It was a bitter lesson in the old prison principle: "Truth does not pay."

Inmates select their friends from among equals and associate very little with their social inferiors or betters. They wait for each other at mealtimes, stand in line together, and choose their own table. It is poor manners to join a table without an explicit invitation. Everybody knows that the "jail house lawyer" eats with the librarian, the "professor," and the "real lawyer." Two income tax dodgers have their meals with an ex-stockbroker. The cliques are not surprising. As in any society, common interests, intellectual affinity and mutual sympathy form the basis for social ties and friendships.

When inmates discuss the "better people" they usually describe them as "men" and "gentlemen"—connoting the highest praise. Giovanni is a real "gentleman." He is reputed to be a wealthy man. He is friendly but distant, ready to do a favor, never gets into trouble, has two or three friends among the "better people." Giovanni is heard attentively when he expresses an opinion on the latest prison rumors, decisions of the United States Supreme Court or a current trial in the Southern District.

"Don't waste your time in jail by talking with your friends only about sex and broads. Listen to men who can teach you something useful." This was the advice an oldtimer gave a young offender. In many ways the influence of people like Giovanni upon the younger crowd is rather constructive. I saw several youngsters whom he taught good manners and advised to get a legitimate job when they were released from jail.

At the opposite end of the social scale from "gentlemen" are the lowest of the low—the homosexuals. The traditional American intolerance toward sex deviation is increased to fantastic proportions in this atmosphere of tension and sexual deprivation. Inmates with a homosexual record are segregated from the rest of the prison population in a special house within single, barred cells like cages where they can be observed day and night by the officer on duty. Other inmates treat them like lepers. Newcomers are often labeled as homosexuals by other prisoners even though they are not so identified by the administration or lodged in special quarters.

Speech mannerisms, posture, facial expressions are considered sufficient clues for identifying a new man as a "fag." Henceforth, he will be referred to as "she" and will be ostracized and victimized. Homosexuals are routinely accused of crimes against the prison code, such as stealing cigarettes, getting others into trouble and committing the contemptible crime of being a "rat," an administration informer.

There are, of course, a number of inmates who sexually use the homosexuals for "free" or for payment in cigarettes, but that does not change their attitude in public. Prison breeds homosexuality just as the outside society breeds prostitution; in both places the respectable citizen hides his guilt and shame by loudly condemning the practice, though sometimes indulging in it.

More conspicuous than the social distance between somebodies and nobodies is the chasm between races. Although the prison is officially integrated, the conflict between whites and Negroes seethes with prejudice, hatred, sexual stereotypes and as much segregation as the prison will permit.

The rows of chairs in the auditorium are divided by a center aisle; on days when movies are shown Negroes voluntarily sit on the right side and whites on the left side of the aisle. In the "honor house" there is a "black" side and a "white" side. If either side is temporarily filled up the newcomer might be forced to take a bed in a hostile camp. But as soon as a vacancy occurs he will tend to move in with his own kind, which may be not only whites or Negroes but Jews, Italians or Puerto Ricans who also usually cluster together with their beds side by side.

Loyalties become increasingly intense and follow clear patterns. They begin with the general loyalty of inmates against the administration, then narrow to the prisoner's own race, to his ethnic group, to his friends and finally, most intensely, to himself. Life in prison frequently requires the sacrifice of some loyalties to others, but the sacrifices must be made to survive in the highly rigid maze of conflicts, emotions and unsatisfied needs.

No culture is complete without its myths and legends. Prison culture rejects the myths supplied by the administration—myths of justice, equality and rehabilitation. Inmates dream of the day when they will be back on the "street" and have a woman, a car, a soft bed or a "real steak with French fries."

There is the myth of a bill in Congress which will allow each prisoner additional "good time" deductible from his sentence, and many men spend their time calculating to the hour when they will be out if the bill is passed. There is the myth of a Parole Board reform that will inform the inmate of the reason for being denied parole; moreover, he will be able to appeal the adverse opinion. There is the myth that inmates will be allowed to spend a night with their wives "like in some places abroad." There are legends of heroic escapes, never recovered "loot," people who "beat the law." Finally, there is the dream of the "last big job" and a trip abroad, beyond the reach of the law where one will live without fear or worry.

In many ways, these hopes seem to contradict each other; they echo a desire for justice and respectability while wishing for more criminal success. The contradictions only reflect the average prisoner's state of mind. He is tired of the endless cops and robbers game. He is tired of fear and anxiety, of eventually being caught and incarcerated.

How to break this vicious cycle of crime and punishment? The question is as acute for the prisoner as for the penologist. Many times I heard the words, "It's the last time. I don't come back again." But neither the speaker, his friends nor the administration believe it. "He'll be back," says the guard opening the gate. "He'll be back," repeat friends after shaking his hand and wishing him good luck. And, of course, sooner or later he *will* be back, another statistical unit in the tables of criminal repeaters despite the progress in penology, despite the theory of rehabilitation, despite the learned seminars on "What's Wrong with Our Prison System?"

And why shouldn't he be back? Prison offered only a system of punitive rules, a staff composed mostly of indifferent guards and values formed by fear, anger and frustration. The inmate leaves prison totally unprepared to face a life of "respectability" in an inhospitable society.

Stigmatized by imprisonment, unable to cope with his social and economic problems, frequently without family and friends, he will sooner or later fall back on the old "connections" and "skills." Then, again behind bars, his experience enriched by the prison culture, he can dream anew of a time when his human dignity will be respected, and when the time spent in prison will lead to a meaningful change in life.

Part 4

SOME EXPERIMENTS IN CHANGE

ABOUT HALF the authors who contributed to sections 2 and 3 called for changes in the criminal justice system. Vorenberg and Wilson, especially, pleaded for administrative experiments which might on a small scale demonstrate the wisdom of making large-scale changes. This section reports on a number of such experiments, ranging from the Family Crisis Intervention Unit of the New York City Police Department to Synanon, a self-help organization where drug addicts help each other get off, and stay off, drugs. All the experiments have been judged successful. Two of them—the bail experiment and the work furlough experiment—have stimulated legislative changes in many jurisdictions.

Perhaps the most significant fact about the Family Crisis Intervention Unit, described here by Ronald Sullivan, a veteran police reporter for the *New York Times,* is that its activities are not concerned with law enforcement in the strict sense of that term. Instead, the unit provides a service and, in so doing, helps keep the peace. Psychiatric treatment and family counseling services are not available to most working-class families. They are too expensive, too intellectual, and too threatening. Moreover, most public and private social welfare agencies close their doors at 5:00 P.M., just when working-class men return home to find that the problems they left in the morning are still there. Police departments are the only social service agencies of any consequence that are open twenty-four hours a day. It is reasonable, then, to expect that the police would be called upon for various kinds of assistance and services, even if they publicly cling to the image of themselves as "law-enforcement officers" and nothing else. Studies of police calls and police activities have shown that the law-enforcement officer is also guide, counselor, therapist, philosopher, welfare agent, and friend. When the New York Police Department explicitly acknowledged the service function of its patrolmen, it began training men to fulfill the function. The Family Crisis Intervention Unit was the result, and the beginning. Since all policemen are likely to be frequently called to the scenes of family disputes, all should be trained to intervene peacefully and effectively. Further, since policemen are frequently called on to render other services, they should be trained to render them, and rewarded with pay raises and promotions for rendering them in outstanding ways.

Policemen, by virtue of their occupational specialization, are opposed to change. The old ways are not only "the best," they are "right" and "true." Suggestions for change are "wrong" and "crazy." Similarly, most judges are not inclined to overhaul the machinery of justice. But Gertrude Samuels, a staff writer for the *New York Times Magazine,* tells how Manhattan's Presiding Justice Bernard Botein has greatly improved the administration of justice merely by keeping a criminal court in operation twenty-four hours a day. Other courts and criminal justice agencies should similarly try to adjust to the needs of their clients, rather than requiring the clients to adjust to them. Earlier, this same remarkable Judge Botein conducted other experiments which proved successful and which also could well be emulated by criminal justice agencies all over the world—substitution of release on one's own recognizance for release on bail; issuing summonses in lieu of arrest; computerization of information regarding the days and hours at which jurors are most readily available for service; civil commitment of mentally ill persons; and "law guardians" for juveniles.

Prisons have changed considerably during their two-hundred-year history. In the United States, the most significant changes have occurred since about 1935, when the Federal Bureau of Prisons demonstrated that a penal institution need not be a place where men merely do time in unsanitary, uncomfortable, and unpleasant surroundings. Further, in the last two decades many prison administrators have come to agree that prisons should somehow engage in "treatment," "correction," or "rehabilitation," as well as in punishment and incapacitation of criminals. But, despite more than two generations of "reform," the conditions of living in many American jails and prisons are still deplorable.

Imprisonment must, of course, be painful. Each criminal law stipulates that whoever behaves in a specified way shall be punished. Punishments once involved physical pain, but now the suffering that accompanies "mere" deprivation of freedom is stressed. The history of imprisonment, in fact, is the history of attempts to substitute "mere" deprivation of liberty for the physical suffering inflicted on the inmates of early prisons. Gradually, the physical suffering has been reduced. Most state prisons, and many jails, now have reasonably good levels of sanitation, medical care, food, and recreation. Brutality, physical torture, and "hard labor" are rare. Most of the physical pain imposed on prisoners nowadays is imposed by fellow prisoners. Moreover, even the degree of deprivation of freedom has been reduced in recent times —as indicated by the invention of probation, parole, honor camps and other "open institutions," and the work furlough system described by Miss Samuels. But the fact is that prisons and jails still exist in order to inflict pain on men by depriving them of their liberty.

The judges who sentence men to jail and prison usually do not know what they are doing. A judge knows, of course, that he has sentenced a man to, say, three years "in prison," just as a policeman knows that a man he arrested "got three years." But judges and policemen—and even prison wardens—ordinarily have little idea of what "in prison" means to the prisoner. A Workshop in Crime and Correction, conducted by three Berkeley criminologists and described here by Richard Hammer, a staff member of the *New York Times*, tried to change this condition of ignorance. By arranging for judges, policemen, correctional officials, and convicts to come together for informal bull sessions and psychodramas, the workshop gave both the criminal justice administrators and the convicts useful insights into "how the other half lives."

But in Synanon there is no "other half." In this organization, former drug addicts are both "inmates" and "officials" or "staff." Synanon has been remarkably successful in keeping addicts off drugs. Some observers believe the success is due to the love provided by the substitute family which is Synanon. Others believe the magic ingredient is the psychotherapy given by members to each other. Still other observers think Synanon's success stems from the fact that each "reformer" is also a "reformee"—by assuming the role of a reformer, each addict necessarily reinforces in himself the anti-drug attitudes that are essential to remaining off drugs. No matter what the theoretical foundation of Synanon's success, this experiment in correctional organization has demonstrated that correctional agencies should try to erase the distinctions between those men being changed and those doing the changing.

Violence, Like Charity, Begins at Home

by Ronald Sullivan

"All I've got for you is a little family trouble at Sixteen-Thirteen Madison." He'll tell you which floor and thank God it isn't the top, and so you'll climb, climb, climb, and all the while you'll be preparing to say, "Listen, what's the matter with you folks? Pipe down, can't you? Oh, shet ep, sister. Look—people are complaining; you're waking up folks in the building. O.K.—so you can't get along. O.K.—so you're drunk too. Now, look, I want you out of here. And quit socking your wife, and if I see you around here again before morning—before you're sober and ready to behave— I'll break your head wide open!"

That's the little speech, the succession of disciplinary directions that you'll be composing as you trudge upstairs; and then you hear the shuddering gasp, and somehow you're through the door before they've opened it for you, and he's standing there alone. The woman is on the floor with her skirts around her middle, and what beautiful red rosy tights she wears—all slick and damp—and the tights are extending themselves into a big evil patch on the floor.

From the *New York Times Magazine*, November 24, 1968, copyright © 1968 by The New York Times Company.

But beyond her he is there. He's very large; he looks colossal to you now. He doesn't have anything on except a pair of striped underwear shorts, and his eyes are rolling. He keeps watching you. He has a bloody bread knife in his hand, and you keep saying "Put it down, put it down—let go that knife," as he comes toward you a step at a time, and as the woman grunts and shifts on the floor in her blood, and still he keeps coming in, you've got to decide, and all in the instant. Do you shoot or do you try to use your stick? Do you try to take the knife away from him? . . . You don't like to be alone, nobody would like to be alone.

MacKinlay Kantor, "Signal Thirty-Two."

THE THREATENED cop in Kantor's novel, like policemen everywhere, had every reason to feel alone. The odds were against him because it seems that violence, like charity, begins at home. According to the Federal Bureau of Investigation, one of every five policemen killed in the line of duty dies trying to break up a family fight. The President's Commission on Law Enforcement and the Administration of Criminal Justice reported last year that family disputes "are probably the single greatest cause of homicides" in the United States. And if policemen don't get killed in a family fight, they still stand a good chance of being bloodied. "There is a strong impression in police circles that intervention in these disputes causes more assaults on policemen than any other encounter," the commission reported in "The Challenge of Crime in a Free Society." In fact, the New York City Police Department estimates that 40 per cent of its men injured in the line of duty were hurt while responding to family disturbances. Moreover, the department estimates that such calls take as much time as any other single kind of police action. "Yet the capacity of the police to deal effectively with such a highly personal matter as conjugal disharmony is, to say the least, limited . . . an activity for which few policemen—or people in any profession—are qualified by temperament or by training," the commission reported.

But that was before an experimental New York City police unit began intervening in family quarrels in upper West Harlem. Despite the high statistical probability of being knifed, shot at, gang-jumped or pushed down a flight of tenement stairs, none of the 18 volunteer patrolmen assigned to the Family Crisis Intervention Unit in the 30th Precinct has sustained a single injury, much less a fatality, in the unit's first 15 months of operation. Moreover, after intervening in more than 1,000 individual family crises—an average of a little more than two a night—the unit has not been involved in a single charge of police brutality, and this is an area in which such accusations are commonplace.

But perhaps just as important, none of the interventions resulted in either a homicide or a suicide. There are no conclusive records in the precinct to show how this deathless record compares with the outcome of family fights in the precinct in previous years. Nevertheless, Police Commissioner Howard R. Leary, the United States Department of Justice and the project's originator, Dr. Morton Bard, director of the Pyschological Center at City College, are convinced that the new unit unquestionably has saved many lives.

There are no records connecting deaths with family fights because no police function is more misunderstood, more underrated, and more grudgingly performed than calls to break them up. Unlike other police activity, such as murder investigations or criminal surveillance, intervention in family fights is commonly regarded at all levels in the Police Department as a thankless job that poses the danger of grave personal risk and the distinct possibility of becoming embroiled in charges of police brutality, with very little, if any, promise of reward. A cop makes detective or becomes a sergeant by the big arrest or the daring rescue—not by breaking up a family fight. It is not surprising, then, that there are few references to the subject in police literature or at police training academies.

Now, however, it seems likely that the apparent success of the Family Crisis Intervention Unit will have an impact on the way policemen are motivated, trained and ultimately rewarded by their departments. In fact, this year's report by the National Advisory Commission on Civil Disorders recommended New York's pilot program as a "model for other departments." The report said, "The commission believes the police cannot and should not resist becoming involved in community service matters. . . . Such work can gain the police the respect and support of the community."

Its importance was pointed up by the Governor's Select Commission on Civil Disorder in New Jersey. After investigating the causes of the Negro rioting in Newark in July, 1967, the commission reported that most complaints of police brutality originated from incidents that began as family-disturbance calls—and that these complaints had been increasing before the rioting broke out.

According to Dr. Bard, outmoded police organization is the silent factor underlying the growing tension between police and community, particularly in the urban ghettos. And the violence of family conflict in these areas is matched only by the indifference of society outside to its existence. Professor Bard emphasizes that only the police, of all social institutions, are present 24 hours a day, every day of the year, to answer the call when family violence threatens.

Thus, with the full support of Commissioner Leary, and $94,736 from the Federal Government, Dr. Bard's Psychological Center began a two-year experiment last year in training police to intervene in family fights. The pilot program, which is scheduled to end next April, does not aim to turn cops into psychologists or social workers. "That's just exactly what we're attempting to avoid," says Dr. Bard, who was a cop himself for a short time in the late nineteen-forties before he became a group worker with street gangs and ultimately a professor of psychology. "We have no intention of creating a family cop, or a family division, or making family crisis intervention an esoteric police specialty. All we're trying to do is give the ordinary policeman a new skill, one that will help him do better what he now does most—and that is help people in trouble." If, at the same time, he can become a primary mental-health resource in the community, so much the better, of course.

The program also is part of a growing revolution involving the training of clinical psychologists and the development of community mental-health programs in the cities. There simply never will be enough psychologists to treat poor persons in the slums, where most of the aggressive behavior and mental disorder is. So the idea at the center is to train psychologists to train other persons to do it.

At the same time, the university is given the chance to break out from its pedagogical shell by turning the surrounding community into a teeming psychological laboratory rather than a hostile environment. What better place is there than Harlem to study marital breakdown, aggression, sadomasochism and the effects of violence on early childhood development? And who is better equipped to study it than the persons who face it every day, like Patrolman John E. Bodkin, a 32-year-old, cigar-smoking, no-nonsense, seven-year veteran and member of the Family Crisis Intervention Unit?

"It was up on 145th Street," he said. "And the couple was from the South. We went in there and I could see right off that this guy was tight, very tight. He was a Negro fellow, about 21 or 22 years old, only up in New York six months. She had called the police because of a dispute—a minor thing. But there he was, a little guy, and he was really tense because when we walked in with our uniforms and our sticks, you could see that his earlier associations with police officers must have been very rough.

"You could see the fear in his eyes, the hostility in his face. His fists were clenched, and he was ready to do combat with us. God knows what he would have done if he'd had a gun or a knife. I moved toward the kitchen table and opened my blouse and I told him in a nice quiet way that I wanted to talk to him, but he's still tense and he's still looking at my stick. Well, the stick is under my arm so I hung it up on a nearby chair, purposely, to show there's no intent here. 'Look, I don't need it,' I'm trying to say to this guy. 'I don't need it because you're a nice guy in my eyes. You don't threaten me, so I'm not going to threaten you.' I've got to show this guy that I'm not a bully, a brute, a Nazi or the Fascist he thinks all cops are.

"So he calms down a little. Then I took my hat off and I said, 'Do you mind if I smoke?' And he looks at me funny. And I say, 'I'm a cigar smoker and some people don't like the smell of a cigar in their house, so would you mind if I smoke?' And the guy says, 'Oh sure, sure,' and you could see he was shocked. I felt he saw a human side of us, that I had respect for him and his household.

"Then the guy sat down and he and his wife proceed to tell us what it was all about. When we explain to her why he's upset, she smiles. 'Yes, yes, yes.' You see, she thinks we're on her side. Then we tell him why he's mad and he smiles. 'Yes, yes, yes.' Now we're on his side. Well, they eventually shake our hands; they were happy and we never had another call from them."

Patrolman Bodkin and the 17 other policemen in the family crisis unit operate in biracial pairs out of the 96-year-old, four-story 30th Precinct station house on the southwest corner of 152d Street and Amsterdam Avenue. The 30th is one of New York's smaller and more insignificant precincts, running north from 141st to 165th Streets and east from Riverside Drive to Edgecombe Avenue. Most of the old apartment houses on Broadway have been taken over by Puerto Rican and Negro families. The remaining whites in the precinct, many of them apparently Jewish, are virtually barricaded in the big apartment houses overlooking the Hudson on Riverside Drive. Actually, the 30th is just what Dr. Bard was looking for: a poor, rat-infested neighborhood, but without the wretchedness of some of the other black precincts in Harlem, one free of big crime and big institutions and one that comes alive every week when the welfare checks roll in.

Like Bodkin, most of the cops in the family unit were already working in the 30th before the program began. None of them was picked because he evidenced a bleeding heart for minority problems. All of them, and this includes the nine Negroes, were used to feeling hated, feared and envied in the ghetto. None of them has a college degree. They tend to be young, in their late 20's and early 30's, because it is very hard to teach old cops new tricks. What Dr. Bard, along with Dr. Bernard Berkowitz, a psychologist with 12 years as a policeman in his background, looked for in choosing from among 45 volunteers were experienced cops who expressed enthusiasm for the experiment and frustration with their present inability to deal effectively with family crises, and who showed every indication of being sensitive to the changing role the police must assume in the cities.

The 18 men, who were released from duty, spent nearly a month with professional psychologists at the center in mutual exploration of the best methods of successful intervention. The psychologists knew all about such things as aggression, trauma, neurosis, alcoholism and all the other behavioral patterns associated with family violence. And that is what they taught the men during the first three weeks of intensive psychological classroom work. But the center's pedagogy and its proclivity for reflective analysis generally failed the psychologists when they departed from the laboratory or the textbook for the explosive, instant-action world of police confrontation with family violence. "No one has a textbook for that. This is where we had to learn from each other," says Dr. Bard.

During the third week, the cops were subjected to three days of family-crisis psycho-skits staged by a group of professional actors. The short plays showed typical family crises and were written without conclusions; the endings were improvised by the patrolmen themselves, who intervened in pairs at the end. For example, in one play, a young Negro actress portrayed a wife who was cowering against the rear classroom wall, away from a tall, husky Negro, playing her wife-beating husband.

"He's going to hit me, he's going to hit me again," she screamed as the two cops burst on the scene and split, one of them going to the aid of the stricken woman, the other confronting the man.

"Whaddaya doing that for?" the patrolman snarled at the man as he pushed him toward a corner of the improvised stage. "That's no way to treat a woman, that's no way for a man to act. You're no man." With that, the Negro actor, even though he knew it was only a play, reacted angrily and moved toward the advancing patrolman, bellowing, "Who says I'm no man . . . ?"

At that point, the play was stopped and the cops and the actors analyzed their respective reactions. For one thing, the cop who confronted the husband was told this is how most cops get hurt— challenging a man's masculinity. Moreover, the cops were told that the wife may very well be a masochist who has spent the day provoking the man into attacking her. He gets an outlet for his aggression; she has the simple pleasure of getting beaten up. The idea, the policemen were told, is to give the combatants alternatives and the help they need to understand why they fight.

But an unsophisticated cop can go only so far, and this is where their fourth week of training came in. They took field trips to various social, health and welfare agencies where experts explained the kinds of help available to poor families in trouble.

Later, the men took part in human-relations workshops where they were prompted to examine, in group sensitivity discussions, their individual prejudices and preconceptions of disrupted family life in the ghetto.

After this, the unit began operating out of the 30th station house in the precinct's special family car. Two members of the unit work each of the day's three eight-hour tours and are dispatched on all complaints involving family disturbances. They also continue their normal police duties—they give out parking tickets and speeding summonses; they patrol a given sector of the precinct; they are expected to respond to any emergency just like any other cop on the beat. At the start, they were subject to considerable jeering from other patrolmen, but their capacity to handle both missions effectively has turned the initial jibes at the station house into inquiries on how to deal with family crises.

Meantime, all of the 18 men continue their training, taking part in six-man discussion groups led by professional psychologists. In addition, each man has a weekly private consultation with a third-year graduate student in clinical psychology. The consultation cuts both ways. The officer reports the way he reacted to a particular family crisis and is given advice on ways he might have responded differently. Some of the students have become intrigued with the research opportunities afforded by these exchanges. One has formulated a research proposal in which he will attempt to measure differences in aggressive threshold stimuli among children of families in which day-to-day violence is a part of the environment. These children will be matched with children raised in nonviolent homes.

Adriaan Halfhide, a 27-year-old Negro cop assigned to the family project, is convinced that 60 per cent of the people in every block in the precinct are aware of the new unit. "We're more aware of them, too," he says. "We go into a family dispute and we can pick up certain signs, statements, gestures, looks and facial expressions that enable us to get a basic idea of what's going on. For example, I notice whether a man is gritting his teeth, whether the veins in his temple are throbbing. Before, I only looked for whether he had a weapon, or whether he was bigger than me. Later, when they just want someone to yell at, someone to use as a butt for their anger, I say, 'O.K., get mad at me.' Then everybody yells at me. But they're all together, yelling together, but at me, and that's groovy."

Halfhide and the other family cops have some fundamental ground rules. They always stay calm; they don't threaten and they don't take sides. They don't challenge a man's masculinity; they don't degrade a woman's femininity. They intentionally give people verbal escape routes to save face. And mother isn't always right—they know about Oedipus complexes. They notice that most family fights tend to break out on Sunday night after a festering weekend of drinking. They say the major causes of conflict are, predictably, money and sex. Families fight more in the summer because it's hot, and more in the winter because it's so cold outside they can't escape one another.

On the back seat of their patrol car the family cops keep two small wooden boxes with card files showing whom the unit has previously been sent to. The file is kept by street numbers so the men on duty can determine immediately whether any other team has called upon a family to which they are on their way. The cards show whether an earlier intervention involved any weapons so that the responding patrolmen can be on guard. The cards have 35 entries, including besides usual vital statistics: "What happened IMMEDIATELY before your arrival? What do *you* think led up to the immediate crisis? (Changes in family patterns?) (Environmental changes, etc.?) Impressions of the family: How long has this family been together? Who is dominant? What is the appearance of the house? Appearance of the individuals? Other impressions? What happened after your arrival? (How did each disputant respond?) How was the dispute resolved? Mediation ( ). Referral ( ). Aided ( ). Arrest ( ). Full details. *Summarize* the crisis situation and its resolution."

Every intervention is different and each of the nine teams reacts differently. Nevertheless, there are some standard procedures. The patrolmen go in together, then split, with one of them going toward one of the antagonists, the second toward the other. Guns are rarely drawn. In fact, the cops often leave their nightsticks in the car. They don't shout, they don't push and they don't threaten to lock up everyone in sight. All the while, the two men are scooping up any knives, scissors or other weapons, putting them where no one can get at them. Windows are checked in case the crisis involves a potential suicide. Children are accounted for.

Generally, the cops attempt to mollify both sides, taking the combatants into separate rooms so they can be questioned without one of them challenging the other's version of the crisis. The cops try to draw out the underlying facts, compare the differing versions and then, in a kind of group therapy, they attempt to explain to the family why it is fighting and recommend ways for it to stop. Normally, the family will be referred to a health or social agency. The cops carry printed slips with the addresses, offer to make the appointment—and in some cases drive the family down in the patrol car.

Many times, interventions do not involve violence. There is, for instance, a five-story walk-up on Amsterdam Avenue, a squalid rooming house taken over by prostitutes and narcotic addicts. But up on the top floor an old Negro couple—she in her late 70's, he in his 80's—were barely surviving in abandoned isolation in a tiny rear room. He was weak from advanced age and malnutrition and had fallen out of bed. She did not have the strength to lift him back. They had no children, no friends, no neighbors and no money. So she called the police and the family unit was dispatched. Instead of just putting him back in bed, which is what a lot of cops would have done, the unit called the Visiting Nurse Service. The V.N.S. told them that they should call a physician. So the cops went out and got one. And the couple are now visited regularly by V.N.S. nurses who make sure they are getting along the best they can.

Violence, though, or the forestalling of it, is the rule—especially as weekends draw to a close and the relief checks are gone, some of them spent on gin. This particular night, Patrolman Bodkin and his partner, Frank Madewell, get the call on the police radio: "Man with a gun at One-Six-Three Street and Amsterdam." They weave fast against traffic and screech up at the address behind three other patrol cars. Upstairs, there are six cops in the third floor hall and a thin, hysterical woman in her nightgown shouting obscenities—alternately through a closed apartment door and at the cops for not breaking it down. "He's got my kids inside, and he's got a gun!" she screams.

From inside, the man roars, "You come in and I'll blow your ———— head off." With that, a burly sergeant pushes by the woman and bangs on the door. "Let's go! Open up or we'll kick it down!" he shouts. "Come right ahead, ————," the man bellows back.

Meantime, Madewell goes back to the car and checks the address in the card file. The couple has quite a file; he is marked as violent and possibly armed. Madewell goes back up and tells the sergeant, who jerks his thumb toward the closed door and replies: "O.K., you're the family cops. You go on in." And slides out of the line of fire.

"First, we used his first name," Madewell recalls. "We tried to con him. I said, 'I can't scream through the door, and besides it's cold as hell out here and all your wife wants is her clothes.' But he just tells me to do you-know-what and I'm sweating. 'You can at least give her her clothes,' I say to him. 'We won't say a word to you; we won't even look. C'mon, it's getting late and we can't stay here all night. Tell me what happened; you're a man, you can tell me. Did she try to put you down?"

"God, I'm talking and talking to this guy, and the other cops are over by the stairs with their guns out. Finally—I can't say how long—I feel the lock give and the door open a crack and we go in and take him."

Later, detectives from the 30th squad determined that the man had attempted to fire a .32-caliber revolver at the sergeant through the closed door, but that the firing pin failed each time to strike the shell hard enough to shoot the bullet. The man said he had stopped trying to shoot when Madewell called him by his first name and started to talk to him.

Or spend the early-morning hours of a recent Saturday on duty with Albert Robertson, a 42-year-old family cop, a Negro with 11 years in the department, most of them in the 30th. He and his partner, William Robison, a nonunit patrolman who has been pressed into family-car duty on this tour, prowl through the precinct's garbage-strewn streets.

The first radio call sends them to St. Nicholas Avenue, where they climb, climb, climb to the sixth floor. At an open door, the young, buxom Negro woman who called the police lets them in and jerks her thumb toward a big man asleep in the bedroom. "Robbie," she says to Patrolman Robertson, whom everyone on his beat seems to know, "he's nothin' but a bum who's been whippin' me for eight years. I want him arrested before he kills me. He beat me somethin' awful before he drank hisself to sleep."

"But, sweetheart," Robertson replies, "you know he'll be out tomorrow. And are you going to give him the bail money?" (It turns out later that she simply wanted to get rid of him for the weekend so she could go to Atlantic City.)

There's another call. And at 150th Street and Amsterdam a woman shouts down from a second-floor tenement window: "Robbie! Robbie! He's got a gun. He's messin' with us with his pistol."

So Robertson and Robison draw their guns this time, and tell the woman to stand back. "Open the door!" yells Robbie. "For what?" the man inside growls. "That bitch is nuts." He finally opens up but he has no gun on him—and they have no search warrant.

Then it's back quickly to a big, run-down apartment house on St. Nicholas Avenue where a man and wife in a shabby basement apartment have been at each other all night. She says: "Look what he done to me; he kicked me in the belly. I want him locked up, officer." He says: "Hell, lock her up, too," and holds out his arm to show where his wife has cut him with a kitchen knife. "I'll go as long as she goes, too; otherwise, you got to fight me."

Carefully, with a look of weariness in his round, good-natured face, Robertson takes off his blouse and cap, lays his black notebook on the hall table, and sinks slowly into the only comfortable chair in the living room. "What's you folks been drinkin'?" he asks. "Scotch," the glowering, heavy-set man answers. "Sweetheart," Robertson says to the woman, "get me a small drink, will you?" Then he takes off his shoes and rubs his arches and wiggles his toes, and the man just sits and looks at him incredulously. The man gives Robertson the Scotch, but the drink has no ice, so Robertson asks the wife to bring him some.

"By this time," Robertson explains later, "they're so shook up with me sitting in *their* chair, sippin' *their* Scotch [he actually never drank it] that now we can find out what they're really fighting about. Before you know it, I'm part of the family."

She tells Robbie that they'd always drink and end up fighting. And it begins to come out, five years of it: He can't stand the dirty dishes, the food left for days on the stove, the messy apartment, and she knows he can't. She says she can't stand his all-night drinking, his playing around, and he knows it, too. So Robbie gives them a little advice—"Look at her side; look at his" —and tells them that next time they want to fight, call him up at the station house and they can fight with him and keep it in the family. He offers Robbie another drink. . . .

The car radio sends Robertson and his partner to Riverside Drive, where a young, attractive Negro woman is standing in the lobby of one of the better apartment houses facing the river. She says she had a fight with her husband and that he won't let her back in to get her baby or her clothes. She said he threatened to kill her, too. Robbie goes up and talks to him, and the man finally agrees to let her take the baby but not the clothes—"because I paid for them." But the cops persuade him to let her have them.

Suddenly, as she's packing, he pushes by Robertson and grabs her, and as they escort her out, he lunges at her again. Then he rushes into the kitchen and comes back with a bread knife. "If she goes with the clothes, you're going to have to kill me tonight. Tonight I got to die," he says. Robertson ignores him. But as they turn to leave, the man moves toward them, waving the knife.

Robertson draws his revolver and tells the man: "Put that away and settle this in court tomorrow." The man keeps coming. Robertson cocks his revolver and says: "Buddy, it isn't a question of me shooting you, but where you're going to get shot." As the man hesitates, Robertson grabs the front door, shouts: "Merry Christmas, happy New Year and a good night to you," and slams the door in the man's face.

"You know what he was doing?" he says later. "He was looking for a little sympathy. And what better way to get it around here than get shot by a cop?"

Sometimes the intervention ultimately fails, as happened earlier this year when a woman, mumbling incoherently, her hands and legs covered with blood, staggered into the 30th station house and threw a bloody paring knife on the desk. Two unit patrolmen, Tony Donovan and Joseph Mahoney, happened to be there and they led her gently to a side room.

"O.K., sweetheart," one of them asked her quietly, "where are you hurt? What happened?" They gave her a cigarette and lit it for her. And as she held it in her trembling hand, she moaned: "He kept nagging me. All day, kept after me. Couldn't stand it no more. Oh, God, go help him."

Six months earlier, the woman had called the police and the family unit had been sent to stop a fight between her and her husband. The unit determined then that both were alcoholics and tried to get them to go to Alcoholics Anonymous, but they refused. However, they did agree to separate, but he came back later. The drinking began again, and the inevitable happened. They began to fight. But instead of calling the cops this time, she had stabbed her husband, nearly killing him.

Or there's the night when Patrolmen John Edmonds, a quiet 41-year-old Negro, and John Mulitz, a tall, 35-year-old Pennsylvania Dutchman, get the call: "A man shot," and Mulitz, who's driving, turns on the flashing red light and uses the siren to get through traffic up Broadway to 163rd Street. The address is not in the car's card file. The dying man, a middle-aged Puerto Rican, is on his back in the bedroom. Part of his intestine has bubbled through his abdomen where the steel jacketed bullet came out. His wife mumbles incoherently to Edmonds: "We have ze argument. He goes into ze bedroom. . . ."

"Maybe if she called us earlier . . . ," Edmonds says.

Then it's another call and Mulitz and Edmonds pull up in front of a sagging tenement on 149th Street where a young, scrawny Negro, his right hand swathed in bandages, comes rushing out screaming that one of his wife's sisters just threw acid on him. It seems that he and his wife had got drunk together earlier. They started to fight, and he put his hand through a bedroom mirror. When he tried to resume the fight after being treated at Harlem Hospital, one of his wife's three monumental sisters (they could have been a beef trust, Mulitz remarks later) heaved him out while another threw a panful of cleaning ammonia on him. In the scuffle, he stabbed his wife in the leg.

When Mulitz tells him that he must be arrested for this, the Negro takes out another knife hidden under his belt and snarls: "I ain't goin', and you can't make me." Mulitz orders him to drop the knife, but he continues to move up the front steps. Mulitz opens his holster and shouts: "Drop it!" but the man just looks at him.

Finally, Mulitz, who towers easily more than a foot over the man, crosses his arms and says: "Listen, you don't have to prove you're a man to me or to your wife and her sisters. I know you're a man; you already proved it to me. Now drop the knife like a good fellow." The man stops, wavers a few seconds, then bursts into tears—and drops the knife.

And one night, George Timmins, 33, and his partner, Ernest Bryant, a 33-year-old Negro who cuts his hair Afro style and wears love beads offduty, pay their fifth visit to a Puerto Rican couple on 145th Street who are determined to destroy each other. This time, the husband has methodically dismantled the family bed and stacked the pieces neatly against the bedroom wall before leaving for his nighttime job. "She's no goin' to mess around in this bed while I gone," he says.

Normally, the man's wife would have tried to kill him for taking the bed apart. In the past 16 years she has opened him up across the chest with a carving knife, shot him on three separate occasions and once has thrown lye on his sexual organs. She is an obvious sadist. He, on the other hand, doesn't seem to mind much and he proudly pulls up his workshirt to show the cops his battle scars. She only glares at him and turns to the cops. "You think he look bad now, ha," she says. "He keeps this up, he's really goin' to get hurt."

Federal officials such as Louis A. Mayo Jr., the 39-year-old program manager of the family-intervention project in the National Institute of Law Enforcement and Criminal Justice, a new agency within the Department of Justice, consider the experiment a success, even though its full results have yet to be evaluated. "We are very encouraged," Mayo said recently. "For a very limited financial investment, there's been a handsome payoff on a cost benefit basis alone—and that doesn't include the personal agony that goes with a homicide."

"Look," says Mrs. Carole Rothman, a petite and attractive 23-year-old graduate student in Dr. Bard's project. "I used to have the typical 'dumb cop' image. I simply couldn't believe a cop had the capacity to figure out the psychological nuances of family conflict. But you should see how fantastically sensitive they really are. They pick up on things that I would miss, and they challenge things I let go by. Now I've become intolerant of people who have cops stereotyped. I see cops as faces, not uniforms."

"If you ask the average psychologist, 'Who becomes a cop?' " says Dr. Bard, "you know what quick, glib answer you get off the top of his head? You get: 'A sadist, a latent criminal, a paranoid.' I have yet to have someone answer: 'Somebody who wants to help.' I suspect very strongly that a significantly large percentage—not all—of the men who seek to become cops do so out of a wish to help. They're idealistically motivated.

"But the police establishment quickly disabuses any such notion. There's no mechanism for a guy to develop along these lines. He learns very quickly that the only way he can make it is to give up this helping aspiration. The system does not reward this kind of behavior and it does not encourage it because its guiding principles are repressive, restrictive and in keeping with the horse-and-buggy days when conflicts were resolved in the middle of Main Street by the man with the quickest draw.

"Some of these guys make a compromise; they go into youth work or rescue service. A significantly large number quit. The ones who stay make more compromises and become the most cynical transmitters of the same values which they themselves deplored when they first came in. Now, a wholly different organizational structure of the police must prevail in which the system addresses itself to the problems that society really has, rather than those which society once had. The way it is now is neurotic.

"Let's face it. The very nature of the cop is to preserve the status quo. And the reason for the confrontation between the police and the intellectual is that, if there is anything the intellectual is for, he is for change."

A former New York City police official said: "It is a fact that until very recently a patrolman who got in a gun battle was immediately rewarded with a promotion to detective. And it is unfortunately a fact that the tradition of rewarding the man who winds up in a violent confrontation is still a very real part of the New York City Police Department and most other departments, too."

Dr. Howard E. Mitchell, director of the human resources program at the University of Pennsylvania, and an expert on police, contends that the day of holding a once-a-year Brotherhood Week at the station house, on the one hand, while beefing up the Tactical Patrol Force on the other, is over. "It's a different ball game now," he says. "The police are going to have to make a lot of changes, and it doesn't take any great intelligence to know that a person trained for riot control is not the one to send out to stop a family fight in a tense community."

In a sense that is pretty much what the Family Crisis Intervention Unit is all about. Or, as Capt. Vincent T. Agoglia, the commanding officer of the 30th Precinct and a 30-year veteran, remarked as he watched his men turn out the other morning: "You've got to have the people in the community on your side or else you can forget about police work. Look at the changes here in the way the community has reacted. We've got families now who come in here and ask for the family cops. Last year, they might have to come in here looking, instead, for the civilian complaint review board. It's not what the police *say,* but what they *do,* that counts."

A Judge with "Disciplined Indignation"

by Gertrude Samuels

AT 9:30 ONE MORNING a few weeks ago, the narrow corridor on the third floor of the Criminal Courts Building in lower Manhattan was as crowded and chaotic as a subway platform at rush hour.

Along one wall stretched a "holding pen"—a long, massively barred cell—with 36 male prisoners. Some 50 had already been processed and sent to the courtroom by the court clerks and uniformed officers who milled in the corridor. All had been booked as suspects on felony charges: assaults (with a knife, a gun, an icepick), burglaries, "1757's" (narcotics violations), some "1897's" (possession of firearms). None had yet been arraigned—much less found guilty.

Outside the bars, investigators from the Department of Probation were trying frantically, in the few minutes allotted them, to get down a few facts about each case. Those facts, about the suspect's roots in the community, his job, his family, were to inform the judge whether this or that man could be safely released without bail until his trial.

Suddenly there was a pause in the uproar to allow a tall, white-haired man to put some questions to the prisoners:

"What time were you arrested?"

"Were you kept in a police lockup?"

At first the accused held back, sullen and suspicious. They slumped against the wall of their cage or remained seated on its iron bench. No one answered. A uniformed attendant urged them, not unkindly: "Listen, fellas, this is Judge Botein. He's trying to help this situation here."

Some reacted to the word "judge." They came forward to speak to him through the bars:

"I was in a police lockup overnight, Judge."

"I been here since 2 o'clock this morning, Judge."

". . . Since 3:30 yesterday afternoon."

". . . Since 8 o'clock."

"Eight o'clock this morning?" the judge asked.

"No, Judge, 8 o'clock yesterday morning. They just put us in the lockup. 'Stay there for a while,' they said."

"This means," the judge asked an officer, "that this man has been waiting for 26 hours without appearing before a judge?"

"Yes."

The judge's mouth tightened with displeasure. He walked down a flight of stairs on which Legal Aid attorneys (they represent the poor without fee) were interviewing clients for lack of space elsewhere. On the floor below, other Legal Aid men were conducting interviews through the bars of two small cells, "feeding pens" adjoining Felony Court, where the first stage of the court process —arraignment—takes place. A young attorney smiled ruefully at the inquiring judge. "It's really submerging us," he said.

Now the judge made his way, with difficulty, through a harried group of uniformed officers into the court. The room, where a black-robed judge sat under the legend "In God We Trust," was jammed—with complainants, private counsel, Legal Aid attorneys, assistant district attorneys, relatives of defendants; with policemen who might be tied up for hours waiting to testify about arrests; with ordinary court buffs who love a circus. The jammed courtroom symbolized the problem: a piling up of cases because the personnel and the courthouse itself were on conventional 9-to-5 hours.

Judge Botein had taken me with him on this inspection tour for a glimpse of some of the conditions that he hopes to correct through a revolutionary experiment—called the 24-Hour Arraignment Court—which is just going into effect. Under the plan, the result of nearly two years of field work by teams of specialists in many stationhouses and many courts, the Manhattan Criminal Court will remain open 24 hours a day so that prisoners can be brought promptly before judges. Judges and attorneys—both prosecuting and defense—will be on duty in shifts around the clock.

The remaining four counties of New York will be studying the Botein experiment closely, for if it works it will be extended throughout the city. Indeed, every major city in the country will be watching, for the problem of booking, arraigning and hearing suspects promptly on criminal charges is national in scope.

Above all, the experiment, which has the strong support of the Mayor and city officials, will, Judge Botein told me, help to reduce the problem of coerced confessions. "A man claims he has been beaten up in a police precinct," he said. "We may strike his confession and erase his conviction and so forth. I asked myself: 'Why not reduce as much as possible the *potential* for this kind of complaint? Why not eliminate police precinct lockups altogether?' That's what the 24-hour arraignment project will accomplish. It just seemed to me that when a fellow needs a friend the most, it's when he's about to cross the threshold of the very first court—his first contact with law and justice." The words reflected his determination not to let convention mire the rights of the individual.

Bernard Botein, Presiding Justice of the Appellate Division for the First Department of New York State's Supreme Court (New York and Bronx Counties), last month marked his 25th year on the bench. He was a trial judge in Supreme Court for the first dozen years; for the remainder, an associate justice and (since 1958) the P. J., as he is irreverently known, of the Appellate Division. It is one of the country's most powerful courts.

What, then, is the P. J.'s philosophy of law? What's wrong with the courts the way they are, and what, in his view, should be done? We were back in chambers when I put the questions—in a large, walnut-paneled, booklined office in the Appellate Court.

Whether in his black robes of office or in the quiet gray or dark blue business suits that he favors, the P. J. looks the part—a tall, lean, handsome man with deep-set gray eyes, wavy white hair and a square, lined face. Now as he began to pace, considering the questions, his jacket came off and he became literally the shirt-sleeved judge of his reputation.

"A judge's philosophy of law is a set of values," he began. "These values take root in his beginnings—are molded and shaped later in life, but somehow, it seems to me, remain amazingly constant. And so, because of my beginnings, which were in poverty, I believe that I started my judicial career with a certain built-in understanding of the plight of the little man caught up in the terrifying net of the law.

"My heart belongs to the so-called lower courts, the criminal courts and family courts, because they deal essentially with people, whereas the so-called higher courts have been too preoccupied with property and money. In other words, I'm more concerned with courts that deal with broken homes and broken lives than with courts that deal with broken contracts.

" 'Does the law work for the people?' I ask myself. It should. Without it, you have anarchy, the strong overpowering the weak without restraint. Regretfully, though, the law too often is still incapable of protecting the weak against the strong—or, more important, the weak against themselves, against their own ignorance and failings.

"The powerful, specifically in the criminal courts, can afford the best lawyers. They are not behind bars. They have no trouble raising bail, and no gnawing anxieties about paying the grocery bills while awaiting the outcome of the charges against them. The weak cannot hire lawyers. If the breadwinner can't raise bail, his family often has to go on relief while he stays in jail awaiting trial.

"The law on the books is theoretically the same for all: for rich and for poor, for powerful and for weak. But the law in action is often quite different. And this has always frustrated and angered me. I still have a capacity for indignation—*disciplined* indignation, I hope, and no bleeding heart. When I react, I like to react in a manner that can be effective."

What are the biggest issues of crime and enforcement?

"The biggest challenge confronting all the courts today," he replied, "is equalizing the position and resources of the poor man with that of the rich man. This is particularly true of the criminal courts, where, in New York City at least, 75 per cent of defendants cannot afford to pay for lawyers. [Most are assigned Legal Aid.] The trouble with law enforcement—and by this, I mean courts, policemen, prosecutors—is that the defendant is usually only a statistic to them. He is not approached as a human being who, if handled as such, might have been saved from either beginning or continuing a life of crime.

"What is fundamentally wrong is that law enforcement is not moving forward to meet the potential offender at the point where he first exhibits symptoms of future delinquency. That is the main problem of law enforcement.

"And the courts, of all the agencies charged with law enforcement, have probably been the least mobile. This is because the traditional stance of the court has been to wait, to receive a case, decide that particular case—that and no more. Until the advent of the Warren Court, we judges were too often content to sit on our status quo. That highest court moved out of the traditional bind with decisions bearing on confessions and counsel for the indigent.

"But Supreme Court decisions are destined to have little impact unless the communities are receptive and prepared to implement them. They're not going to cure all the evils by a long shot —there are too many areas which cannot be reached by courts functioning in their judicial capacity alone. It is a beginning.

"And that is why I find my most challenging responsibilities require me to come off the bench—to cross the threshold of the court, go out into the community and try to find out whether the problems that bring people into court can be averted. For this reason, I am working constantly with experts in the medical, social and other sciences, who, in this collaboration of many disciplines, can give me answers that are unobtainable from the legal profession."

The 24-hour arraignment experiment is the newest of many experiments in social justice that have engaged Judge Botein in recent years. They have included the question of bail, the issuance of summonses in lieu of arrests, the commitment of mentally ill persons, the jury system itself, law guardians for juveniles in trouble, and a series of studies on the complex problems of alcoholics, drug addicts and homosexuals.

"The Botein projects are revolutionary," says one veteran observer of the courts, "in the way that they are upsetting the status-quo thinking among judges and lawyers, and, most important, in the way that the initiative is coming from a high-ranking personage usually too far removed from the hurly-burly of the courthouse—a Presiding Justice."

"I'm not a rare person—a lot of judges feel the way I do about the law and justice," the P.J. insists. "It's only that I'm in a position today to do something about it. It's not enough to have the indignation. You have to have the power to move. I have that now."

What he meant was that there was not much he could do about his ideas—though he had been talking them up for many years—until a little more than four years ago. Then, on Sept. 1, 1962, the first major court reforms in the city and state in more than a century brought the day-to-day functioning of the lower courts in his jurisdiction under his Appellate Division. Where there had been largely autonomous judges, there is now one body of judges —and Botein's Appellate Division is free to assign them from one court to another. This means that where there is a slack in one court, the judicial manpower can be used where it is needed. Above all, the reforms eliminated the fragmentation of jurisdiction in the so-called social courts, the Family and Youth parts.

Today, the Appellate Division over which Botein presides is quite possibly the busiest judicial body in the country. His own court hears only appeals from civil and criminal courts; except for a limited right of appeal to the Court of Appeals (the highest in New York State), its decisions are final. But in addition to his own court, the P.J. "rules" the State's Supreme, Surrogate's, Criminal, Civil and Family Courts—a total of 311 judges in 26 courthouses staffed by more than 6,500 nonjudicial employes. The Appellate Division covers every legal action from the simplest breach-of-contract or negligence case all the way to problems of corporate reorganization and to murder.*

In Criminal Court alone, during the calendar year of 1965, there were 4,152,621 new cases, and 2,490,270 dispositions. (A large number were traffic cases.) Family Court, with 45,099 new cases and 408,912 hearings, also accounted for nearly $31-million of support payments for families and children.

Ever since court reorganization, the P.J. says, he has been wearing two hats: one as a sitting judge in Appellate Court; the other as administrator. Indeed, his great gift, says one colleague, is as an administrator: "This is an innovator who works for his courts." And Aryeh Neier, director of the New York Civil Liberties Union, says warmly: "Judge Botein is the best we have. Without Judge Botein, I think it would have been very difficult to create the impetus behind the drive for the 24-Hour Arraignment Court, and for the bail and summons reforms."

The P.J. often works in the background, preferring to let the initiative for a project come from a public-spirited citizen or a city official in order to get results. Such was the case with the Manhattan Bail Project, which proved so successful that it has been copied by major cities throughout the country.

For some years Judge Botein had been watching the studies of Prof. Caleb Foote of the University of Pennsylvania Law School on the idea of reforming bail practices. Foote wanted to see whether people unable to afford bail could be released on their own recognizance until trial—that is, on their honor, or what lawyers call being R.O.R.'d.

That idea was still incubating when an outraged citizen, Louis Schweitzer, no lawyer but an engineer and philanthropist, came into Botein's office expressing anger and puzzlement at having seen youths held behind bars in the Brooklyn House of Detention

---

* The Appellate Division also has a Second Department—Brooklyn, Queens, Staten Island and certain suburbs—whose Presiding Justice is George J. Beldock.

because they could not afford bail. He had an idea, he said, of raising a fund, to which he would contribute a large sum of money, to provide bail for the indigent. Instead, Botein countered, why not set up a foundation whose legal staff could show a judge that a man with roots in the community, with a job and a family, could be trusted on his honor to show up for trial?

Thus, the VERA Foundation (now the VERA Institute of Justice) was born—named for Schweitzer's mother—and with it the Manhattan Bail Project. Law students on VERA's staff went into jails and checked defendants' previous criminal records and the current charges. Following a point system to evaluate whether a man is a good parole risk, the student sent a summary of the information to the arraignment court with an R.O.R. recommendation if warranted. (Their work has now been taken over by the Department of Probation.)

In the first 30 months of the project, 2,300 defendants were R.O.R.'d—only 1 per cent of whom failed to appear for trial. In the same period about 3 per cent of those who could afford bail failed to appear for trial.

"I was nudged by an enlightened citizen, Schweitzer," Botein says candidly. "The President has now signed the Bail Reform Act of 1966, affecting Federal bail practices. It is the proudest experiment that I have ever been connected with."

On another, related project—that of the summons—Botein again preferred to remain in the background in order to get results.

Working closely with VERA's executive director, Herbert Sturz, he sought approval for the police to issue simple summonses to persons accused of misdemeanors, instead of locking them up. This, he felt, would not only eliminate arrest, with all its damaging consequences, but it would also free the cop on the beat to continue on his beat.

The then Police Commissioner, Michael J. Murphy, balked at the idea. The judge nevertheless reflected that "if a hard-nosed cop like Murphy would take the initiative on this project, that would be better than a judge taking it." So he called a conference in chambers and decided to appeal to the Commissioner's civic pride.

"Look, we're going to have a national bail conference in Washington," he said to Murphy privately. "There will be 500 delegates there from all over the country. And one of the important topics is going to be a handmaiden of bail reform and that is the substitution of summons in lieu of arrest. I would be very proud," he went on, choosing his words deliberately, "to have the Police Commissioner of my city deliver the all-important paper on the worth of this approach rather than to turn to the Police Commissioner of Cincinnati to deliver it." (Botein had received some tentative offers from Cincinnati, and he was not above using the bait.)

Murphy threw up his hands with a laugh. "All right, we'll do it, Judge."

"And once he made that decision," Botein added with fervor, "Murphy backed it up all the way. He supported the project wholeheartedly, and helped it to succeed."

Of Judge Botein's many projects, perhaps those affecting jurors have been the most popular. The jury system, he philosophizes, is at the heart of justice, but the hardships it works on the ordinary citizen must be minimized so that it can be preserved.

As far back as when he sat as a calendar judge in the Supreme Court, he established a new system of deferral of jury service, under which a person who could not act as a juror at the time he was called could arrange with the clerk of the court for service at a more convenient time. In this way he created a pool of jurors to be relied on for some particular time—"and they would be willing jurors as a result of this kind of consideration."

Later, when he and Leland Tolman, his Department Director of Administration of the Courts, began working together in the Appellate Division, they adopted a computerized system for calling up, interviewing and processing jurors, to speed up the work —a system now copied widely. Not long ago, with the help of community and business leaders, who do not like having their employes sitting around jury rooms when they are not sitting on cases, Botein pioneered an experiment under which jurors may simply remain available on telephone call at their places of business or homes.

This sampling of the Botein projects reflects what many regard as a hotbed of court experimentation, because nothing on this scale is going on anywhere else in the country. Chief Assistant District Attorney Alfred J. Scotti, some of whose cases have gone to Judge Botein on appeal, says: "He's a man with a great respect for the law. But he doesn't look at the law in a purely abstract manner; he makes you aware that human beings are involved. Cardozo was like that, too."

And Judge Hilda Schwartz of Civil Court, who has had long service in the Family and Youth parts, says: "Tone is vital in the court setup. The tone that Judge Botein has set is social justice. It runs like a theme through all the courts. This to me means more than just concern with the rights of the individual. It's concern also with the rehabilitation of the wrong-doer, and with allowances made for the immaturity of the young."

The problems of the poor are far from theoretical to this judge who grew up on the Lower East Side of New York. He was born May 6, 1900. His father died when he was 6, and he worked his way through Morris High School. At 14, he had a newspaper route; later, he held jobs in a clothing factory and a florist shop. One summer, he worked as a copy boy on the old New York Sun and when he moved to a $25-a-week job in the clipping library, he was temporarily imbued with ambitions to be a reporter. By then, he was working nights and attending City College during the day, until overwork resulted in a breakdown. Later, he worked in an insurance office to help pay for his evening studies at Brooklyn Law School.

After some private practice, he got a job as an Assistant District Attorney for New York County (1929–36). Gov. Herbert Lehman made him his chief trouble shooter, whereupon Botein fell out of favor with Tammany Hall by uncovering stock swindles in the state's business. As a result, Tammany opposed him when Lehman named him a State Supreme Court Judge in November, 1941. But next year he won election to a full, 14-year term on that court; Gov. Thomas E. Dewey later assigned him to the Appellate Division (justices of the Appellate Division are usually selected from among the trial judges of the Supreme

Court), and in 1958, Gov. Averell Harriman appointed him Presiding Justice. The P. J. gets a higher salary than the Chief Justice—$41,500 compared with Earl Warren's $40,000.

The judge lives with his wife, the former Marian Berman, an attractive, forthright woman, in a seven-room apartment on Fifth Avenue. They have two sons—25-year-old Stephen, who is doing advanced work in American history at Harvard, and 22-year-old Michael at Cornell Law School—and a granddaughter, Hilary, nearly 2. The judge used to be an ardent golfer and fisherman, but today his chief hobby is his family (mostly at quiet dinners at home or at the theater).

His ambitions to write never dimmed. He co-authored "The Slum and Crime." His "Trial Judge" (1952) has been translated into 14 languages. His recent (1963) "The Trial of the Future" poses challenges to the judicial process.

The other evening he carried home, in addition to papers on his projects, the appeals briefs on three criminal cases (robberies and murder), several accident cases and a complex real-estate case and a brief on an employe in a city department who was seeking reinstatement. As a sitting judge, in a recent four-day period he heard 56 appeals and more than 100 motions.

On a typical morning, he is driven to court in a black Mercury chauffeured by a court attendant. Mondays are "case conference" days for all eight Appellate Division judges; they sit in their conference room, hung with portraits of their predecessors, to decide the previous week's cases. Tuesdays to Fridays, the calendar usually starts at 2 o'clock, in the ornate Appellate courtroom.

Twice a week, Judge Botein visits other courthouses, always giving advance notice, since a lower court is likely to be staggered at finding "God" in its vicinity. He has a steady stream of telephone callers, notably Administrative Judge Saul S. Streit of the Supreme Court, Herbert Sturz of VERA and Hyman W. Gamso, the clerk of his own court.

Behind the scenes, he works closely with Tolman, who oversees the day-to-day workings of the division, the assignment of judges, development of projects and the like. Tolman is a veteran lawyer and an enthusiastic activist, like his boss.

Proposed new breakthroughs were on their minds the other late afternoon in chambers.

"You know, I've got a whimsical idea about that Bowery-derelict project," Botein said to Tolman. With Sturz, Botein wants to create not only a decent drying-out facility for alcoholics, but also some long-term medical and psychiatric treatment for them outside the criminal process.

"Maybe it's not so whimsical. We're getting about $400,000 for this facility from the city, but we need about $200,000 more. I've been thinking: How about going to some big liquor concern to put up the rest of the money? Certain large distillers could sponsor a program that would *diminish* drinking by those who can't hold their liquor. I'm serious."

Tolman grinned. He knew the P. J. was serious.

The judge was equally serious about sponsoring a program to experiment with the voluntary, civil (as opposed to compulsory) treatment of what he calls "status offenses"—the chronic alcoholic, the narcotics user and the adult, consenting homosexual—"for they are all accused of crime that is essentially related to their status. Some day I hope all three will be out of the criminal lexicon, because what is happening is that they are being punished for their illnesses."

Another potential breakthrough, still only a gleam in Botein's eye, concerns the sense of helplessness that besets the average person brought to a criminal courthouse. His team of experts is toying with the idea of having a case aide—someone with social-work background but not a lawyer—stay with the defendant, from the moment that a lawyer is assigned by the court, as a sort of "guide to the perplexed." The case aide would go to the family, explain what had happened, go with the wife if necessary to the Welfare Department to guide her through its labyrinths, visit the man's employer in an effort to hold his job. If the man was sentenced, the case aide would keep in touch with him in jail—acting, in short, as a liaison to preserve his dignity and salvage for the community as much of human values as possible.

"We can no longer cope with the need for change in the old leisurely fashion," Judge Botein summed up. "This is where social justice comes in for one form of social justice is *preventive* justice. By that, I mean that skilled and trained people can help as many persons as possible never to come in conflict with the law —or, if they do, to help them to make it the last such episode in their lives.

"Our society is so resistant to change that people who are privileged to be in positions such as I occupy are duty-bound to initiate the change process. Who else will do it?"

The judge has had his failures—one of the worst being his inability to eliminate the superfluous Surrogate's Court. He wanted to place it inside Supreme Court, and at least transfer control over adoptions to the Family Court, which has protective social services. He also lost the fight to eliminate upstate justices of the peace, many of whom have no legal training.

And there are certain public officials who are dismayed by his social philosophy, who believe that it tends to "coddle criminals" at the expense of public security. District Attorney Aaron E. Koota of Brooklyn says: "Judge Botein is recognized throughout the country as a progressive jurist. However, I am always concerned, entirely aside from Judge Botein, with the general tendency on the part of some of our courts to weight the scales of justice by hypertechnical decisions heavily in favor of the criminal suspect, to the detriment of decent, law-abiding citizens."

Not long ago a prisoner, who had for two years been in jail for several offenses, sought an appeal on one count. He received an indifferent letter from his assigned counsel, telling him not to worry about the appeal, that "we can take our time." The last thing any prisoner wants to hear is that his lawyer will take his time while he languishes behind bars. He wrote to the P. J., petitioning for a change of counsel—which he promptly got from the judge, whose wrath, expressed in a letter, brought an immediate reform in one legal division.

The last letter to Judge Botein from this prisoner says it for many:

"I really dont know the Correct words to express how greatful I am to the honorable court and your honor. All I can say, is I truely thank you. And that my faith, which was beginning to fail as to receiving Justice, is restored."

Working Their Way
Through Jail

by Gertrude Samuels

JAMIE JOHNSON, a 29-year-old Sioux Indian, rises at 6 o'clock, showers, dresses in a rough work shirt, blue jeans, work boots. He make his bed, breakfasts, clears away the dishes, dons a yellow construction helmet and, by 7:30, stands waiting in the road. A friend picks him up in his old Buick and they drive together to work, where they start promptly at 8 as $125-a-week machine operators for United Concrete Pipe Corporation.

Johnson works all over the yard, stacking, patching and repairing pipes. He operates a forklift. A tall, placid man with watchful eyes, he lunches on salami and ham sandwiches, milk and cake. The one indication that Johnson's status is different from his co-workers' comes when he smiles tolerantly at a friend's joke to "come out for a beer" after work. Johnson will not and cannot, and his co-workers know it. For Johnson is a prisoner of Santa Clara County's jail system, serving 60 days with a $200 fine for petty theft and driving without a license. At 4:30, he must reverse his schedule: ride back to jail, check in at the sheriff's office, return to barracks, shower and dress in prison blues.

From the *New York Times Magazine*, November 14, 1965, copyright © 1965 by The New York Times Company.

Johnson is one of 94 prisoners (their real names are withheld) currently enrolled in a rehabilitation program known here as Work Furlough. Furlough is simple in theory and simple in practice. It allows selected groups of sentenced prisoners to leave jail daily to work at jobs in the community at standard wages and return to confinement after working hours.

Instead of serving "dead time" behind bars while his family goes on relief, Johnson is supporting his wife and four children, paying the county for room and board, meeting his union dues and paying off his fine. There is even something left over, after his personal expenses, which is being held in trust until his discharge. And when he comes out, he will have a job.

One of the oldest such programs in the country, Work Furlough in Santa Clara County is in its eighth year. Nearly 2,500 prisoners have taken part since its inception and this year there have been close to 450. Los Angeles County now has a similar scheme, as do agencies in at least 24 other states and many European countries, but the idea has made little headway in New York State. (Governor Rockefeller recently signed a bill to allow Family Court judges to send delinquent fathers in nonsupport cases to jail for parts of days and on weekends, thus permitting them to work, but its scope is limited to this particular class of offenders.)

The basic objective is to build a bridge, of self-respect and responsibility, between abnormal prison life and normal community living. As Louis Bergna, Santa Clara County's forceful young District Attorney, told me: "For years, the theory has been to stick the offender in jail and forget him—in short, to throw away all his responsibility to family and society. I think this program, by taking away only some of his rights, still gives the offender the chance to behave like a good citizen."

The brain behind Work Furlough is George K. Williams, the County Rehabilitation Officer, a civilian. But he could not have handled his job without the militant support of the sheriff's department, and notably of Capt. James Geary (who has a degree in sociology) and many judges. The County Board of Supervisors created his post back in 1954 to coordinate a program of rehabilitation among prisoners in the county jail and farm. A Navy lieutenant commander with degrees from Oregon, Stanford and Pennsylvania Universities, Williams, then 34, had worked with German prisoners of war, trying to de-Nazify them and change their attitudes. Now the sheriff virtually told him, "Go out and rehabilitate my prisoners."

At first, Williams devised a traditional program of counseling, education and recreation, but was dissatisfied with the results. He was working with able-bodied men who remained idle while their families went on relief. He read about Wisconsin's so-called Huber Plan where, as far back as 1914, legislation had given local judges the power to sentence selected offenders to jail, but to "furlough" them during the day to jobs in local businesses. Williams studied that program with growing enthusiasm.

This, he felt, was something that had a concrete value: money saved, for taxpayers and offenders; families supported; individuals on their way to self-respect.

Williams launched his experiment with 26 prisoners. There was uneasiness in some courts and in the community. Yet six months later, in June, 1957, under the impetus of the experiment, the California State Legislature enacted the Work Furlough Rehabilitation Law (Section 1208 of the Penal Code). An enabling act gave the county the option of appointing as its administrator either the sheriff or the Adult Probation Officer. The sheriff was appointed, but he assigned Williams to administer the program. In the next seven years, Williams expanded and refined it, until by February, 1965, 2,373 prisoners had been furloughees.

Santa Clara County, with a population of 850,000, lies some 30 miles south of San Francisco in a valley of rich orchards and big industry. And although visitors are reminded that Work Furlough is strictly an extension of jail, the atmosphere at Elmwood Rehabilitation Center, where furloughees are in custody, is anything but that of a jail.

Situated on 200 acres, a few miles from the county seat of San Jose, with spectacular views of the Santa Cruz and the Sierra Madre Mountains, the jail is a compound of sparkling white, Spanish style buildings and low, modern structures with walks shaded by palms and pines. Prisoners on their way to the library and dormitories pass by peacocks who live on the grounds.

Throughout the nation, jails are demoralizing and negative institutions; this ranch—as the inmates call it—is certainly designed to encourage their aspirations.

Elmwood Rehabilitation Center is a special kind of open prison —an honor camp. There are no cells. There are guards, but they are not armed; there are no guns and no watchtower. There are security precautions—head count, bed check—but they are not designed to prevent escapes. The gates are wide open. There is a cyclone fence around the compound, but, officials say, only to keep the curious out and not the prisoners in. The prisoners can, in effect, walk out any time they choose, but few have escaped (under 1 per cent).

Men selected for the center are carefully screened on the basis of their past arrest record and performance in custody. The total prison population varies from 500 to 600 men, and all must work at something on or off the grounds—flood-control projects, maintenance of public parks and buildings, raising vegetables for county institutions, etc.

The élite of the population are the furloughees. They live apart from the other prisoners, in their own two dormitories. Of the 94 men currently in the furlough plan, all but a handful are white, about a third of them Mexican-Indians. The rest are Negroes and Indians. Their offenses include armed robbery, burglary, grand theft, forgery, assaults, drunk-driving and non-support. Those convicted of narcotics offenses are not usually acceptable as they are considered too unreliable.

Most prisoners are anxious to go out on a paying job, although with budget limitations, only 18 to 20 per cent are accepted. The selection process is flexible and realistic. The prime goal is to rule out prisoners of "dubious stability" or poor security risks.

The majority of furloughees are misdemeanants serving short terms (30 to 90 days). But felons, including several sentenced for manslaughter, have also been placed by county courts in the program. Each case is judged on its merits.

The screening process by rehabilitation officials includes personal interviews, an evaluation of the whole "criminal profile," including the offender's past arrest record, evaluation of family and job status, psychological tests.

If approved by the rehabilitation staff, the case goes to the sentencing court, with a request for modification of sentence to admit the prisoner for Work Furlough. Often at this stage, the judge wants the prospective furloughee back in court; he feels it is more meaningful if the man in black robes actually sentences the offender to the program.

Over the years, the furlough office has developed lists of firms and farms which take furloughees. Williams has found that for the employed man who lands in jail and is qualified for furlough it is desirable, monetarily and psychologically, to get him back on the job, earning the same salary, as soon as possible. Thus, when Jamie Johnson's employer was told how Work Furlough operates, he said he would hold Johnson's job for him. Within 10 days of his sentence, Johnson drew his first week's pay as a furloughee.

Men who are jobless can, through family, friends or attorneys, secure job interviews and a rehabilitation officer will transport them to prospective employers or otherwise help in securing them jobs. If a furloughee is a member in good standing of a union, he is allowed to go unescorted to the union hiring hall in San Jose to seek or be placed in a job—another radical advance in penology.

No training is done at the ranch. Willams and his staff help the unskilled find "stoop labor" jobs—gathering harvests, pruning, weeding on farms. To help a furloughee begin work, a loan of up to $20 may be made to him by the ranch to pay for work clothes, tools and transportation to work. The loan is repaid out of his first pay check.

The wages he earns must go (by weekly check) to the furlough administrator who keeps account sheets for each worker. The administrator makes disbursements—to the wife or parents; to satisfy debts or fines or restitution; to defray personal expenses. The furloughee is charged $3.50 a working day for room and board at the ranch. (Since it costs $3.56 daily for the ordinary prisoner, a furloughee in custody thus costs the county only 6 cents a day.)

For his part, the furloughee always carries with him a copy of his agreement with the furlough office, which contains the rules of conduct. Failure to obey them results in disciplinary action and removal from the program. He must wear civilian clothes on the job and is forbidden to go to taverns or to drink, to make unauthorized telephone calls or visits to his family. He must "go to and return directly from" work, and not return with purchases (to avoid contraband).

The psychology behind the furlough system is to induce prisoners to accept the responsibility for their decisions—something quite different from the position of the man doing straight time, who is told when to get up, when to eat, when to work. But it is not too pleasant to put in a full day's work and then have to return to jail every evening.

In fact, about 15 per cent of furloughees are "busted" each year for infractions. One got drunk and visited his girl friend— and landed back in Santa Clara's maximum security jail. His employer said sadly: "It sure throws you off. He was one good worker, and I couldn't see how he could miss."

If a man is missing for only a few hours, it is considered an "escape" and, therefore, a felony. Since the program began, there have been 23 escapees—under 1 per cent. Most were found. Some went to state prison; others got extra time at the county jail.

But the average furloughee knows he is on his honor and is anxious to do his job and keep his job. Williams is always on the go between the courts, the district attorney and the places of employment, for one of his main concerns is his responsibility to the community. Spot checks are made on furloughees at work— and to interest employers in more jobs for candidates.

At 45, George Williams is a husky (5 feet 11 inches, 170 pounds), hard-driving man, with graying hair, penetrating eyes and an incisive manner. A mutual respect between Williams and the furloughees is evident—as he mingles with them on the grounds or goes over their problems in his office—and this is rare in a prison setting. His three assistants, all college graduates, are also specialists.

"People are actually anxious to get our men," Williams says wryly, "because there's no absenteeism, and the men come to work well rested, well fed and without a hangover."

At United Concrete, Johnson comes off the forklift to tell Williams: "It's a real good program. If I were just in jail, I would have lost my job here. All my bills would have piled up and I would be ruined."

Out of the weekly $125 that he grosses, Johnson pays the county $17.50 room and board for five working days; sends $35 to his wife; satisfies his fine at $25 a week; pays the union $6.50 a month dues; retains $10 for personal expenses. The remainder, about $20 after taxes, goes in his trust fund. When the fine is paid off, an extra $25 will go to his wife.

Johnson is the second furloughee placed by Williams in United Concrete. Bob Empey, the manager, tells Williams enthusiastically: "You're sure as heck saving money for the taxpayers with this program of yours. These men are good and willing workers. And actually"—he laughs—"we're safer with them than the average guy. We know where they are at night."

Williams says warmly: "Without employers like you, we obviously couldn't succeed with this program. We appreciate your cooperation."

Another furloughee is 18-year-old Harry Simms, an eager, gray-eyed youth with braces on his teeth. After committing a burglary, he had been thrown out by his father. The boy stole from a store where he was formerly employed: $75 in cash, a radio and a television set and a pickup truck valued at $1,200. All but $35 was recovered. The court sentenced him to 6 months but consented to his placement in Work Furlough because of his youth.

Bob Miller, a wholesale drapery manufacturer who was recently elected to the San Jose City Council, gave Simms a job of trust involving access to money. Simms earns $1.60 an hour. He says earnestly: "All these people went to a lot of trouble to get me in this program, and I owe something to them—to myself too."

Out of his long experience with youths in trouble, Bob Miller told Williams: "A person will be very hesitant to violate a trust, not because he fears you but because he doesn't want to."

Not all sheriffs would agree. In fact, there is a good deal of antipathy to the idea in certain sheriffs' departments. When, for example, that remark was quoted to one deputy sheriff, he retorted, "That's garbage!"

"As a policeman, I think there should be punishment for a

crime," he went on bitterly, "and I can't see putting felons, especially habitual felons, on a furlough program. Punishment is the deterrent. A criminal belongs behind bars."

The worth of the program is reflected partly in the statistics. Since February, 1957, the 2,373 furloughees (to February, 1965) achieved these earnings and savings to taxpayers:

Wages earned:	$1,212,780.35
Disbursements:	
Family support	$ 554,314.03
Fines paid	9,663.64
Room & Board	298,011.39
Personal Expenses	182,126.94
Misc. including trust funds	168,664.35
	$1,212,780.35

But the program must be measured in more than dollars. Captain Geary says: "If we can send them back holding up their heads, we can hope that there will be less possibility of their returning. Given the staff and facilities, I feel we could handle three or four times the number of men in this program."

Judge Robert Beresford, the senior judge of Municipal Court, who has sent many prisoners into Work Furlough, says: "I feel that this modern approach to penology should be more broadly used in the land. Policies should be designed so that on his release the offender should not be a threat to society or prepared to repeat his offenses."

Some critics argue, however, that the offender who is given jail with a "work furlough" proviso would have been as good a candidate for straight probation and should not be in jail at all.

In reply, Williams says: "Many have already failed on probation. This is a compromise. It's less harsh than actual confinement, and yet a great deal more confining than simple probation. The courts are in a quandary sometimes. When you punish a man by putting him in jail, whom are you punishing? Him? Or his wife, his parents, his children?"

What deeply concerns Williams, Geary and many judges

is the lack of scientific research on the rehabilitative effects of Work Furlough. Williams has applied to the National Institute of Mental Health in Washington for funds for this crucial research. He would enlist the aid of sociology professors in San Jose State College to get the answers—"it may take years to find out"—to such questions: What does Work Furlough do for the individual offender when he returns to society? Is the recidivist rate lower in this program than it is in conventional jails? Does it have a lasting effect on the individual's attitude toward society?

It is generally accepted that many thousands of prisoners do not need the expensive, close custody of prison cells and walled-in yards. Yet there persists the historic, punitive attitude toward social outcasts: judges, D.A.'s, custodial officials still fear the risks of new penological techniques. Then, too, the public must be educated to the advantages of the program. Many taxpayers believe in strict incarceration of lawbreakers (at least until it touches their own families) and employers hesitate to become involved in radical rehabilitation programs.

There are also practical problems: Furloughees mean casework, minimum custody away from the prison population (to ease security safeguards), and extensive bookkeeping facilities for their accounts—calling for additional staff and higher budgets.

Many California counties now use Work Furlough, yet even Los Angeles, which leads the country in such penological reforms as work-and-education camps for delinquents, hesitated until last year to try the experiment. Now, after several months' trial with 70 prisoners, the program is so "operationally feasible and economically advantageous to Los Angeles County" that the chief probation officer has recommended a broader program for the coming year.

But New York still lags miserably behind. Our jails remain overcrowded with prisoners doing dead time. One official at Women's Prison in Manhattan told me, not long ago: "We teach our prisoners merely to be good inmates. By not giving them responsibilities and jobs in the community—to which they have to return—we defeat our own purposes."

That is what society forgets, or doesn't want to remember: that virtually all prisoners return to the outside world. The real question is, should they be encouraged to come back with some degree of respect for themselves or with bitterness toward society?

San Jose's venerated poet, Edwin Markham ("The Man with the Hoe"), gives one answer in his famous quatrain:

> *He drew a circle that shut me out—*
> *Heretic, rebel, a thing to flout.*
> *But love and I had the wit to win:*
> *We drew a circle that took him in!*

Role Playing:
A Judge Is a Con,
A Con Is a Judge
by Richard Hammer

FOR NINE days this summer, the grassy, groomed and venerable campus of St. John's College in Annapolis was the scene
of a remarkable confrontation. The college kids and their professors were off on vacation, and the "great books"—the core
of the St. John's curriculum—had been laid on the shelf. In
place of the faculty and students were 21 convicts from three
state prisons and about 100 lawyers and judges, prosecutors,
policemen, prison officials and state legislators and some "interested citizens." Before the nine days ended, the participants had
been enlightened and, in some cases, emotionally scarred by
their experiment, a "Workshop in Crime and Correction."

This was anything but a gathering of dreamers and bleeding
hearts concerned over the failures of the prison system. Those
failures, of course, are beyond argument. The "correctional institutions," as they call themselves these days, neither correct nor
rehabilitate; more than half, some say more than 70 per cent, of
those released from the nation's prisons end up behind bars again,

From the *New York Times Magazine,* September 14, 1969, copyright ©
1969 by The New York Times Company.

and what they usually learn behind those bars is how to make better "hits," how to be better burglars or bank robbers the next time they walk free. The non-prisoners at the workshop were not ignorant of these facts, but they lacked an appreciation of the personal and emotional realities behind the statistics. That appreciation was provided in psychodramas, seminars, all-night bull sessions and in hours spent as "inmates" themselves in three Maryland prisons.

The workshop had the best "establishment" credentials: It was financed with $67,000 from the Social and Rehabilitation Service of the Department of Health, Education and Welfare and was sponsored jointly by the Maryland Governor's Commission on Law Enforcement and the Administration of Justice and the National College of State Trial Judges, which claims the membership of more than 4,000 jurists in all 50 states.

Directing the conference were the Berkeley Associates, a consulting organization formed by three Californians whose experience in the prison system has left them disillusioned. They are: Dr. David Fogel of the University of California at Berkeley, a heavy-set, bearded, emotional sociologist who worked seven years in the Marin County jail system; Dr. Richard Korn, a U. of C. criminologist who resigned after three years as a psychologist at a New Jersey prison farm "when I found one night that I could lock up my assistant, a prisoner, in his cell and walk away without feeling anything," and Douglas Rigg, a public defender in Berkeley, a former associate warden at San Quentin who once resigned as the warden of a Minnesota state prison after his reform efforts led to charges that he was "coddling convicts."

Given the workshop's credentials, the conference organizers found it easy enough to round up participants among the professionals. Finding the right convicts, however, was another matter. Berkeley Associates did not want a group hand-picked by prison administrators, but a representative sampling of both men and offenses. Above all, they sought the right to select the 21 convict participants themselves. Ultimately, they settled for a compromise: Prison officials chose a group of more than 100 inmates from which Berkeley Associates picked the 21 they wanted.

The convicts came from three institutions in Jessups, Md.— the Maryland House of Correction, a medium-security prison with a reputation as little more than a warehouse for men convicted of anything from nonsupport to murder and rape; The Maryland Correctional Camp Center, a minimum-security institution where some inmates are on a work-release program, and the Patuxent Institution, a maximum-security prison for "defective delinquents," all of them serving indeterminate sentences.

Some of the 21 men chosen for the workshop were serving terms as short as two years, others had been sentenced to "life plus"; some had been behind bars for only a year, others for 20 years or more. Their crimes ranged from possession of narcotics to burglary to rape and murder. One participant was even an alumnus of death row; his sentence had been commuted to life shortly before his date in the gas chamber.

As a group, the participants were not entirely representative of Maryland's 6,000 convicts. They were articulate and intelligent, with considerable insight into themselves and others. Most of them seemed to retain some hope for a future life beyond the walls. As the workshop progressed, however, it became evident that most of the participants from the outside world looked upon the *con*-sultants (as they called themselves) not as a select group but as a random sampling of the prison population. The effect of their words and actions during the conference was thus generalized—and magnified.

A typical day began at 8 A.M. as the convicts, dressed in casual sports clothes, arrived at St. John's by bus. More than one prisoner was amused at the thought of breakfasting with the judge who had sentenced him—a judge dressed in Bermuda shorts and a flowered shirt.

The business session usually opened with a speaker after breakfast, then a psychodrama, a brief play in which the magistrates and the miscreants were the cast, sometimes playing their real-life roles and sometimes trading roles. The scene was always one having to do with the judicial process: a disciplinary hearing for a policeman accused of having used abusive language, a grand jury session, a parole hearing, the arrival in prison of a new con. Fogel or Korn set the scene and the actors improvised as the plot developed. Members of the audience were allowed to interrupt if they thought the portrayals lacked realism.

Later in the day, the workshop broke up into seven groups for discussion and more psychodrama. After the prisoners had returned to their cells for the evening, the "outside" participants heard another speaker, then attended informal bull sessions that typically lasted until 4 or 5 A.M.

In the first days of the workshop, there was a tentative feeling, a sparring for openings, an evident wariness. The cops sat in a back row, isolated; the judges sat together; the cons sat in a group. A psychodrama about a policeman's use of a racial epithet produced only yawns and bored rustling.

What broke the conference open was a psychodrama on prison life. Fogel set the stage: The action was to be the arrival in prison of a new con, a first offender sentenced to four years for assault. To play the new con Fogel selected a young, blond correctional officer who looked indeed as though he could be in that position. The inmates who processed him into the prison were played by real cons. The only other roles in the play were two prison officials, a guard and a counselor, played by men whose real-life roles these were.

The drama began as "Scag," a black inmate who supposedly worked as a runner in the prison storeroom, led the new con, "Frank," from the storeroom, where he'd been issued prison clothes and other gear, to the tier where he would be locked into a cell.

SCAG: You know anybody here, anybody can help you?
FRANK: (shaking his head): No, I don't know anybody.
SCAG: Not nobody at all?
FRANK: Nobody. I don't think I belong here.
SCAG (laughs): That's what everybody says. You know, you gonna need some protection.
FRANK: Protection? From what?
SCAG: Man, you is gonna be approached.
FRANK: What for?

SCAG: Man, I ain't got to tell you.
FRANK: Well, I don't want any part of it.
SCAG: You ain't got no choice.
FRANK: If they come to me, I'll fight.
SCAG (laughs): You can't fight three-four men at a time.
FRANK: What can I do?
SCAG: Man, you can avoid it.
FRANK: How?
SCAG: You can pick somebody to protect you. . . . You got any money?
FRANK: No. But I've got a ring and a watch.

Reaching the tier that contains Frank's cell, Scag holds a mumbled conference with Slim, a black inmate assigned as a runner in the tier.

SCAG: We got a new chicken here.
SLIM: Yeah, what we gonna do with him?
SCAG: I'll tell you. I'm gonna play his friend. You make him think he's got to turn to me to protect him from you.
SLIM: Yeah, that's right, I'll scare him right to you and we'll split what he's got. Only don't do like you did the last time and hit me when you're protecting him.
SCAG: Don't worry, we'll play this cool.

As Scag leaves, Slim explains prison life to Frank, telling him that he can order once a week from the commissary and that he must come out of his cell immediately when the bell rings for a meal or an exercise period in the yard or he will be locked in again. Slim offers to give Frank a pack of cigarettes in exchange for two packs after Frank has received his order from the commissary. Then a bell rings and Slim patrols the tier, chanting, "Yard time. Yard time."

The scene shifts to the crowded prison yard, and when Frank appears there are whistles. "Say, man," says one con, "that's a real sweetie." Another yells: "Hey, baby, I think you need a protector." The action then moves back to the cell tier.

SLIM: Where you been?
FRANK: In the yard.
SLIM: How come you didn't tell me you was going?
FRANK: I did.
SLIM: Man, I says you didn't! You callin' me a liar?
FRANK: No. I thought. . . .
SLIM: Man, you want to go someplace, you tell me. Whenever you go someplace, you don't go without you let me know, dig?
FRANK: Why are you jumping all over me?
SLIM: Man, you is askin' for it. I gonna come in that cell with you and lock the door you don't watch out.

Scag suddenly appears, telling Slim to leave the new inmate alone. After Slim wanders off, Scag offers to take Frank into the yard during the next exercise period and walk around with him, explaining: "That'll let everybody know I'm protecting you." He says it will cost a carton of cigarettes a week. Frank says he will think about it and stays in his cell during the next few exercise periods. A few days later, against Slim's urgent advice, he insists upon seeing an officer.

FRANK: It seems there are all these guys who want to be my buddies. They want to protect me. But they want cigarettes and they seem to want my watch and ring and shoes, too. And they seem to be able to do anything they want and nobody stops them.
GUARD: When did all this start? When did they approach you?
FRANK: As soon as I got in here.
GUARD: Can you identify them?
FRANK: I'm afraid. I don't want it to get back to them.
GUARD: Well, anytime you want to tell me anything, you just ask. I'll come. You just ask. We'll protect you.
FRANK: I'm scared to tell.

The realization that the guards cannot effectively protect him sends Frank back to Scag. At the next yard call, they go out together and Scag introduces Frank to other cons, among whom blacks outnumber whites by more than two to one.

Fogel interrupted the action to ask several of the convicts what they were feeling as Frank was being introduced. Among the answers were these:

"I'm feeling that colored guys have all the goodies. I feel like they must feel out in the streets. I'm a minority in here, and I'd like a crack at that goody."

"I don't care what Scag or the rest of the black guys do as long as they don't touch my man."

"I've got a feeling of fear. I know what happens to young cons like him; it happened to me."

"He's a white boy, and I don't care what happens to him."

The action resumes in the office of a counselor with whom Frank has requested an interview.

FRANK: I've had some weird things happen since I came in here. There's a lot of homosexuals running around loose and they all seem to be looking at me.

COUNSELOR: Well, what would you like us to do?

FRANK: I don't know. I think I'm more afraid of the inmates here than I am of the institution itself, and I thought it would be the other way.

COUNSELOR: What do they want?

FRANK: Everything I've got. My watch, my ring, my shoes, all my personal possessions. Can I send them home?

COUNSELOR: Yes. If you give them to me I can have them sent home for you.

FRANK: They want my tail, too.

COUNSELOR: I'm afraid I can't send that home. You want to tell me who these guys are who are doing these things to you?

FRANK: If I tell you, what will happen to me?

COUNSELOR: We'll try to protect you.

FRANK: How?

COUNSELOR (bursts out): I'll adopt you! . . . Seriously, the only assurance I can give you is close supervision.

The psychodrama ended there, amid shouts and cries from the convicts in the audience. "Man, you can't give him no protection. He'll have boiling coffee thrown at him even if you lock him up in solitary," said one. "He ain't got no assurance. You think his only salvation is in protection and custody, but that won't work. Somebody'd get to him."

"Maybe you'd put him in B-3, where they keep all the sissies," said another con, "and then he'd be branded one, and he'd be branded a rat, too, and that wouldn't be no protection."

"There's a million ways to get to him," a third convict warned. "We'd be in contact with him and that would be that." Another added:

"Nothing anybody can do will make any difference because it's a jungle we live in. The only ones who can do anything for him or against him are the other inmates."

One of the prison administrators asked the actor who had played Slim, "Would you protect him for a guaranteed parole?"

Slim stared at him. "For a guaranteed parole? Man, I guess so."

Another con leaped up: "And who would protect Slim? Then who would protect the next guy and the next? You gonna let us all out on parole to protect this one guy?"

As more members of the workshop joined the discussion on prison life and its purposes, one inmate rose and asked: "What's rehabilitation? I've never seen it. We come in laborers and go out laborers. All we learn in here is how to make [license] tags, and there ain't no place outside where you can make tags. We're the same guy when we go out, and that's where it's at, baby."

The psychodrama had shaken the workshop. For many in the audience—judges, policemen, lawyers and even some prison officials—it was the first good look at what goes on behind the walls and at criminals as real people. Save for the criminal himself, almost everyone's contact with the problems of crime, correction and justice is severely limited. The average citizen's only glimpse of crime occurs when he is a victim, and even then the contact is usually just the discovery that something is missing from his home or car; the policeman's contact with the criminal begins with the arrest, often a dangerous and charged confrontation, and ends at the station house or in the courtroom; the judge and attorneys see the criminal only when his behavior is circumscribed, when he is wearing a face that is often not his real one; prison officials see him only as a number, and parole officers only when he has finished his term and is again a free man.

The disclosures made in the psychodrama—of homosexuality, rackets, brutality and fear—therefore came as something of a shock to many. In the smaller sessions later in the day, emotions ran high and every suggestion brought sharp probing and searching questions.

A discussion of prison apprenticeship programs, for instance, remained optimistic until the convict participants gave their point of view. The training program in printing, they said, was limited to those serving sentences of at least 15 years; it was a five-year program, and—since parole is often granted when one-third of a man's term is served (though it is possible after one-fourth of the sentence)—men serving shorter terms might leave before their training was complete. Convicts sentenced to less than 15 years could enter the program only if they agreed to forgo parole until the training was over. Further, since the apprenticeship program was given only at the House of Correction, an inmate had to agree to remain there and not accept transfer to a minimum-security prison farm where he might be eligible for an occasional weekend home leave.

When prison officials complained that they did not have the money to buy some necessary equipment for a course, the cons said that most of what was needed could be bought through Army surplus for less than $100.

And, of course, there was always the problem of food. "How can we feed these guys decent meals," one official asked, "when all the state allows us is 61 cents a day per con for meals?" You can't feed them very much or very well on that, it was agreed, just as you can't "rehabilitate" them totally when the state budget comes out to less than $2,000 a year for each con. But, one judge wanted to know, isn't at least something good possible—say, ice cream on occasion? "How can we give them ice cream," the official asked, "when it costs about 8 cents a brick wholesale? That's more than 10 per cent of the daily food budget. It's just impossible." The prisoners replied that Army-surplus ice-cream makers could be bought for less than $75—and that one of them could produce ice cream for an entire prison at less than a penny a serving.

Even if all the equipment were available, the prison officials declared, it would still be difficult to do anything about training the inmates to use it. There was a major problem in getting outside instructors to teach because of low salaries. How about using the expertise of the cons? "We don't trust the prisoners to run the programs," said an administrator. "Whenever we've tried it, we've had a bad experience. Rackets have developed—you know, prisoner-teachers selling grades, things like that. So we don't feel we can use them."

"Man," one inmate said, "you'd better realize that the only way you're going to help prepare us to make it on the outside so that we don't come back in is by beginning to show you trust us a little. That's the name of the game. If you don't trust us at all inside, you ain't going to trust us outside, and we know it, and you're going to have us right back with you."

"Why the hell should we trust you?" asked one official. "Look what happens whenever we start trusting you guys. Look at the jungle you guys live in."

"You know you ain't never trusted us one little bit," the con replied, "and maybe that's why we do what we do in there, because there ain't no trust. And you're right, prison's a jungle. But who's really responsible for it, us? Or all you people who dump us in there and want to forget about us until it's time to let us back into society, until we've served out our time?"

The cons challenged one another as well as the prison system. When one of them complained that the state was charging him $2.50 room and board plus his transportation costs from what he earned on the outside in a work-release program, another snapped: "Man, when you get out, who the hell is going to give you free room and board? Are you a ward of the state or are you a man? You better learn to pay your own way; you're going to have to if you ever get out."

Behind all the criticism was the evident desire to transform prisons from schools for crime into institutions that would produce men able to adapt to society. The cons quickly dispelled the idea that they sought to turn prisons into pleasant resort hotels. They had committed crimes, they agreed, and society had a right to punish them. The point was that if the system was to be successful it had to be more than just institutionalized punishment.

The emotions released by the psychodrama were heightened the next day when the conference adjourned behind prison walls. A third of the delegates went to each of the three prisons, where most of them were led on tours by the inmate conferees, unhampered by guards and officials. And at each of the prisons, three or four of the outside workshop members, including a couple of judges, were processed as though they were new inmates. The convicts and guards who processed them were—officially, at least —unaware that they were not real prisoners, though it was evident that word had leaked out.

While the rest of the outside visitors entered the prisons through the main gates, the men chosen to be pretend-convicts were handcuffed and shackled together, put on prison vans and driven into the processing areas. There they were checked in, stripped and made to sit naked on wooden benches while being interviewed. Then they were forced to undergo a flashlight examination under the arms, between the legs, in all the hairy parts of the body—"we're looking for crabs, narcotics, you know, things like that," said the inmate-clerk conducting the examination at one of the prisons. The new "convicts" were showered, given prison clothes, mugged, fingerprinted and asked other detailed questions about their lives. Then they were led to cells and locked in.

When the doors closed, one "convict," an elderly white-haired state representative, sank onto his cot, put his elbows on his knees and buried his head in his hands. "I can't tell you what this did to me spiritually," he said later. "I knew that any time I wanted to get out, all I had to do was yell and they would come and let me loose. What if I had known that I couldn't get out, that I was to be locked in there for years?"

A judge who had sentenced scores of men to the prison through which he was processed suddenly pretended to be a mute. Later, he was to say that he had enjoyed the experience, but those who saw him doubted it. He was certain, he said, that he had been spotted, "and I didn't know whether I was going to get a knife or just be pointed out to everyone else." Within a couple of hours, he asked to be released from his cell.

When another judge left his cell for lunch, a knife was planted in it by one of the few guards who was in on the pretense. The judge was pulled out of the lunch line and thrown into solitary confinement in the "hole" next to a black convict who was lying on his cell floor, his legs in the air, screaming, "White mother-f——s, white mother-f——s. . . ." (The judge later said he had not heard a word.)

After a half hour in the hole, the judge was brought before a five-man disciplinary board, none of whose members knew that this was all a pretense. The judge was dressed in prison slacks and shirt, white socks without shoes; his hair was tousled, his face distraught.

The board chairman asked, "Do you know why you're here?"

"They told me you found a knife in my cell."

"That's right. Can you tell us how it got there?"

"No, I can't think how."

"Did you bring it in with you?"

"No. Somebody must have put it there."

"When did you get here?"

"This morning."

"Do you know anybody in here?"

"No."

"Does anybody in here have anything against you?"

"No."

"Then why would somebody have planted a knife in your cell?"

The judge, knowing that he was innocent, was sentenced to 30 days in the hole.

One of the civilians who went to the House of Correction was later to describe the place as being "like a decayed military school." There was no morale, he said, and there were no screens on the windows; there were razor blades in his cell, splinters of steel in the food, a total lack of communication between the cons and the staff, and everywhere he looked "there were flaming faggots making assignations."

Perhaps one of the most concerned men of all, however, was a high-ranking police officer who was visiting a prison for the first time in his 18 years on the force. He met a prisoner who seemed familiar, talked with him and discovered that he had first met the man many years before, when the convict was 11 years old. "He was a truant and I happened to be at school that day and I talked with him. And then the next day, I got a call and went to a house and there was this little boy. He had had an argument with his mother and stabbed her in the side with a paring knife. He hadn't done much damage, but it was pretty serious. Anyway, he kept getting in trouble, but I never had much time for him, there were always other things. Now he is in for life, for murder, for cutting up someone into eight pieces." The policeman paused and looked around. "I wondered if maybe I couldn't have done something, back then, to have prevented all this. But I'll tell you one thing: I'm going to be a better cop because of this. And I'll tell you something else: Nobody's going to work for me for 18 years without going into an institution this way again. Every man under me is going to spend a day in prison."

"This is a jungle," said one of the judges. "And if all the guys inside come out as they have to live in there, pretty soon we're all going to be living in that jungle. We'd better do something and we'd better do it damn fast."

How did the cons react to the tour through their homes? "I'll tell you," one inmate said the next day, "the guys inside all look at us as traitors for revealing what's been going on. They're telling us, and some of the guards are telling us, 'This thing will cool off and then we'll see about the guys who've opened up on us.' "

And how did the prison administrators react? "We have lousy prisons and no one in the administration will disagree with you," said one. "But where are all of you when we need help? I don't think anybody gives a damn." Another official commented: "Nobody around here understands us; nobody appreciates what we're doing. We're sitting on the lid of a garbage can keeping the garbage off the streets."

Korn tried to pull the reactions together and get at some of the basic truths behind the conferees' experiences of the previous few days. "We do know," he said, "how to deal with the people we love and the people we hate and the people we don't give a damn about, despite all the myths. We protect and defend the people we love. And the people we hate we turn over to the people we don't give a damn about, to people who hate them. We turn animals over to animals to cage them."

What we ask of people we put in prison, Korn said, is conformity, something we do not want for ourselves or anyone we love. In prison we want men to conform to rules that have no meaning. "We call it correction," he said, "but it is not correction."

Korn laid out some of his ideas for a solution, which he called a new-careers program. Under it, the massive institutions would be gradually dispensed with, giving way to community-based and neighborhood correction centers. The inmates would be given responsible, meaningful jobs, often working with youthful offenders in an attempt to stop the young men from becoming professional criminals.

During the last days of the conference there were hundreds of resolutions for action—supporting conjugal visits in prisons, urging improvements in the food, backing the idea of neighborhood correction centers, even making the St. John's Council on Crime and Correction a continuing organization that would meet again to try to reform the Maryland prison system.

There was a graduation ceremony, including diplomas for all those who had attended, and a commencement address. The speaker was Petey Green, a former long-term convict who is working in a new-careers program in Washington. Society has to make use of the talents of the prisoners, Green said over and over again. "And how can you say these guys ain't got no skills when they can reach over and lift your wallet without you feeling it? Who's going to be a better store detective than an ex-booster? Maybe the stores ought to think about hiring somebody like that."

It's not hard to motivate the cons, Green said, if you do it the right way. "Why, when I began to change and got to working in the prison school, there was this one guy, a bank robber, who kept telling me he'd rather play basketball than come to school. So I told him, 'Man, when you went into that bank, they had a big sign sayin' this bank is guarded by cameras. But you couldn't read, and that's how come you got busted.' That guy became one of the best students in the school."

And then, when Green had finished, the cons went back to prison and the free people went their separate ways.

The end of the conference, though, did not mean the end of the campaign for better prisons. The St. John's Council continues, with task forces meeting weekly to work out reform recommendations requested by a joint legislative committee on corrections.

The convict who played Scag in the psychodrama was paroled on July 28, has a factory job and is applying for a scholarship to study penology at Catonsville Community College. The inmate who played Slim is scheduled to face a parole board soon and, if he is released, may get an $8,000-a-year job—about which he has not yet been told—working with fellow ex-cons. Several other inmate-participants in the conference have won paroles since June and still others have been transferred to minimum-security prisons.

So far, the resolutions of the workshop have not been abandoned. One convict from each of the three prisons attends a weekly meeting, and interest among the inmate-participants remains high. Some of the judges, policemen and legislators are more concerned than they were before the workshop. They seem to agree that what is at stake is not the coddling of criminals but the very fate of society. This is, however, a short-range reaction. Whether the St. John's workshop will lead to anything permanent remains a question.

Where Junkies Learn
to Hang Tough

by Gertrude Samuels

"HANG TOUGH." With pure grit, through mutual help and in truth-telling sessions that are often savage inquisitions into their private lives, a group of former drug addicts are learning slowly to "hang tough"—to stay with it and not give up—in their struggle to make a clean break with their past on "the street." The slogan is boldly lettered on life preservers which decorate their communal houses. It is at the core of a unique social movement which, for more than seven years, has been trying to restructure the lives of addicts—the movement called Synanon (pronounced SIN-a-non).

At the parent house in Santa Monica, a nondescript three-story, red-brick building on a Pacific bay, one senses the impact of the slogan on a new member. It is Saturday night, the weekly open house to which the community is invited. A tall, 18-year-old boy, scrubbed and neatly dressed, stands on a small balcony overlooking the sea. He had been shooting dope since he was 13 when his probation officer back in Orange, N. J., told him to "try Synanon." Just two months ago, he arrived here, in torn and dirty clothes, sick with anxiety and withdrawal pain.

The boy, "clean" now, stares out at sand and sea, and says

with a twisted smile: "I've had bad moments, doing without the
dope. It's tough adjusting to the rules here." He struggles to
frame a thought honestly. "I could split—like leave—any time.
I've thought of it."

He gives a short laugh. "But no one's been able to help me—
out there. I think . . . I'll be all right now."

What the boy is really saying is that though members are
expected to "hang tough," the door to Synanon swings both ways.
This is a private foundation, and its people come in voluntarily.
They are addicts, but they have not been committed—as to a
prison or a hospital. They are free to leave at any time.

Since 1958, 1,180 drug addicts have come voluntarily to Synanon. Of these, 40 individuals have graduated—i.e., gone back
into the outside world with Synanon's approval to make new
lives for themselves. Some 40 per cent have split—as the boy
said—i.e., because they were unable to take the Spartan, drug-
free life. Most of these have gone back to "the street" and drugs.
Some have returned to Synanon. As of this writing, there are 537
persons—men and women, boys and girls, aged 17 to 61—enrolled in the movement.

Synanon maintains six establishments—all in the West, except
for a small house at Westport, Conn. (There is also an information center in Manhattan.) Of the members, about half have come
from New York. More than three-quarters have been whites; the
remainder Negroes, Puerto Ricans and Mexican-Americans.

The present racial imbalance has an economic explanation. In
the early days, Synanon took addicts as they came—off the streets
and out of prisons, without a penny. It still accepts a number
this way. But, faced with the problem of finding new houses for
its growing population, Synanon increasingly has been asking addicts—or their families—to pay their own transportation and to
contribute according to their means—usually a donation of $100
to $500. Many addicts have told Synanon bluntly: "If I had that
kind of money, I'd use it for dope."

To the "square" (outside) society, Synanon's accomplishments
may seem small, but they are impressive to anyone who knows
how difficult it is for professionals and law-enforcers to help even
one drug addict to lead a normal, productive life.

New York City, with the country's biggest drug problem—50,000 to 60,000 addicts—has no Synanon live-in facility. This writer came to the West Coast to study the movement.

Synanon had its start in a seedy Ocean Park, Calif., flat and a $33 unemployment check. The flat and the check belonged to Charles E. (Chuck) Dederich, a one-time business executive. To understand Synanon, one must first understand Chuck—for he created Synanon out of his own grinding need.

Chuck is a massively built man with a massive ego. Until eight years ago, he was a disordered person and an alcoholic. Now he is father-figure and teacher to his "family of addicts," for that, he says, is what he has created: "An autocratic family structure similar in some areas to a primitive tribal structure that demands that members perform tasks as part of the group."

He looks and acts the part of a patriarch. His powerful 5-foot 10-inch, 220-pound frame is topped by short, stiffly upright hair. His face, craggy and pockmarked, thrusts up aggressively and seems quizzical because of a slight facial spasm. He rarely smiles and is rarely silent. His intense, erratic moods, when he hurls ridicule and abuse, can shake friend and foe alike.

In casual clothes, slipping his bare feet in and out of his loafers, Chuck can be loud and arrogant, and sometimes gentle and patient, as he puts direct questions and insists on direct answers—whether he is dealing with legislators and judges or a bottom-of-the-barrel junkie. His wry humor flashes, though: "A lot of people have to listen to me now when I talk—and I talk most of the time."

Chuck was born 51 years ago in Toledo, Ohio, the oldest of three sons of a Roman Catholic family. He was 4 when his father, an alcoholic, was killed in an automobile accident, 8 when a brother died, 12 when his mother, whom he adored, married a man whom he hated—all of which helped to make Chuck a hell-raiser early in life. He drank heavily before he graduated from high school, and dropped out of Notre Dame after 18 months because of poor grades. In the next years, he lost good jobs through his drinking, and wrecked his two marriages. At 43, he joined Alcoholics Anonymous.

In A.A. he tried to find himself, by involving himself deeply with others in similar trouble. The torrents of his ideas and words seemed to help. He turned his Ocean Park flat into a sanctuary for alcoholics.

Since his student days, Chuck had been stimulated by a large body of philosophy—Freud, Emerson, Thoreau, Buddhism, Lao-tse. In particular, he believed in a concept of Lao-tse: "By enabling man to go right, disabling him to go wrong." Intuitively, he began to search for a way to put his ideas to some purpose. He discarded A.A.'s emphasis on religion, and, as he counseled other men, began to create his own methodology.

Soon addicts began to show up for his meetings. Chuck gave them vicious "haircuts" (tongue lashings) for their "stupid behavior," and, in crude seminars, encouraged them to "let go" their hostilities. Even a subculture has ideas of caste, however, and the alcoholics dropped off as the addicts came in.

Chuck has never been on drugs and did not know much about addiction, but he came to believe that "narcos" probably knew more about their illness than the Establishment—the law-enforcers, psychiatrists, judges and doctors who could punish or detoxify them, but who could not make them want to stay clean.

It seemed to him that dope fiends—as they frankly called themselves—needed a tough, disciplined, drug-free environment with a dash of T.L.C. ("tender loving care"). He decided to devote himself to one group under one roof.

With that flair for invention that characterizes all his techniques, Chuck called his group Synanon after an illiterate junkie stumbled over such square words as "seminar" and "symposium," gave up and called them "synanon." On Sept. 15, 1958, Synanon was incorporated as a non-profit California foundation, with 40 members.

They first rented a storefront building, then chipped in enough money to lease their present headquarters: an old armory, once a beach club, in Santa Monica.

From those dubious beginnings, through trial and error, Chuck and a nucleus of Synanon officials developed their approach to addicts. Synanon's theory is this:

The addicted person is not an adult, and it is futile to try to cure him with adult procedures. He is, emotionally, a compulsive, inadequate, stupid child, whose character disorder has made him completely dependent on drugs. With heroin, he has been able to escape the painful realities of life. He may appear to be a mature person, standing 6 feet tall and with a deep, resonant voice, but, in Synanon argot, "there is a little baby kicking around in his gut, dictating every move that he makes." Or as Chuck puts it:

"Crime is stupid, delinquency is stupid and the use of narcotics is stupid. What Synanon is dealing with is addiction to stupidity."

To treat this character disorder, Chuck has created a therapeutic community. In it, he demands allegiance to the family and right conduct in place of allegiance to the fix. At daily seminars, members sharpen their desire for learning on any subject. Every member in Synanon has a job.

Essential to the treatment is a variation of psychotherapy called attack therapy. Three times each week, Synanon members meet in small groups for violently outspoken discussions that they call "games," or "synanons." In the games, they release pent-up hostilities and attack the thoughts and deeds, of themselves and others, that they feel have broken them down all their lives.

Synanon believes that the only persons who can help the addict-child to mature are ex-addicts. They understand the addictive personality as psychiatrists, social workers and law-enforcers never can.

No one can "con" another in this "family." Nor is there any talking down to one another in the "we-they" attitude of professionals toward dope fiends, which seldom works. The newcomer has the living examples of "clean" ex-addicts before him every day—showing what he can aspire to, including the jobs they hold.

What motivates addicts to come? There is no single explanation. Some come with the idea of getting far away from home, for what is sometimes called the "geographical cure." Some come because they have a friend in Synanon or have read about it.* The most important reason is that every addict, at one time or

* There are two books on Synanon: "So Fair A House," by Dr. Daniel Casriel, and "Synanon: The Tunnel Back," by Lewis Yablonsky.

another—usually when his habit is so great ($30 to $50 a day)
that he is tired of stealing, hustling, cop harassment—simply wants
to get off the street. He is not thinking in terms of whether
Synanon will work. He just wants to stop running for a while.

New addicts usually arrive with all their jailhouse attitudes. They
resent Synanon for, they feel, taking their dope away from them.
They are skeptical about the abstaining dope fiends they see
around them, and secretly try to figure what the gimmick is:
"Who's got the dope?"

They are expected to arrive "clean"—that is, free of drugs.
But many arrive experiencing withdrawal pains. No pain-reliever
except aspirin is given here, but the "cold-turkey" withdrawal is
far less painful than in a jail cell. The withdrawal is supportive,
on a couch in the living room, where ex-addicts provide food, egg-
nogs and, above all, empathy.

Now the newcomer is initiated into rigid rules of right conduct:
no drugs, either on or off the premises (for the first few months
he is accompanied by a senior member); no violence; no foul
language, except in the synanons to release hostilities as part of
therapy; no promiscuity or homosexuality. Whoever breaks the
rules is tossed out.

One hefty Lesbian arrived in men's trousers and a mono-
grammed shirt, and insisted on using the men's toilet. Chuck
snarled: "In here you will act and dress like a woman. I don't
give a damn if you have sex with a sheep, but we will not have
this sort of thing in Synanon." (She stayed, and began to wear
dresses for the first time in her adult life.)

Everyone in Synanon has a job. To help the new arrival adjust
to the rules, there is an initial "honeymoon period"—two or
three months of bland acceptance by the rest of the house. He
gets menial tasks in the kitchen or office and learns to mouth the
jargon to help his adjustment: to "go through the motions" (behaving decently, though he may feel rotten), to "stay loose"
(be prepared to change his ways), to accept a "haircut" if he
misbehaves.

In the second stage, if he is making progress, he is promoted
to such jobs as canvassing the community for contributions—

usually of food, clothing or other goods—or working in the group's warehouses or the small workshops that Synanon has set up.

In the third stage, after 18 months to two years, members who are mature enough can move into managerial work. They run the organization, help with expansion plans and fill hundreds of speaking engagements at colleges, professional and business organizations and churches. No fees are charged. No salaries are paid at Synanon. All that members receive is $1 to $5 a week of pocket money—which goes largely for cigarettes.

In the parent house at Santa Monica, where 180 are in residence, one can observe the theories and techniques in action.

Inside, the walls are plastered with cuttings and photos from the national press. Offices and a small auditorium for seminars, or "town-meetings," are on the ground floor.

Upstairs is a large dining and living-room area, which is used also for seminars and entertainment. Chuck's private suite is here. (He has now married for a third time. His wife, Bettye, is an ex-addict and colored; they have adopted a colored child.) The suite, which doubles as Chuck's office, has the same unsettling charm as the rest of the house: Nothing matches; sofas, chairs, carpets and tables, contributed by the community, are serviceable, but the impression is Chaos Colonial.

On the third floor is an open, comfortable dormitory for men. Adjoining the main building, on the beach front, are cottages with separate quarters for men and women. Nearby, on a modest residential street, is a house for married couples. There have been 28 "Synanon marriages," performed by ministers who support the movement. Several babies have been born in Synanon (an addict's baby is often born addicted; these children were born clean).

Some 7,000 donors in the community help support this house —with everything from flints for cigarette lighters to truckloads of meat, milk and canned goods and the trucks for making pick-ups.

The other afternoon a seminar was led by John Maher, 22, who has become an example—a "role model"—for many other members as he has climbed in the Synanon hierarchy. Little more than two years ago, John was the terror of West 84th Street, known to every cop on the beat as Whitey the Priest.

A gang boy since he was 14, John has been in practically every institution, reformatory and prison in New York State; he has tried the Government's Public Health Service Hospital in Lexington, Ky. He was always back on drugs within the hour of reaching the street again.

He had heard about Synanon while doing time for robbery on Rikers Island, and agreed to try it. He came straight from jail.

Today, John, baby-faced and wiry, is a "Wizard." Each Synanon house has a Wizard—really an extension of Chuck—whose job is to counsel members when they get "sewed up tight" (deeply troubled). John has attended Santa Monica City College and, last fall, went back to New York for a television and speaking tour.

Everyone in the seminar has a past that competes with the Wizard's. Here is Florrie, 46, from the West Seventies in New York—but chiefly from penitentiaries, mental hospitals, Lexington and city jails. Twenty years on drugs, a hardened prostitute, tough and verbose, she has been in Synanon only two weeks. She came straight from Women's Prison in Manhattan, with the help of Synanon's legal adviser, John Ciampa, who had received a pleading letter from her while in prison.

"Say there's a certain X here—an unknown, whatever it is," she told me, "that they want to achieve in a person. I'm selfish and I'm tired. I want it, more than anything else in the world right now."

Here is Gary, a fair-haired, married young man of 22, raised on a ranch north of San Francisco. "You don't have to be from the cities to get hooked," he says quietly. Gary has been here three months, and says: "The way I see it, there must be something here for me—with so many people who stay clean."

The focal point of life here is the synanon. Groups of 7 to 10 meet three evenings a week for this leaderless type of psychotherapy. One or two staff leaders, called Synanists, dominate a meeting to move it along, but the attack therapy is used by everyone in the "game."

This is a sort of emotional dumping ground where the Synanists lean on their own experience—what Chuck calls "gut-level insights"—to force out of the others the truth about themselves. Members ridicule, exaggerate, rant and curse—at one another, at themselves, at society—to effect a catharsis of their emotions.

In a basement room, one synanon comprised two former street-gang members from New York; four women from New York, Chicago, Los Angeles and Bridgeport, Conn.; and two Synanists, Lee and Jerry.

One gang boy had split and come back in. Synanon makes "splitees" really plead to be taken back, and uses devices to humiliate them for a period (shaving off a man's hair, putting a stocking cap on a girl). This boy hates the menial job he has been demoted to, and says bitterly: "I'm not a follower, I'm a leader."

Lee yells: "You've still got one foot out the door, man—because you haven't decided yet to give up the f— stuff!"

"Yeah, you're right, O.K., O.K.," the boy says, "but I just want to start moving again in Synanon. I feel this waiting around. . . ."

"F— your feelings," sneers Jerry. "You only know one thing, man, the things you did before you came to Synanon: how to hit a man with a pipe; how to shoot up. You're a leader in that, man, but that's the image you've got to let go."

The third-degree goes on for some minutes. Then, as the strategy calls for, Lee's tone softens, and he builds the boy up before they turn to another member: "Don't you think if you talked to the people you work with, you could get to know them, just as you have to get to know your fears?"

The verbal attacks—on pride, on lies, on resistance to the program—are transferred to each one in turn, tearing at their defenses in the language of the street to get them to "stand naked," figuratively, and see for themselves why they are at the bottom.

It all seems to have been a prelude to the savage attack that opens on Virginia. Her "honeymoon period" is just over. A tall, slender blonde in a white jersey, plaid slacks and loafers, she has been sitting, chain-smoking, silent and fearful during the encounters.

"Virginia, you going to sit through every synanon and not say anything?" Silence.

"Virginia, when was the last time you got mad at someone?"
"Well, Saturday. . . ." She gives a genteel cough. She speaks in educated, well-modulated tones. She tries to stare down her attackers.

"Where you at, Virginia?" . . . "You think you're smarter, better than we are?" . . . "You're always 'up tight,' trying to impress everybody. You're a phony!" . . . "What are you, Virginia?" Silence.

"Why you so goddam superior? How do you feel about someone like Sandy—feel superior?" (Sandy has been a prostitute.)

"No, because in my own mind . . ."—she struggles to be honest—"what I was doing to myself was a little bit worse."

"Come on, now," Jerry says roughly, "level with us. We've all been prostitutes, pimps, thieves, hookers. You're right in the middle of it."

"I feel I am being honest. I don't feel one has to scream, to throw things. . . ." She stops, white-faced.

The boy gangster who had been originally attacked opens on her: "You've been a dope fiend. You got your drugs from the doctor. You were living with this man, yes? So this was your old man and you were shacking up with him."

She sits silent, trying to smoke, trying not to break, as the inquisition mounts. They will not let her be silent. Haltingly, she lets down some defenses. They force out that she has had two husbands and two children; that she used barbiturates and morphine before heroin. Just before coming to Synanon, she had tried to kill her mother—by throwing a bottle at her.

"Ever since that day, Virginia," Sandy says, "those feelings are buried deep in you. You know that. Until you let go and scream and carry on in these synanons, you'll be storing up all these feelings until you maybe take it out on someone here. Are you ashamed?"

Virginia is shaking, but she seems amazed that, though they know her story, they do not reject her.

"You can't really feel ashamed," she says, "when it's someone you hate."

They still pursue her. The boy gangster says sarcastically: "You're very well-composed. You act the lady. You can drop the pose. You were being kept by the doctor. You were selling your body to him for the f— stuff. Pardon my language, but that's the truth?"

The girl stares at him. She crumbles at last.

"Yes."

Except for the San Diego house, which has the warm support of the Mayor and the courts, every Synanon facility has had its troubles with the community. In Westport, Santa Monica and San Francisco, court battles have raged over zoning ordinances and the like, largely induced by homeowners who fear having a "horde of junkies" on their doorsteps. In 1961, Chuck spent 25 days in Santa Monica jail—the only time he has ever been imprisoned—accused of running "a hospital" without a zoning permit. But the Saturday-night open houses are attended by college students and professors, lawyers, doctors, psychiatrists, journalists, businessmen and housewives; they bring their children. A dozen doctors and dentists have donated their services to Synanon. Why do they care?

Dr. Jack D. Wax, whose offices are in the Melrose Medical Arts Center in Hollywood, says warmly: "Because I think we're beginning to see a form of solution to this problem that had no solution before—certainly not at Lexington."

Among the donors, or "Synanon Sponsors," are the Arnold Siegels. He heads the Kohler Automotive Company of Los Angeles, and has guaranteed all the liabilities that Synanon may incur from a gas station that 12 members run in Santa Monica. His wife, who has been a psychiatric social worker, says:

"In all my former work, we were never able to help a drug addict. Here I see a society in which there is a feeling to one another that's missing outside: protective in the beginning; then supportive, as it helps people find, perhaps for the first time, a family environment in which they are free, at last, to find themselves and grow up."

In San Francisco, near the docks, Synanon has leased and revamped an immense, 100-year-old warehouse called Seawall. Unions provided workers and materials, without cost, to put on a roof and make it habitable. The 85 ex-addicts who live and work there—many are artists and musicians—hope to make it a National Art Center.

The potential of this center is described by its best-known

"square"—Joe Zirker, artist and sculptor, a university lecturer whose work has been shown in a dozen museums. He turned down an offer from Stanford University to move with his wife into Seawall, bringing with him all his equipment—lithographic press, stones, inks and handmade papers. He will train apprentices in the art of lithography, and hopes to attract other artists.

A short, mild, precise man, Zirker told me: "Synanon suits my artistic needs. Every artist has a dream of space and time to do his work, and an environment that does not put pressure on him. I have this freedom at Synanon. And I find I am in tune with this very moral society of people who are striving to rebuild their lives."

An hour's drive from Seawall into a lovely Rivieralike setting brings one to the only property that Synanon owns—a large, rambling house with annexes on Tomales Bay. Here Chuck envisions a Synanon City of 900 acres—a community for 5,000 drug addicts, with resident complexes, buildings for seminars, art studios and shops, meeting halls, a theater, an administration building, a library. It would cost $3.5 million.

"I dream of a Synanon house in New York, where the biggest addiction problem is," says Chuck, "similar to that in Santa Monica. And, a short distance from New York, another Tomales Bay–type of community for thousands of addicts. I would populate it with non–New Yorkers. One obvious reason is that if you put a little real estate between a person and his problems, he's not apt to run home to mama so fast.

"There are schools for lawyers, journalists, dentists, carpenters," he went on, "but there doesn't seem to be any school for basic character, for learning how to live."

There is no set date that tells a member when he is well, strong enough to live on the outside again. After a long haul, usually lasting into the third year, he may develop confidence and self-respect to such a degree that he will think he is ready to "graduate." Quite often, the group will discourage him from leaving. Sometimes it is because the others do not feel he is ready for the "square" world; more often, it is because Synanon is frankly making a concerted effort to hold on to members who have grown up in the movement.

This is a building period for Synanon. Officials point out that it takes years of intensive effort to train administrators and organizers, whom they will need for their expansion plans.

Thus, there are many like 22-year-old Merv Weinstein of Brooklyn, who has been here for two years and expects to stay on and work in Synanon. "I'm no longer concerned with cure or noncure," he reflects. "That's all past history now. I think in terms of completing myself as a human being. Synanon is so much a part of me now that wherever I am, in one sense, I'll never leave. This is my home."

I have personally known several Synanon graduates.

One is Nadine, a slender young blonde whom I met in 1962 at the White House Conference on Narcotics and Drug Abuse. A Synanon resident then, she had come with fellow members to tell their stories to the law-enforcers, judges and professionals, but few listened.

Nadine had started on marijuana in the eighth grade, and heroin at 17. She met her present husband, Bob, in Synanon. He had been on drugs for 13 years, and had done penitentiary terms. At his request, the San Diego jail had paroled him to Synanon. Bob was in Synanon for 18 months, Nadine for two and a half years.

Today, in Los Angeles, they have their own home. Bob earns $6,500 a year as a taxi driver. Until recently, he also worked nights as a gas-station attendant. They are about to buy a five-bedroom house in San Fernando Valley, large enough for their four children—three from Nadine's first marriage to a seaman, who also was a drug addict, and their new baby.

Sometimes they go to Santa Monica to help others by their own example. Bob stumbles as he tries to express what Synanon has done for him: "Just say . . . it's made a whole new life for me."

Nadine adds sadly: "My former husband committed suicide last year. If only he had tried Synanon. . . ."

Another is James (Jake) Ross, who went on drugs while in the Navy and was an addict for eight years. An ascetic man, college-educated, he had tried private psychotherapy for a year without success when he entered Synanon. He stayed for 23 months. Today, Jake is an editor in a New York publishing house.

How do graduates stay clean? Jake answers: "Drugs no longer

have any more meaning for me than the average individual on the street—less, really, because the ordinary person may have a morbid interest in drugs, which was what started me on them. I find that I use and value many, many things I learned in Synanon as tools in my everyday life, getting along on my job, in my married life, in human relationships generally."

Synanon and many experts say that its methods are workable. But there are professionals and community leaders who oppose its approach. To them, the fact that there have been but 40 graduates means that this is the limit to which Synanon can rehabilitate. A therapeutic community, they say, should aim at reintegration with the larger society. Otherwise, all that is happening is that one sort of dependency (on Synanon) is being substituted for another sort of dependency (on drugs).

On the law-enforcement side, the California State Department of Correction and certain judges and legislators say that "criminals" and "patients" cannot become their own therapists and doctors. Many courts have refused to recommend parole of addict-prisoners to Synanon, and contend that Synanon is frustrating their efforts to maintain control over parolees.

Yet no Synanon house has been closed by the authorities. And, say the movement's supporters, in money terms the savings to society are impressive: Synanon costs about $3 a day per person; jail $15; hospitals, $20 to $25. But Synanon is more than statistics.

Senator Thomas J. Dodd of Connecticut, chairman of the Senate Subcommittee to Investigate Juvenile Delinquency, has said: "There is indeed a miracle on the beach at Santa Monica, a man-made miracle that I feel can benefit thousands of drug addicts."

Judge Leland Lazarus, the senior judge of San Francisco's Superior Court, who lived for many days at Synanon "to see that things were not being misrepresented," told me: "It not only gets people off drugs, but it makes real human beings out of them again."

Vincent A. Starace, Deputy Borough President of the Bronx, who also lived at Synanon to see for himself, told Mayor Wagner last fall: "The transformation [of former] addicts was marvelous, hard to believe unless you saw it."

Chuck Dederich is aware of the flaws in Synanon. He is particularly concerned with the 40 per cent who split—for them, since they go back to the street and drugs, clearly some humane approach must be found.

"We could improve our holding power," he says, "if we had more decent places to live. What is the alternative to Synanon? The hospitals? The jails? With the proper understanding and financial help, we could turn this population of 500 people living without bars, without shooting dope, improving each day, into 5,000 people, and 5,000 into 50,000.

"The country would like to forget our people, to sweep them under the rug. Society always wants to take a kid from the slums and put him in a penitentiary to 'cure him.' Then it sends him back to the slums to 'straighten out.'

"Well, I would feel that nothing had happened to a member, that I had failed, if after living here, he went back to live in a slum. Synanon is the only real 'slum clearance' in the country."

Part 5

SOME PROPOSALS
FOR CHANGE

THE THREE articles in this section propose radical modifications
of three different parts of the criminal justice system. Generally
speaking, the authors find that, from the viewpoint of some significant part of the public, many of the wheels in the machinery
of justice are unnecessary, counterproductive, or irrelevant.

Charles Hussey, a London newspaper editor and writer, shows
that almost all the criminal justice processes—arresting, convicting, sentencing, and punishing—have little relevance for the
criminal's immediate victim. The official action taken against a
criminal by the state is taken on behalf of all the people, not the
victim. Criminal cases are headed *People vs. Jones* or *State vs.
Jones.* A person whose interests are damaged by a criminal must
initiate a civil suit in order to recover the damages. Civil cases
involving suits for recovery of damages are headed *Smith vs.
Jones.* In other words, if I am hit on the head by a robber, or if
my television set is stolen in a burglary of my home, the fine,
imprisonment, or other punishment imposed on the offender only
satisfies my vague need for revenge and for social order. So far

as getting my doctor bills and hospital expenses paid, or getting a new television set, the state's official action is irrelevant. As a remedy for the criminal law's irrelevance to the immediate victim of crime, England in 1965 began compensating the victims of violent crime, but not the victims of property offenses. Even under this progressive plan, however, the compensation awarded to a victim remains irrelevant to the criminal, just as the official action taken against the criminal remains irrelevant to the victim. In the United States, restitution to the victim often is officially required as a condition of probation, making the official action relevant to the criminal and the victim alike. But this concern for the victim and for the possible rehabilitative effects that restitution might have on the criminal has not been regularized or systematized by statutes.

The various branches of our court system are not integrated, court personnel are not well trained, courts are badly managed, and the rules of criminal procedure are outmoded. These conditions, in combination, make the court system somewhat irrelevant to anyone seeking systematic justice in it. Arthur T. Vanderbilt, Chief Justice of the Supreme Court of New Jersey, proposes reforms that would correct this state of irrelevancy. Similar proposals were made before Justice Vanderbilt made his plea, and many have been made since. Warren E. Burger, Chief Justice of the United States, in 1970 called for reforms similar to those proposed by Justice Vanderbilt in 1957. Chief Justice Burger asked, basically, that modern management techniques be substituted for the "purely mechanical operation of the courts."

There seems to be little possibility that the court system, or any part of the criminal justice system, will be reformed by the participants themselves. They have too much at stake. As Justice Vanderbilt so wisely observes, reform of our outmoded judicial structure can be achieved only if there is an aroused public opinion, followed by intelligent and effective action. Legislators are not likely to get excited about court reform until their constituents give court reform a high political priority.

Dr. Ralph S. Banay, formerly head of the psychiatric clinic at Sing Sing prison, closes the discussion by arguing convincingly that prisons—and the entire system of imprisonment—are irrelevant to the reclamation, reformation, or correction of criminals. In Part 3, M. Arc showed how prison workers' attempts to "enforce the law" are self-defeating. He called for better personnel. But, by definition, imprisonment requires criminals to live in strange and abnormal circumstances. It is impossible to turn the key in a prison cell therapeutically. Perhaps, then, even the best prison personnel will not be able to change prisons significantly. Should this be the case, prisons will remain irrelevant to the correction of criminals and irrelevant to the direct victims of crime.

Prisons incapacitate criminals for varying periods of time, rendering them unable to commit many crimes against persons who are not also prisoners. The escape rate is low. But within any prison the crime rate is high, indicating that prisons are even somewhat irrelevant to inmates who need protection from the crimes of other inmates. Prisons also punish criminals effectively. As we noted in Part 4, men are deliberately sent to prison so they will suffer. It should not be surprising to find, then, that suffering is rampant in even the most "modern," "enlightened," and "progressive" correctional institutions. The pain stemming from loss of liberty should not be underestimated. Further, imprisonment deters some unknown portion of the general public from crime. The prison's ability to incapacitate, punish, and deter is not in question.

The issue is this: Can an organization which does not rehabilitate and which merely inflicts some kinds of punishments on some kinds of criminals some of the time be tolerated in a democratic society? This question should be asked about the entire so-called "system" of criminal justice as well as about each of the organizations that comprise the whole—police departments, prosecutors' offices, courts, probation departments, prisons, parole bureaus, and so on. We must stop looking backward to what happened on the day of the crime, which now determines almost all the official actions taken against a criminal. We must instead look forward to the possible effects which various courses of action—punitive or correctional—might have on the criminal and on the rest of us.

Britain Pays the
Victim of the Crime

by Charles Hussey

A FEW WEEKS ago a 50-year-old British post office worker was hit on the head with an iron bar by a member of a gang making a raid on postal property. The injury was not serious—he had three scalp wounds—but for three months he suffered from emotional tension and a raised pulse rate. The assailant was neither identified nor traced. The post office worker was awarded £160 —about $450—out of state funds.

He was one of the first of 59 victims of violent crime to receive an award from the Criminal Injuries Compensation Board set up by the Conservative Government last August, a month or two before losing office. In the board's six months of operation it has paid out the United States equivalent of $31,000 in Government money, as solace for injuries and compensation for loss of earnings or increased expenditure. It is an entirely new departure in social security in Britain—and indeed throughout most of the world. Only New Zealand, a pioneer of social security, is known to be experimenting with this kind of compensatory scheme.

In the past, the victims of criminal assault in Britain did not get a penny, unless the criminal was captured and had legitimate personal means on which a civil claim could be based. This often meant hardship to the victim, as dramatized in the classic case of a man named Richardson. He was so severely beaten that he became blind and suffered other permanent injuries. The criminals were caught and sentenced. Richardson sued them for compensation and was awarded damages of more than $33,000. They were unable to pay, so Richardson took them to court. The judge ruled that each should pay 70 cents a week. Thus it would take 442 years to pay off the damage, and even worse, Richardson had to pay $800 legal costs.

This was one of the cases on which Margery Fry, the famous British penal reformer, who died in 1958, based her arguments 10 years ago when she opened her campaign for state compensation for the victims of criminal violence. Miss Fry was one of the great spinster reformers of Britain, like Florence Nightingale and Eleanor Rathbone, to whom we owe family allowances. She was a vivid, brown-haired woman full of energy and high principles, daughter of the first Quaker to take a judgeship and descendant of John Howard and Elizabeth Fry, the 18th- and 19th-century pioneers of prison reform. She combined crusading fervor with remarkable political skill. Though she became the bane of reactionary chiefs of police, she had the ear of the Home Office and a faithful following of members of Parliament.

Miss Fry opened her campaign in the columns of the heavyweight Sunday paper, The Observer, and the perky, now defunct London evening paper, The Star. She started with the proposal that criminals should contribute toward the compensation of their victims as part of the redemptive process of imprisonment. (This was a principle endorsed by the U. N. Congress on the Prevention of Crime and Treatment of Offenders, held in Geneva in 1955.) But she went far beyond that. In presenting her case she drew upon an argument of the philosopher Jeremy Bentham (1747–1832):

"It is old-fashioned now to quote Bentham, but on the tendency of criminal law to pay scant attention to the needs of the victim, he puts it well: 'Punishment, which, if it goes beyond the limit of necessity, is a pure evil, has been scattered with a prodigal hand. Satisfaction, which is purely a good, has been dealt out with evident parsimony.' He held that 'satisfaction' should be drawn from the offender's property, but 'if the offender is without property . . . it ought to be furnished out of the public treasury, because it is an object of public good and the security of all is interested in it.'

"Is Bentham's proposal useful today? Clearly, so far as offenses against property go, any scheme for state insurance would be wrecked by the ease with which it could be defrauded. But crimes of violence against the person are a different matter. Few people would voluntarily wound themselves to obtain a modest compensation, and the risk of successful deception is negligible.

"The value of the proposed compensation would not be economic alone. There is a natural sense of outrage on the sufferer's part, which the milder aspect of our modern penal methods only exacerbates. The young hooligan goes to a course of training in Borstal [reformatory], while the shopkeeper he has 'coshed' nurses his grievance with his broken head, gaining perhaps some solatium for a day's work lost giving evidence.

"After all, the state which forbids our going armed in self-defense cannot disown all responsibility for its occasional failure to protect."

With arguments such as this, Margery Fry was able to persuade R. A. Butler, as Tory Home Secretary, to give the first official response to her campaign. Five years ago he presented to Parliament a Home Office memorandum on "Penal Practice in a Changing Society." This cautiously suggested that if there was to be a new look at penal methods, it must be concerned not only with the obligation of society and the offender to one another, but also with the obligation of society and the offender to the victim. The memorandum recognized that as a rule "society alone can effectively compensate" and proposed that a Home Office committee should be set up to examine the Fry thesis.

Four years ago, this committee presented its report. It came down on the side of a special court which would grant compensation on the basis of common-law damage; in fact, the kind of damages which would have been awarded by civil court if the victim had sued his assailant.

And yet, the committee said, there must be certain differences. It felt there should be no compensation for loss of happiness, no "exemplary" damages, and it excluded all motoring offenses unless the automobile was used as a weapon.

As so often happens, the Government, having commanded and got its report, took no action. Two Labor members, Carol Johnson and Reg Prentice, made three attempts to introduce legislation but the Government would not find time for it.

Then "Justice" got to work. This is a voluntary body dedicated to law reform and headed by some of the greatest lawyers of the day (including Lord Gardiner, the new Lord Chancellor). Justice set up a committee under the chairmanship of the Earl of Longford, a high-minded Catholic reformer who is now Labor's leader of the House of Lords.

It reported in favor of a scheme of compensation, and about the same time a committee of Tory M.P.'s under the chairmanship of a future Attorney General reached the same conclusions, though it prescribed a different form of tribunal.

In 1962 Lord Longford opened a debate in the House of Lords. There, as in Commons, were no arguments against the *principle* of state compensation; the discussion was about the basis on which compensation should be awarded. Labor inclined to the view that the injured person should have a legal right to claim from the state. The Conservative view was that the state could not be liable at law for its failure to protect a citizen against a violent assault, but that it did have a moral obligation to provide financial help and solace as an act of grace.

The most significant speech was made by one of the Lords Justices of Appeal, Lord Denning. He thought there were too many anomalies to make state compensation a matter of right. He could see no consistent principle of entitlement. He did not see how it was possible to blame the state "which provides the best police force in the world."

Summing up, he proposed that, instead of legal entitlement, there should be ex gratia payments. Lord Denning's view has triumphed. The present system, now in its experimental phase, is making payments not on a legal but on an ex gratia basis, on principles established not by law but by the Home Office.

The office of the Criminal Injuries Compensation Board is a modest setup in Woburn Place, half a mile from the Law Courts. Its secretary is a solicitor, David Harrison. Its chairman, Judge Kelly Carter, is a senior official referee at the Law Courts. There are six members of the board, all lawyers, doing a part-time job at $60 a sitting day. So far the board has been working in complete secrecy, publishing each month only the barest details of the cases and the awards.

Since the board was set up last August, 190 applications for compensation have been made, and about two-thirds are still being processed. This is the procedure:

People who have been assaulted learn from the police or their doctors or the Citizens' Advice Bureau that they may be able to claim compensation if their injury has caused them either three weeks' loss of pay or losses and expenses amounting to at least $150. They are then sent an application form which requires them to answer such simple queries as these:

Has the offender been prosecuted? What were your injuries? What is the name of your doctor? At what hospital were you treated? How much loss of earnings did you suffer? The form provides 13 lines for a description of the attack.

The board staff checks the facts with the police and medical authorities. And then one of the six members of the board makes an award or rejects the claim.

Many of the cases are simple, such as these:

Man, aged 24, assaulted in street by a stranger. Butted in the face and punched on the head and body. Fractured nose, broken teeth, bruised and cut lips, stomach disorder, shock. Admitted to hospital—fracture reduced under general anesthetic. In-patient for seven days. Loss of sense of smell, probably temporary. Off work three weeks.

Assailant charged and fined—no blame attached to victim.

Compensation $570, including $120 net loss of earnings and out-of-pocket expenses, after taking into account payments from public funds.

Man, 53, hit over the head with a bottle and cut on the hand with a knife during a quarrel on private premises. Treated in hospital as an out-patient and six sutures inserted. Off work four weeks.

Assailant charged and placed on probation. No blame attached to victim.

Compensation $150, including $54 net loss of earnings and out-of-pocket expenses, after taking into account payments from public funds.

The police are hopeful that the compensation experiment will encourage members of the public to act when they see crimes being committed. If they are injured, they now stand to get payment as well as police gratitude. Here are two such cases:

Man, 24, stabbed late at night in a struggle while attempting to arrest one of two men he found tampering with a window of the house next door. One-inch stab wound in lower chest, abrasion on left shoulder, and small laceration on the scalp. Hospital treatment as an out-patient—three sutures inserted in stab wounds. Absent from work for four weeks to recover from nervous shock. No permanent ill effects.

One of the two men was caught, charged and convicted of attempted burglary. The second man was not traced. No blame attached to victim.

Compensation $225, including $105 net loss of earnings and out-of-pocket expenses, after taking into account payments from public funds.

Man, 58, aroused in the night by his dog barking, to find two youths attempting to break into an adjacent shop. The youths ran away, and the victim and his dog gave chase. One of the youths rounded on the victim and struck him with a stick, causing bruises across the ribs and down into the abdominal muscles. Treated by own doctor. Stiffness and pain for two weeks and full recovery after a further four weeks. No permanent injury. The youths were not caught.

Compensation $279, including $54 out-of-pocket expenses, after taking into account payments from public funds.

Cases of sexual assault on women also rate compensation, as in these instances:

Girl, 17, sexually assaulted and robbed in the street at night. On examination after the incident, the victim's condition was found to be consistent with her complaint of rape. She also had extensive bruising and abrasions of face and hands, and was in a condition of extreme distress. No permanent ill effects. Absent from work for three weeks.

Assailant convicted of rape and larceny and sent to prison.

Compensation $450. No loss of earnings or out-of-pocket expenses.

Woman, 36, assaulted by a stranger while walking home from work on a public footpath through a wood. Black and swollen right eye, burst mouth and nose, cracked cheekbone, bruising of neck and shoulders. Hospital treatment as out-patient. Fit for work after eight months, but still suffering from nerves and minor ill effects.

Assailant charged with indecent assault and placed on proba- tion. No blame attached to victim.

Compensation $480, including $105 out-of-pocket expenses and loss of earnings, after taking into account payments from public funds.

In the following case the compensation award was compara- tively high:

Man, 27, passenger in a car, threatened by a group of men, one of whom smashed a window with a belt. Victim was struck in the face, causing a rupture of the left eye, which had to be removed; also a fracture of the lower orbital margin and lacer- ations of eyelids. Hospital in-patient for six days. No residual disability apart from loss of eye.

Assailant charged and sent to prison. No blame attached to victim.

Compensation $6,000. No loss of earnings—past or prospective.

If the applicant is disappointed with the award, he can appeal to the board and three members will hear his case. The proceed- ings are informal and the witnesses are not on oath. So far, there have been three such appeals. Here is one in which a substantial change was made: The applicant, a woman aged 63, was escorting her crippled sister through a subway passage when an assailant snatched her handbag, causing her to fall to the ground. She suffered a dislocation of the right shoulder and severe bruising. She was detained in hospital three days. On discharge her right arm was immobilized in a sling. At first she suffered severe pain. When the sling was discarded, the movement of the shoulder was restricted but gradually increased. She received physiotherapy treatment as an out-patient.

Applicant had retired from her employment. Her injury prevented her from carrying out her normal household duties and from looking after her sister.

A single member of the board awarded applicant $150, including $6 out-of-pocket expenses. Applicant appealed the award as inadequate. The board obtained a fresh medical report which showed that the injury would continue to affect her for another 12 months and would leave behind a permanent limitation of movement.

At the date of the hearing applicant's out-of-pocket expenses amounted to $15 and the board added $600, making a total additional award of $615.

All actions by the board will be carefully watched by members of Parliament and students of justice to see that the cases are handled fairly and with reasonable generosity. So far there has been a good deal of warm public support for the principle of compensation, especially in view of the rise in crimes of violence —eight times more frequent than before the war.

However, there is criticism as well, and many problems must be solved. Some of the leading members of the new Labor Government have attacked the plan. Lord Gardiner, for instance, charged it was put together quickly for electoral reasons, and he and others have found that it contains a number of anomalies.

One example of this was offered by Sir Frank Soskice, now Home Secretary, when he was still a member of the Opposition. If, he said, a ruffian should crack an old man on the head and steal his life savings, the victim will receive compensation for his skull but not for his financial loss. Also, the Home Office committee was alarmed at the prospect of compensation for the "undeserving."

Suppose the innocent wife of a gangster got beaten up when protecting him against assault by fellow criminals? If the state compensated the innocent wife, would it not be effectively helping the criminal husband?

Some Conservatives believed the system invited fraud—especially in the case of sexual offenses. Suppose that after an alleged rape, a woman voluntarily associated with another man and a child was conceived. Who could say whether the pregnancy was the result of violence?

There are also those who think it unfair that a claim cannot be made for injuries when the assailant is a member of the household. A woman attacked by her son-in-law could not claim compensation if he lived with her but she could if he lived next door. A daily cleaning woman could file a claim if raped by the father of the household but a resident maid could not.

Still, there are answers to the criticisms—and those in authority emphasize that the plan is in the experimental stage. Its limitations, they say, are intended to protect the state against fraud, to exclude people who have brought trouble on themselves by provocation, and to restrict payments to a decent minimum during the experimental period. Nobody knows what the cost is going to be. Margery Fry's researches suggested that compensation would cost only about $450,000 a year—but that was eight years ago. Since then money has lost some of its value and there are more crimes of violence.

As it operates now, the board assesses claims on the basis of common-law damages and makes lump-sum payments. Where the victim is alive the rate of loss of earnings allowed is not to exceed twice the average of industrial weekly earnings as determined by the Ministry of Labor—about $50 a week. Therefore, top rate cannot exceed $100 a week. Where the victim has died, no compensation will be payable for the benefit of his estate. But his dependents can make a claim that will be judged on the dead man's income—subject to the $100 maximum.

Since the board is working in secrecy, we shall not know until it presents its annual report what its exact policies are in working out the terms of compensation. Publication no doubt will reopen the question of how the board should approach various problems, and possibly lead to changes in the present system. However, the Labor Government will not, I believe, be in a hurry to amend the scheme radically. It will watch the experiment, and it is always open to the Home Secretary to make minor modifications without going to Parliament.

Brief for a Better
Court System
by Arthur T. Vanderbilt

THE NEW YORK Legislature adjourned recently without taking favorable action on the bills for court reform on which the Temporary (Tweed) Commission on the New York Courts had labored for four years. The proposals of the commission, well intended though they were, were so watered down in a vain attempt not to lose any possible source of support for its program that the result was a mere shadow of genuine court reform. This is characteristic of every movement for judicial reform in its initial phase.

I speak with the utmost sympathy for the public-spirited members of the Temporary Commission, for I, too, wasted an unconscionable amount of time and energy over ten years as chairman of the Judicial Council of New Jersey in endeavoring to draft constitutional amendments to improve the outmoded judicial system in that state.

We, too, sought to retain the support of the leaders of the bench and the bar. We likewise consented to the watering down process in an effort to appease the advocates of the status quo,

From the *New York Times Magazine,* May 5, 1957, copyright © 1957 by The New York Times Company.

only to have our proposals passed one year in one house of the Legislature and then defeated in the other house (and vice versa the next year). After ten years of this painful education in the process of court revision, we decided that our credulity was being imposed upon by the vested interests of the bench and bar.

Then, under the leadership of Gov. Charles Edison, we decided to forget compromises. A constitution revision commission of seven set about drafting the best judicial article within our power. When it was in due course turned over to the Legislature for consideration, that body had a field day. Fortunately, the proposed constitutional amendments as "revised" by the Legislature were defeated at the polls and we were free to start over.

Accordingly, after fourteen years of struggle, we then decided to do what had been done in England almost a century before— to carry the battle to the people and ignore the judges, the lawyers and the politicians. People from every walk of life were organized in committees. Their influence was so great that the Legislature could not ignore them; under the leadership of Gov. Alfred E. Driscoll, it provided for a Constitutional Convention and a new Constitution was adopted in November, 1947—seventeen years after the beginning of our struggle—by a popular vote of three and a half to one.

As a result of our experience, I hazard a guess that real judicial reform will not come in any large jurisdiction by any other method than direct appeal to the people. What happened in England and, much more recently, in New Jersey, proves it. The stage is now set in New York for such a campaign. I can well understand the discouragement today of the members of the Temporary Commission, but I venture to repeat what I said after the years of battling in New Jersey: "Manifestly judicial reform is no sport for the short-winded or for lawyers who are afraid of temporary defeat." It will not be necessary to walk around Jericho seven times and blow the trumpets; all that is needed to tumble down the walls of the present inadequate court system is to let the people know how really simple judicial reform actually is.

It is so simple that any high school student can understand its essential elements. The first requirement is an integrated set of courts. The second requirement is the best possible judges, lawyers, and juries. The third is an effective businesslike organization of the courts, with responsible leadership. The fourth is a flexible system of rules of procedure promulgated, not by the Legislature —which is already overburdened and which cannot be expected to be expert in these matters—but by the judges of the court of last resort, with the aid of a Judicial Conference. This conference would be made up of the ablest and most unselfish judges and lawyers as well as some lay members who, I have found, are adept in asking embarrassing questions which very much need to be answered if we desire to have a judicial establishment geared to the demands of the times.

A Simple Court Structure

It is characteristic of an immature system of law that it is beset by a multiplicity of courts. Lord Coke in his classic "Fourth Institute" describes over 100 different courts; Holdsworth, in the first volume of his monumental "History of English Law," even more. All the courts that any American state really needs, however, are three:

(1) A general trial court with state-wide jurisdiction over every kind of case. This court may and should have a considerable degree of specialization within it, with specialized judges in law and equity, probate and divorce matters. However, every judge of the court should be authorized when occasion requires to try every other kind of case. There should be no jurisdictional conflicts among courts.

(2) There should also be a local court for the trial of minor cases, civil and criminal, and for the holding of defendants for action by the grand jury. In some states it has been found advisable to divide this local court into two, one civil and the other criminal.

(3) There must, of course, be an appellate tribunal to review questions of law from the trial courts and from the administrative tribunals. In the larger states there must be an intermediate court

or court of appeals, the number depending upon the volume of appellate business in the particular jurisdiction.

Very few of our states have achieved this ideal of the three-court system. The degree to which they have progressed in this direction is one measure of their judicial civilization. New York State now has twenty-one kinds of courts. Such a system is needlessly complicated; I defy most lawyers and most judges, for that matter, to define the jurisdiction of so many courts.

Such a multiplicity of courts creates confusion that frequently results in cases being determined on the basis of jurisdictional technicalities rather than on their merits. Unnecessary compartmentalization reduces the/flexibility of the judicial system and its ability to adapt itself to the constantly changing nature and volume of litigation. Inevitably the more different kinds of courts, each with its own clerical staff, the greater the cost of operating the courts. A simple integrated court structure eliminates jurisdictional conflicts, permits the most efficient use of the available judicial manpower, and reduces the administrative overhead necessary for the proper operation of the system.

The Best Personnel

We are primarily concerned with the caliber of judges, jurors, and lawyers—though all other court personnel are also important to the operation of a sound judicial system.

What constitutes a good judge? If I may quote myself:

"We need judges learned in the law, not merely the law in books but, something far more difficult to acquire, the law as applied in action in the courtroom; judges deeply versed in the mysteries of human nature and adept in the discovery of the truth in the discordant testimony of fallible human beings; judges beholden to no man, independent and honest and—equally important—believed by all men to be independent and honest; judges, above all, fired with consuming zeal to mete out justice according to law to every man, woman, and child that may come before them and to preserve individual freedom against any aggression of government; judges with the humility born of wisdom, patient and untiring in the search for truth and keenly conscious of the evils arising in a workaday world from any unnecessary delay."

Judges with all of these attributes are not easy to find, but which of these traits dare we eliminate if we are to hope for evenhanded justice? Good judges can after a fashion make even an inadequate system of substantive law achieve justice. On the other hand, judges who lack these qualifications will defeat the best system of substantive and procedural law imaginable.

The method of selecting judges is crucial. It may come as a surprise to many people that the popular election of judges is unknown anywhere in the world outside of several of the American states, such as New York, and in Soviet Russia and its satellites.

This issue is basic. Not a year goes by but that The New York Times, for example, editorially decries the farce of popular elections of judges. Former Gov. Alfred E. Smith, who was generally conceded to be one of the ablest students of government this country has ever produced, disposes of the issue in a single sentence:

"In the long run [the elective system] means the selection of judges by political leaders and the ratification of their selection by an electorate who are not really in a position to pass upon the legal and other abilities of the individual."

Such a master politician as Edward J. Flynn, formerly chairman of the Democratic National Committee as well as chairman of the Democratic State Committee in New York and for many years Democratic leader of the Bronx, frankly admits the effects of the popular election of judges. Not long before his death he wrote a book entitled, rather ironically, "You're the Boss." His description of the sinister contacts between the political leader and "his" judiciary is shocking, and the more so because he confesses to a realization of its iniquity. He wrote:

"Political leaders have always maintained, not only in New York but throughout the entire United States, that they have the right to speak on behalf of a client to a judge on the bench. Ethically it is wrong; but practically the custom has always existed and it would be difficult to eradicate."

Nor are the conditions any better in the rural areas. Only recently Judge Harvey Uhlenhopp addressed the Iowa State Bar Foundation in this frank language:

"The situation is even worse in the country. The lawyers control the nomination of the judges, and in many rural counties one of the lawyers is politically prominent who holds the delegation in his hand. You ought to sit in this spot: on one side of the table in a close case is a political nobody. On the other side is a man who controls your job. It is a farce to call this a system of justice where the employer of the judge is on one side of the table. That is your rural system."

If the people of a state are not ready to consider the appointive system, especially where appointees are chosen on a bipartisan basis as in New Jersey, they should at least have the American Bar, or California, or Missouri, Plan—as it is variously called—submitted to them. Under this system the influences of partisan politics are kept at a minimum since the candidates for judicial office are first chosen by a nominating commission, composed not of party representatives but of representatives of the bench and the bar. Then, after a brief trial period the judges run on their own record without any opponent, with the public voting upon the simple question: "Shall Judge A be continued in office on his record?"

In cases where juries are used, they are, within their sphere, quite as important as the judges themselves. What will it avail a litigant to have the best possible judge and the ablest lawyers in his case, if there are dishonest or unintelligent jurors in the box?

Strangely, there are those who carry their notions of "democracy" and equality to the extreme of asserting that everyone has a right to be a juror, and that a litigant or an accused has the right to have a jury chosen at random from the populace. But if we look at the administration of justice as a practical matter vitally concerned with affairs touching intimately the welfare both of private citizens and the state, can we possibly say that there is a place on the jury for convicts, the illiterate, or persons mentally or physically unfit? Obviously not, if justice is to be done.

To be effective, a jury must constitute a cross-section of the honest and intelligent citizens of the county and be imbued with a sense of the solemnity of their function and determined to perform it.

Jury panels should always be selected by the judges (provided, of course, the system of judicial selection in use insures judges free from politics) or by commissioners selected for this purpose by the judges, and such Jury Commissioners should be chosen on a bipartisan basis and should be entirely divorced from politics. It is shocking to learn that the jury lists in at least twenty-four states are still made up by political officers, which means that in such states there is always the danger and generally the reality that the jury panel will be selected with political considerations in mind.

I remember the reply of a United States Senator to my plea to him years ago for his support of a bill authorizing the courts to appoint Jury Commissioners to select the jury panels; he had no objection to such a method of selection in civil cases, but he would tolerate no change in the political selection of jurors in criminal matters—one could never tell when one would need help!

The ability, conscientiousness, and integrity of the Jury Commissioners in any state are measured by the competence and suitability of the persons whom they select for jury service. As the word "selection" indicates, the process of choosing jurors is not an arbitrary or mechanical function, but a task requiring the exercise of judgment, discretion, and good faith on the part of those in whom the responsibility for selection is vested. In New Jersey our Supreme Court has instructed its Jury Commissioners that their selection should be controlled by the following considerations:

(1) All names should not be selected from the same source (such as a tax roll, election list, or directory); (2) sources should be so coordinated as together to include all wards and municipalities in the county; (3) sources should be included which are likely to produce the names of persons possessed of intelligence, morality, integrity, and common sense; (4) economic and social status, including race and color, should be considered only to the extent necessary to assure that there is no discrimination on account of them; (5) political affiliations should be completely ignored; and (6) unsolicited requests of persons who seek to have their

names placed upon the jury lists and unsolicited recommendations of names should be accepted with extreme caution.

To obtain real justice, we must also have lawyers who are competent, industrious, and courageous, always mindful of their professional obligations, as epitomized in the Canons of Professional Ethics, to present the facts to the court and jury and to argue the law to the court—for the law in operation is necessarily the joint product of judge, jury, and counsel.

Raising the standards of the bar in any state is something which cannot be accomplished merely by the passing of a statute or the enactment of a rule of court. It requires that law schools throughout the country continue to increase their educational standards and to devise ways and means of inculcating in their students a deep sense of professional responsibility; it calls for the fixing by the court of last resort in the state of high standards for admission to practice and for continued vigilance both on the part of the courts and of the bar associations to see that those few lawyers who ignore their professional obligations are dealt with in the interest of protecting the public.

Businesslike Organization

It is difficult to conceive of any state-wide business concern operating without an executive head and with no administrative organization. Although the courts in every state are the equivalent of a substantial business concern, few of them are equipped for proper administration.

Most of all, every judicial system requires a judge as administrative head, especially to assign the judges of the trial courts to the courts where they are most needed and to the kind of work that they can best do. The chief justice of each state should be the administrative head, but in populous states, such as New York, he should be able to call on the assistance of the presiding justices of the Appellate Divisions of the Supreme Court.

It is almost inconceivable that a large trial court like the New York State Supreme Court should not have any one judge who is charged with administrative responsibility or power. In New Jersey, with such administrative help, the output of the courts was increased 98 per cent in a single year.

In addition to the administrative office and administrative judge, there should be a local presiding or administrative judge selected by the chief justice in every locality where there is more than one judge. His duty would be to supervise day-by-day operations in such localities.

Being in the courthouse, he is in a position to make sure that administrative policies decided on by the court of last resort are put into effect. He can confer directly with the other trial judges, with the trial lawyers and the prosecuting attorney in the interest of keeping the calendars current. It is his responsibility to assign individual cases to the individual judges for trial and to keep the business of his courts flowing.

If the judges charged with administrative responsibility are to discharge their responsibilities adequately and intelligently, it is essential that they have the assistance of an administrative staff. While the need for such assistance would seem obvious, it was not until 1939, when the Administrative Office of the United States Courts was established, that such assistance was provided for the courts in any jurisdiction in the United States.

Since then, various kinds of administrative offices have been established in seventeen states to aid the business of the courts, particularly in collecting statistics as to the work they do. The thought is gradually becoming apparent to judges and lawyers alike that what we need is live statistics that reflect the current state of affairs rather than dead statistics which are embalmed in annual reports published a year or two after the event.

An administrative office of the courts should get from each judge a weekly report of his judicial activities and a monthly report from each court clerk on the status of the calendars and thereby be able to furnish the administrative judge with up-to-date information so essential for the proper exercise of his administrative duties. An administrative office can also render valuable service by taking care of the business or housekeeping affairs of the courts, including the supervision of the work of the clerk's offices, and effect substantial economies by the introduction of modern business methods.

Simple Rules of Procedure

All procedure should be merely a means to an end, and that end should be to aid in the attainment of substantial justice. In many states in this country judgments based on technicalities of procedure have been very common. This is because the rules of procedure for a century or more have been prescribed by inflexible statutes passed by the Legislature. The late Attorney General William D. Mitchell, who was chairman of the Advisory Committee on the Federal Rules of Civil Procedure, has said that "the New York Code demonstrates to the highest degree the deficiencies inevitable in statutory codes of procedure. It is too long, with too much detail, and too many traps for the unwary, and with too much emphasis on mere forms and modes of procedure."

In striking contrast are the Federal Rules of Civil and Criminal Procedure, which are simplicity itself. Under them, reversals on technicalities are practically unknown.

The Federal Rules of Civil Procedure have been adopted in ten states and substantial portions of the code have been adopted by many more, but New York State is not one of them. This led Mr. Mitchell, as late as 1949, to say: "The situation today in New York resembles that in the United States Senate faced by the American Bar Association for so many years. A few stubborn men in key positions have succeeded so far in defeating efforts for this reform."

It is true that a committee appointed by the Temporary Commission is working on new rules of procedure. But even if the committee produces the best rules in the world, the cause of justice will be little advanced because the Legislature still retains the right to tinker with the rules. The "few stubborn men" to whom Mr. Mitchell referred must be forced—and they can be forced—by the will of the people to surrender in the interest of promoting the administration of justice.

The four great objectives of court reform I have described were won by the people in England many years ago, and in New Jersey only ten years ago. There, even the stubborn surrendered to the will of the people. The people can, and I trust will, prevail in New York State under the leadership of the public-spirited members of the Temporary Commission on the New York Courts.

Should Prisons
Be Abolished?

by Ralph S. Banay

THE PRISON, as now tolerated, is a constant threat to everyone's security. An anachronistic relic of medieval concepts of crime and punishment, it not only does not cure the crime problem; it perpetuates and multiplies it. We profess to rely upon the prison for our safety; yet it is directly responsible for much of the damage that society suffers at the hands of offenders. On the basis of my own experience, I am convinced that prisons must be abolished. In their place I would substitute a new kind of institution which would release men for service to the community rather than, as now, for rebellion against it.

Prisons make and install time-bombs in the personalities of the men and women confined in them. That these bombs will explode in time is almost certain. Sometimes prisoners "explode" inside the prisons in incredibly savage riots which destroy millions of dollars worth of property and take many lives. More harmful, nearly every prisoner, after release, will "explode" individually against the society that has imprisoned him. For it is our own fault and folly that prisons are designed only for retribution and expiation; they are not equipped for reclamation or reformation.

The recent siege by four convicts in the Massachusetts State Prison, Boston, is glaring proof of the lack of wisdom in treating seriously disturbed personalities with standard prison disciplinary measures like prolonged solitary confinement and severe restriction of privileges. Individuals who are so treated are unable to use their remaining intellect for self-preservation or to cope with their violent aggressive tendencies.

Consider the prison's lineage and relationships. The idea it represents runs like a black thread through anthropology, mythology, theology and social history—the expulsion from Eden, Prometheus bound to the rock, labyrinths, the dungeon, inquisitions, the stocks and the ducking stool, torture and mutilation, Siberia, Belsen. The penalty of banishment and confinement, inspired by man's inhumanity to man, epitomizes perhaps the most severe and damaging injury the human spirit can suffer. "Let the punishment fit the crime" is an effective yardstick—so long as you are measuring vindictive retribution. But if our aim is to prevent crime and remold criminals, the prison has just the opposite effect.

Advocates of the punitive principle argue that modification or elimination of prisons would amount to an invitation to crime in that it would remove the fear of imprisonment that is believed to work as a deterrent upon potential criminals. The short answer to that theory is that such fear patently has never kept prisons from being crowded, largely by persistent offenders who are sent back to them again and again.

Of the 172,729 persons in state and Federal prisons at the end of 1953, more than 60 per cent were repeaters. The total prison population at that time was 5,355 larger than at the end of 1952 and represented the highest year-end prison population since 1940. In the same year, state institutions released on parole or some other form of conditional release a total of 34,032 prisoners. And 9,080 of them—more than a fifth—violated their conditional release and were sent back to prison. In New York City alone municipal institutions for correction in 1954 received 110,057 inmates, but more significantly, nearly two-thirds of them were repeaters.

It is apparent then that the only type of offender on whom

fear of imprisonment might work is the casual or accidental felon who is impelled into a misdeed by force of circumstances or by some pathological complexity in his emotional make-up. But he usually acts so spontaneously that the consequences of his offense do not have time to sink in.

That fear of prison is a virtually negligible factor in the psychology of the deliberate or habitual criminal is attested by the addiction of repeaters to further and more serious crimes. The typical case-hardened prisoner, with his rationale fixed at an adolescent level, with unlimited ego but no insight, spends much of his time in prison elaborately plotting his next job. He is profoundly convinced that he is smarter than justice and will beat the law the next time. So the crime that put him in prison is endlessly reviewed and analyzed with his fellows there, to spot the "mistakes" that led to his capture and to plot the "perfect job."

Prisons fail because the very experience of imprisonment, of being caged like an animal, has a deeply damaging psychological effect. If society kept these people in cages indefinitely, as it does dangerous animals, it would be acting more consistently. But it releases 98 per cent of all prisoners, after subjecting them to an environment that has made them many times more anti-social and distorted than they were before.

The prisoner lives under a harsh "spotlight" that is never turned off. Guards watch his every movement and "stool pigeons" among his fellow prisoners are always ready to report his talk and actions. Prisons breed, or reinforce, the most cynical attitudes toward the law and any code of private or public morality. The prisoner soon learns that the world he has entered is just as evil as the outside world where he has failed. The worst types of inmates, bullies and would-be "big operators," dominate the scene; they can even influence, cajole or control some members of the custodial staff.

Although programs of work and industrial training have become widespread, most prisoners are still idle a good deal of the time, and the programs bring them little benefit. Civil service overseers are paid out of the profits of these programs, so naturally they organize the work with a view to maximum gain. The welfare of the prisoners who do the work is simply not considered. At times, influence and bribery by inmates determine job assignments.

Many prisons operate impressive-looking educational programs, complete with classrooms, teachers and textbooks, but the educational achievements are more apparent than real. Since the prisons are unable to get enough qualified teachers, they use some of the better-educated inmates as instructors. Apart from the question of competence, inmates are not likely to look up to these teachers for either intellectual light or ethical guidance. The reaction is more likely to be: "He's only a 'con' like me."

Under favorable circumstances, we have the means of getting to the basic emotional factors that underlie delinquent behavior, and of treating them successfully. We can carry out a program of rehabilitation that is one in actuality, and not in name only. This program can be carried on only outside prison walls—that is, in a new kind of institution. No such institution now exists, but it would be a practical and wholesome investment to bring it into being at the earliest possible moment.

It would be an institution so acceptable that persons subject to antisocial impulses would go to it voluntarily—as a patient now goes to a hospital—for professional guidance in the eradication or amelioration of the emotional disturbance. A large percentage of those whom we label as criminals can be reclaimed for useful, stable lives through techniques now available.

At these hospital-like institutions, teams of experts (psychiatrists, physicians, psychologists, social workers and teachers) would pool their skills to reach and extirpate from the personality of the offender the roots of the behavior that had forced the community to exile him. It would be the task of these teams to make the offender's stay there bring forth positive fruit for him and for society.

There must be, too, another kind of institution for those who, because of age or emotional characteristics, are not receptive to therapy. They would be committed to custodial institutions, to be held there indefinitely under appropriate security conditions. Suitable work or activity would be provided for them in an environment as far as possible non-punitive. Even here the worst aspects of the prison should be eliminated, as much for the sake of society's ethical self-respect as in recognition of the fact that even the worst offenders were born to human brotherhood and that many of them are unfit for it through circumstances beyond their control.

To the argument that therapeutic facilities should be superimposed on the present prison system, the reply is simply that it has been tried and it does not work. Any attempt to treat delinquents seriously in prison is hamstrung by hostile forces. The prison psychiatrist is in effect isolated from both staff and inmates. The ingrained attitude of custodial personnel is that their charges are social pariahs, vicious and irreclaimable, and that such rehabilitative measures as psychiatric treatment are wasted.

Even the prisoners, in this stagnant environment, strongly resist treatment. Most of them would rather be labeled as criminals than as emotionally impaired persons. The psychiatric patient is disdained and ridiculed by his fellow inmates. Moreover, prisoners look upon the psychiatrist as a member of the administration and therefore an enemy.

Divorced from the prison environment, rehabilitative therapy is immeasurably promising. The literature of psychiatry already contains numerous accounts of the intensive and successful treatment of delinquents whom enlightened judges and magistrates have put into the hands of psychiatrists and social workers, rather than in prison. In my own observation, persons guilty of such diverse crimes as arson, burglary, forgery, homicide and assault have responded favorably to systematic treatment, and afterward have remained socially adjusted.

Let no one suspect that this is merely an appeal to turn criminals over to psychiatrists and thus cancel their penalties. The belief that psychotherapy alone is a magic wand for the cure of criminal conduct has not been substantiated. Experience has shown that complex emotional difficulties often may be traced to obscure physical conditions that have remained undiscovered under incomplete methods of observation and procedure. In any event, just as pain and other physical symptoms reveal ailments and the need for medication or surgery, aberrant conduct, including criminal behavior, often is a natural signal of a condition, perhaps profound and complex, that calls for correction.

Although every prison offers opportunities for religious worship and many prisoners attend church services regularly, prison is barren ground for the flowering of religious impulses. Most prisoners lack the necessary emotional depth and moral values. It is usually under the whiplash of fear or panic (in the death cell, for example) that a prisoner clutches at the hope that religion offers him.

If the prison system has failed so blatantly in its purposes of protecting society and reclaiming the wrongdoer, why has society not junked it long ago? Part of the answer is that, although society pretends it wants only protection against the criminal, it is much more strongly motivated by the primitive impulse to punish the criminal. Psychologically, this vindictive feeling toward the offender is understandable. Society's desire for revenge, based on a pattern as old as man, grows out of its own fears and insecurities. By punishing the criminal, society hopes to prevent the expression of its own criminal impulses.

None the less, we can hardly afford the luxury of this psychological mechanism, which only aggravates and inflames the problem of crime. A more realistic attitude would be in keeping with the progress recorded in other social fields.

Newly won scientific knowledge of the causes of criminal behavior offer some effective tools for the constructive handling of offenders. The old penal philosophy leans on the assumption that the criminal must be either insane, and therefore not responsible for his acts, or sane, and therefore completely responsible. It does not recognize that there can be many gradations and varieties of emotional disturbance causing delinquency.

The delinquent we encounter in penal institutions today is usually an emotionally disturbed person, with marked destructive tendencies, who acts out his disturbance at the expense of society. He is full of resentment and hatred. His view of reality, as it affects him, may be far from accurate. Yet, erratic as is his conduct, it is highly unlikely that he is insane.

In prisons, the outlook for most of these delinquents is for their most destructive and rebellious tendencies to be sharpened and brought to a pitch. The already vindictive behavior pattern will become hardened and set.

To those who still hanker after punishment of the offender, no matter what the social consequences, I would say that the therapeutic approach involves suffering for the offender, too. After all, hospitals are not generally regarded as havens of pleasure. Not only would the offender still be deprived of his freedom, but the therapy itself would call for arduous emotional and physical effort on his part over a long period of time.

The notorious shortage of competent personnel for existing corrective institutions prompts a question as to how a scientifically trained staff could be recruited for the proposed new treatment centers. This obstacle is not insurmountable, for the project would have to start with one or more pilot institutions and develop gradually. Psychiatrists, who are too few in number for the work already awaiting them, would form only a part of the "teams" that the institutions would require for their broad-gauge medical and social undertaking.

One person in every hundred is in jail at some time each year. So there is no doubt that the field is enormous, but the staff-training requirement would not be prohibitive in a program of gradual transition. Schools of social work have considered just this kind of training, but have hesitated to undertake it without assurance of employment opportunities.

A Commissioner of Correction once said to this writer in discussing prison therapy: "Doctor, our job is just to keep these people *in*." As a doctor interested in social dilemmas, I should like to say it is time society gave more thought to keeping people from *going in* in the first place and to preventing their *going back* thereafter.

Suggested Reading

Abraham S. Blumberg, *Criminal Justice,* Chicago, Quadrangle Books, 1967 (paperback).

Donald R. Cressey, ed., *The Prison: Studies in Institutional Organization and Change,* New York, Holt, Rinehart and Winston, 1961.

Robert O. Dawson, *Sentencing: The Decision as to Type, Length, and Conditions of Sentence,* Boston, Little, Brown, 1969.

George Edwards, *The Police on the Urban Frontier,* New York, Institute of Human Relations Press, 1968.

Ronald Goldfarb, *Ransom: A Critique of the American Bail System,* New York, Harper and Row, 1965.

E. Adamson Hoebel, *The Law of Primitive Man: A Study in Comparative Legal Dynamics,* Cambridge, Mass., Harvard University Press, 1954 (Atheneum paperback).

Wayne R. LaFave, *Arrest: The Decision to Take a Suspect into Custody,* Boston, Little, Brown, 1965.

Edwin M. Lemert, *Social Action and Legal Change: Revolution Within the Juvenile Court,* Chicago, Aldine, 1970.

Lewis Mayers, *The American Legal System,* rev. ed., New York, Harper and Row, 1964.

Frank W. Miller, *Prosecution: The Decision to Charge a Suspect with a Crime,* Boston, Little, Brown, 1969.

Norval Morris and Gordon Hawkins, *The Honest Politician's Guide to Crime Control,* Chicago, University of Chicago Press, 1970.

Donald J. Newman, *Conviction: Determination of Guilt or Innocence Without Trial,* Boston, Little, Brown, 1966.

Philippe Nonet, *Administrative Justice: Advocacy and Change in a Government Agency,* New York, Russell Sage Foundation, 1969.

Herbert L. Packer, *The Limits of the Criminal Sanction,* Stanford, Calif., Stanford University Press, 1968.

Roscoe Pound, *Interpretations of Legal History,* New York, Macmillan, 1923.

Richard Quinney, ed., *Crime and Justice in Society,* Boston, Little, Brown, 1969 (paperback).

Stephen Schafer, *Restitution to Victims of Crime,* London, Stevens and Sons, 1960.

Edwin M. Schur, *Crimes Without Victims,* Englewood Cliffs, N.J., Prentice-Hall, 1965 (paperback).

Thorsten Sellin and Marvin E. Wolfgang, *The Measurement of Delinquency,* New York, John Wiley, 1964.

Jerome H. Skolnick, *Justice Without Trial,* New York, John Wiley, 1966 (paperback).

Edwin H. Sutherland and Donald R. Cressey, *Criminology,* 8th ed., Philadelphia, J. B. Lippincott, 1970.

Austin Turk, *Criminality and Legal Order,* Chicago, Rand McNally, 1969.

Lewis Yablonsky, *Synanon: The Tunnel Back,* Baltimore, Penguin Books, 1967 (paperback).

Index

A Note on the Editor

Donald R. Cressey, one of America's leading criminologists, was born in Fergus Falls, Minnesota, and studied at Iowa State University and Indiana University. His books include *Theft of the Nation; Delinquency, Crime, and Differential Association; Other People's Money; Principles of Criminology; The Prison;* and *Delinquency, Crime, and Social Process.* He has done research in a police department, a district attorney's office, and five different prisons. He is now Professor of Sociology at the University of California, Santa Barbara.

NEW YORK TIMES BOOKS published by QUADRANGLE BOOKS

AMERICAN FISCAL AND MONETARY POLICY
edited with an Introduction by Harold Wolozin

AMERICAN FOREIGN POLICY SINCE 1945
edited with an Introduction by Robert A. Divine

AMERICAN POLITICS SINCE 1945
edited with an Introduction by Richard M. Dalfiume

AMERICAN SOCIETY SINCE 1945
edited with an Introduction by William L. O'Neill

BLACK PROTEST IN THE SIXTIES
edited with an Introduction by August Meier and Elliott Rudwick

CITIES IN TROUBLE
edited with an Introduction by Nathan Glazer

THE CONTEMPORARY AMERICAN FAMILY
edited with an Introduction by William J. Goode

THE CORPORATION IN THE AMERICAN ECONOMY
edited with an Introduction by Harry M. Trebing

CRIME AND CRIMINAL JUSTICE
edited with an Introduction by Donald R. Cressey

EUROPEAN SOCIALISM SINCE WORLD WAR I
edited with an Introduction by Nathanael Greene

THE MEANING OF THE AMERICAN REVOLUTION
edited with an Introduction by Lawrence H. Leder

MODERN AMERICAN CITIES
edited with an Introduction by Ray Ginger

MOLDERS OF MODERN THOUGHT
edited with an Introduction by Ben B. Seligman

NAZIS AND FASCISTS IN EUROPE, 1918-1945
edited with an Introduction by John Weiss

THE NEW DEAL
edited with an Introduction by Carl N. Degler

POP CULTURE IN AMERICA
edited with an Introduction by David Manning White

POVERTY AND WEALTH IN AMERICA
edited with an Introduction by Harold L. Sheppard

PREJUDICE AND RACE RELATIONS
edited with an Introduction by Raymond W. Mack